Design for
Life

D1518622

Stuart Walker's design work has been described as life-changing, inspiring, disturbing and ferocious.

Drawing on an extraordinarily diverse range of sources and informed by creative practice, *Design for Life* penetrates to the heart of modern culture and the malaise that underlies today's moral and environmental crises.

The author argues that this malaise is deep-seated and fundamental to the modern outlook. He shows how our preoccupation with technological progress, growth and the future has produced a constricted view of life – one that is both destructive and self-reinforcing.

Based on over twenty-five years of scholarship and creative practice, he demonstrates the vital importance of solitude, contemplation, inner growth and the present moment in developing a different course – one that looks squarely at our current, precarious situation while offering a positive, hopeful way forward – a way that is compassionate, context-based, human scale, ethically motivated and critically creative.

Design for Life is an intensely original contribution that will be essential reading for design practitioners and students. Written in a clear, accessible style, it will also appeal to a broader readership, especially anyone who is concerned with contemporary society's rising inequalities and environmental failings and is looking for a more constructive, balanced and thoughtful direction.

Stuart Walker is Professor of Design for Sustainability at Lancaster University. His design work has been exhibited in Australia, Canada, Italy and the UK, including the Design Museum, London. His numerous books include *Sustainable by Design*, *The Spirit of Design* and *Designing Sustainability*, also published by Routledge.

Praise for **DESIGN FOR LIFE: creating meaning in a distracted world**

This book adopts a wholly new approach to design, one that gets right to its heart. Rooted in values, beliefs and creativity it adopts a rhetorical approach to its subject, blurring the boundary between designing and thinking about design.

Penny Sparke, Professor of Design History, Kingston University

In this stunning book, Stuart Walker's sensibility explores deep and complex dimensions of design thinking and doing, shedding light on the role of intentions, priorities and values.

Maria Cecilia Loschiavo dos Santos, Professor of Design,
University of São Paulo

Our society expects and needs a new wisdom for developing our lives in more meaningful ways. In this book, Stuart Walker opens the door for dialogue on wisdom in design. It is a wisdom permeated by creativity, the human imagination, intuition and comprehension.

Takeshi Sunaga, Professor of Design, Tokyo University of the Arts

Praise for Stuart Walker's previous books with Routledge

DESIGNING SUSTAINABILITY: making radical changes in a material world

Quite simply, this is the best book on the key issues that engage us – values, culture, the environment, beliefs, making a better world – that I have ever read. It is utterly original, deeply rooted, supremely pragmatic and splendidly visionary

Martin Palmer, Secretary General,
Alliance of Religions and Conservation (ARC)

A seminal contribution to the profession of design that begins with the heart and mind of the designer and the values most important to human flourishing

David W. Orr, Oberlin College, Ohio

Joyfully and patiently Stuart Walker shows us how to design spiritual satisfaction into the everyday so that we, and the Earth we inhabit, may be whole again

Sara Parkin, Founder Director and Trustee, *Forum of the Future*

There is no doubt that this book is a powerful and spiritual tool for a better way of living. Education at its best!

Design Magazine, Portugal

THE SPIRIT OF DESIGN: objects, environment and meaning

I have read and referenced The Spirit of Design, *and am much appreciating* Designing Sustainability. *They are very welcome – I know of very little else that makes such links between design, behaviour, mindsets and the future of the planet!*

Jules N. Pretty, University of Essex

I find your work deeply philosophical ... what you have to share is special because the objects you use serve as a symbolic language for a deeply relevant human ethic that is so vital right now

A.Wyma, South Africa

Your two books Spirit of Design *and* Sustainable by Design *have been very influential for me and have corresponded to my desire for meaning*

R. Brual, Kwantlen Polytechnic University, Canada

SUSTAINABLE BY DESIGN: explorations in theory and practice

Definitely to be on the booklist of any product design course

Jack Ingram, Birmingham Institute of Art and Design

A fascinating book that takes the reader on a journey that is both diverse and full of surprise

Jonathan Chapman, University of Brighton

A sensitive, thought-provoking book that explores fresh possibilities

Alastair Fuad-Luke, Aalto University

With beautiful images to back up his words, Walker tutors, suggests and inspires...this book is a must for students and designers, its thoughtful approach also makes it an interesting read for anyone who's excited by the current shift of play

Sally White, Resource

Design for Life

Creating Meaning in a Distracted World

Stuart Walker

Routledge
Taylor & Francis Group

LONDON AND NEW YORK

First published 2017
by Routledge
2 Park Square, Milton Park, Abingdon, Oxon OX14 4RN

and by Routledge
711 Third Avenue, New York, NY 10017

Routledge is an imprint of the Taylor & Francis Group, an informa business

British Library Cataloguing-in-Publication Data
A catalogue record for this book is available from the British Library

Library of Congress Cataloging-in-Publication Data
Names: Walker, Stuart, 1955- author.
Title: Design for life : creating meaning in a distracted world / Stuart Walker.
Description: New York : Routledge, 2017. | Includes bibliographical references and index.
Identifiers: LCCN 2016040132| ISBN 9781138232464 (hb : alk. paper) | ISBN 9781138232471 (pb : alk. paper) | ISBN 9781315312538 (ebook)
Subjects: LCSH: Design–Philosophy. | Social ecology.
Classification: LCC NK1505 .W35 2017 | DDC 745.4–dc23
LC record available at https://lccn.loc.gov/2016040132

ISBN: 978-1-138-23246-4 (hbk)
ISBN: 978-1-138-23247-1 (pbk)
ISBN: 978-1-315-31253-8 (ebk)

Typeset in Univers
by Saxon Graphics Ltd, Derby

To the people of Ebbw Vale,
my hometown

We should not be pushing out figures
when the facts are in the opposite direction.

Aneurin Bevan, MP
Ebbw Vale, South Wales

Contents

x

Figures
and tables

All designs, photographs, diagrams and tables are by the author

Figures

Tables

Acknowledgements

First, I would like to thank my wife Helen. As for my previous books, she has edited the text and given me wise insight, immeasurable support and her love. I also thank my colleagues and students whose conversations and questions have helped me shape and refine many of the ideas in this book. Many thanks to the Arts and Humanities Research Council and the Arts Council of England, who have provided me with new opportunities for learning, and to the ImaginationLancaster Design Research Centre and Lancaster University. I am grateful also to all those at Routledge who have offered advice and assistance in bringing this book to publication.

Abbreviations and acronyms

CE	Common or Current Era
CNC	Computer Numerical Control
CSR	Corporate Social Responsibility
HCD	Human Centred Design
IMF	International Monetary Fund
UCL	University College London
UNEP	United Nations Environment Programme
UNESCO	United Nations Educational, Scientific and Cultural Organization

Prologue

Conventional academic forms of writing are especially suited to intellectual argument and reason, whereas images and evocative texts are expressive of values and can stimulate emotional connections and responses. All these modes are used here. Through investigation and critique on the one hand, and synthesis and creative expression on the other, the reader is asked to examine their assumptions and to contribute to a different course. Clearly, this approach is values-based. This is unavoidable when dealing with creative expression and design. It is also necessary if we are to make decisions based on what we believe to be good and right. Values-based arguments are essential if we are to create a material culture and ways of living that are fairer, less damaging and more meaningful. Today's grotesque and widening inequalities in wealth and opportunity and the exploitation of people can, perhaps, be addressed through international agreements and legislation. However, many aspects of today's consumption-based society cannot and should not be dealt with by the law, but they still require our attention and consideration. Traditionally, for example, most human societies have frowned upon traits such as envy, greed and selfishness. In Western culture, there is a long history of teaching that encourages humility and care for community, and denounces leaders who allow social injustice and inequality in favour of the privileged few. But in many ways, consumer society encourages all these social ills through the constant supply of novelty and status-oriented goods combined with invidious marketing techniques that incite socio-positional competitiveness. These are values-based issues, and if we are to confront them, values have to be at the heart of the discussion and central to design discourse and practice.

The approach I have taken employs rhetoric because through such means the arguments can be much richer and far more comprehensive than if they were based solely on reason and evidence. As a result, they are better able to address the whole person. Rhetoric, or persuasive argument, has a number of forms. *Deliberative rhetoric* draws on expert opinion and human values, as well as evidence, to build the case for a particular course of action. *Forensic rhetoric* draws on similar sources to argue for accountability and justice. *Display rhetoric* is concerned with matters such as goodness, beauty, honour and virtue, or indeed their opposites, and is particularly apt for the field of design because, as the name suggests, it is the rhetoric of demonstration and display. These three types of rhetoric, as originally defined by Aristotle,[1] allow us to address issues that cannot be captured solely through intellectual argument or evidence-based methods. For instance, *virtue* includes such things as self-control, magnanimity, justice, technical skill and practical wisdom, the social virtues of amiability and sincerity, and contemplation or speculative wisdom, which includes insight and deeper questions about the meaning of life.[2] These considerations allow us to take into account not just the rational mind but also the intuitive mind, and the ensuing propositions and contentions can embrace logic, ethics and emotion.[3]

The discussions and arguments presented in the following pages draw on work from a wide range of fields, including philosophy, technology, environmentalism and religion. This breadth of inquiry is important because design is, essentially, an integrative discipline that brings together a multiplicity of issues and influences, makes connections and develops a unified, creative outcome. This is combined with creative practice in the form of objects, images and evocative texts. Blurring the boundaries between design and art, these are not necessarily practical products. For me, object creation is a way of informing, synthesizing and expressing ideas about the nature of the modern condition. Collectively, they aim to demonstrate why significant change is needed – by visualizing, for example, the kinds of things we have lost and the sense of anxiety and meaninglessness that results from our distracted consumer lifestyles. Through humour, satire, joy and pathos the objects may elicit surprise, tranquillity or unease but in all cases they invite reflection.

Unlike the sciences and the social sciences, the main purpose of design is not to examine and analyze an existing condition or produce evidence that verifies a theoretical proposition, although developing a basis for design intervention may certainly make use of such approaches. Design is an imaginative, creative discipline; it is concerned not with what already exists but with what might exist. The main task is to consider the interrelationships, accordances and conflicts among a large number of factors and, on this foundation, engage in the deeply immersive process of visualizing imaginative responses. Collection and analysis of empirical data may be necessary but this is never more than a means to another end. Unfortunately, in many contemporary design studies, this stage often seems to take over. The focus then becomes diverted from creative development and synthesis, and the resulting design outcomes are either cursory or absent altogether – the end product being restricted to guidelines, frameworks or toolkits. But this is not design and it does little to advance the kinds of synthetical thinking, tacit knowledge and development of expertise that are essential to design practice.

The crucial feature of this integrated process of thinking-and-doing is that it connects motives and tangible actions; this constitutes a distinctive contribution of design. When pursued through a combination of reasoned arguments and creative expression, it can be summed up as *reflective design* or *design praxis*, which is neither reflection alone, nor practice alone, but the two together as an interrelated unit. Reflection on priorities, intentions, values and meanings informs the imaginative act and the creative outcome, be it a text or an object. Reflection on the outcome allows consideration of how those priorities, intentions, values and meanings have been synthesized and expressed, whether or not they are effective, or if further development is needed. In addition, for an environmentally responsible, socially just and personally meaningful approach to design our motives have to centre on understandings of goodness, beauty and virtue. This will only occur if we are prepared to consider and perhaps alter our values and priorities. But change is not achieved by motives alone. Motives have to be translated into actions and, in design, motives find expression through the creative act. Similarly, we cannot achieve lasting change by actions alone. If they are not rooted in appropriate motives, our actions will be formulaic and hollow. And if our motives and actions are to be consistent with deeper considerations of meaning-seeking and human flourishing, we must reject approaches and attitudes that foster selfishness, envy, avid competitiveness, acquisitiveness and greed. If we hold on to these, our patterns of behaviour and reactions to the world and each other will be markedly different from those motivated by attitudes of selflessness, cooperativeness, kindness, generosity and moderation.[4] To strive to live by these latter values is not naïve or idealistic, it is entirely pragmatic because it not only cares for other people and the world as a whole, it also makes our own lives more meaningful – it is to be rooted in the good and to have a more balanced sense of our physical, social and spiritual selves. Consequently, design that is motivated by such values will be expressive of one's identity, a sense of belonging, and truly living. In other words, it will be design for life.

1

The Subject personal involvement and positive charge

Wisely improve the Present. It is thine.

Henry Wadsworth Longfellow

If design is to make a substantial contribution to contemporary culture, it has to move beyond instrumental solutions for what are often rather trivial problems. From furniture design to household goods, from electronics to services, design's conventional but slender aspiration of creating delight and pleasure in the use of worldly things offers little more than interminable novelty. This zeal for designing the future has created forever new, forever changing and therefore forever unattainable material dreams. It is a fool's game that diminishes us as it lays waste the earth. Design has to reach beyond such devices of desire that disable and disconnect us from each other and the world itself.

Today, design needs to address quite different questions – not of what and how but of why. When we ask why, further questions arise – about priorities, values and meaning. To search for answers, we must look not to the world of inanimate things and rationalized utility but to the world of real encounters and lived experiences. It is here, in the *life-world*, that we contend with fundamental issues of truth and goodness, which may have no definitive resolution but nevertheless are at the core of what it is to be human. This book represents an attempt to explore these deeper questions and their implications for material culture. In this journey, design plays a key role, not least because it is both a creative process and a mode of expression. Therefore, it can be fundamental in informing our understandings, developing different perspectives and conveying concepts and ideas.

For better and worse, we live in a technologically sophisticated world and it has led to ways of life that are blessed with huge benefits. These benefits, however, are accompanied by huge costs, but it is pointless to yearn for some idealized past that never actually existed. The world is now technological and we cannot un-invent it even if we wanted to. As Lanier has said, *"The earth is not a linear system, like a video clip, that can be played in forward or reverse"*; after we've learned to get through climate change, the world will be different, more artificial.[1] And yet, we are not one-dimensional beings. There are many aspects of personhood and many needs not furnished, or even addressed, by our current approaches to design. While we may live with, profit from and enjoy the use of technologies, we still need to engage with other people and directly experience the real world – to touch the earth, taste the wind and feel the rain. Such experiences are restorative and nourish our ability to empathize. This implies a type of design that reminds us of who we are and where we are, about what we are doing and how our actions can be in harmony or conflict with others and the world. This kind of design is not part of corporate capitalism or techno-science. It is about other things, other ways of being ourselves, other priorities, and other aspects of our personhood, and it helps us see more conventional, utilitarian approaches from a different perspective. It is concerned with meaning, intuition, silence, reflection, localization, harmony, nature and time. It is a kind of design that reveals and critiques, reintegrates and replenishes. And it is a kind of design that releases us, at least temporarily, from the intrusions, pressures, hype, noise and busyness of our connected, preoccupied lives. Unchecked, this can create a frazzled, frenetic forgetting, because such ways are entirely incompatible with more contemplative modes. Through many small acts, in which design can play a part, we change the world and as we do so we too are changed. Slowly and imperceptibly our worldview is transformed – from one that is increasingly diminishing of the human spirit and destructive of the natural environment to one based in values and ideals and a belief in the common good; one that is rooted, forthright and hopeful.

2

REFLECTION

The intention of much of my earlier design work was to create possibilities that could be considered for adoption or adaption and so I referred to it as *propositional design*. It is a term that places the focus on what is yet to come. Like modernity itself, the underlying notion is one of progress and the future. Similarly, *speculative design,* which tends to concentrate on emerging technologies, also suggests a concern with the future. *Critical design* seeks to challenge norms and conventions through such means as satire, but its focus is again on emerging technologies and their future implications. None of these adequately describe the kind of design work included in this book, which is concerned with the present. While it is natural to think ahead, in reality, the present is the only place where we can act and make a difference. The here and now is ours, the future is for those we will become.

Today, we hear much talk of design futures, even though foresight is notoriously myopic. We know less about the future than we do of the past and even that, as L. P. Hartley told us, is a foreign country.[2] This preoccupation with the future is an evasion. It is not just a distraction from the present and a means of avoiding responsibility for our actions, it also prevents us from being fully in the present, looking at it squarely, recognizing our presumptions and confronting our biases. By contrast, when the focus of design becomes the present, it can reflect back to us who we are and what we are doing. Disquieting as this may be, it can throw light on established norms and allow us to see ourselves from a new angle. This we can call *reflective design*, not only because it holds a mirror up to us but also because it invites pause and thoughtful consideration of our suppositions. Using design in this way allows us to fully engage in the now, to question and perhaps change our priorities and to make different, hopefully better, choices. Hence, this is not design for an alternative future, it is alternative design for a complementary present – within and coexistent with technological culture. It is a form of design that transcends material utility and responds to another, inner facet of our humanness. It focuses our attention on deeper things by questioning, disrupting and offering fresh interpretations. The concern is with creating a material culture capable of contributing to life in a meaningful way, which implies a material culture that provides for our practical, social and spiritual needs in ways that are not just considerate of others and the natural environment but are also virtuous. In this endeavour it is important to recognize that, whereas practical and social needs align with traditional understandings of inner values and ethics, today

3

the natural world is also a critical concern because its degradation affects both our physical and spiritual well-being.

If we are to extract ourselves from the narrow grip of modernity we must develop new understandings and new ways of doing things – ways that are better, fuller and more caring of each other and the natural world. We cannot do this without first recognizing the inadequacies of our current outlook and in this, design can make a creative contribution. Scholarship in design, if it is to say anything interesting and useful, has to incorporate the creative process of designing because this is the vital core of the discipline. It is a core that involves much more than objectivity, empirical evidence and instrumental rationality. To do creative work we must engage in ways of thinking that are capable of integrating myriad, often conflicting, elements into an holistic outcome. Conventional wisdom in academic research suggests that the subject under investigation is best viewed from a position of objective detachment; a neutral position free of subjectivity and bias. As will become evident in Chapter 6, in recent times this notion has been shown to be misguided. Indeed, as Bouteneff notes, *"some of the best research and insightful observations come from those who are deeply and personally involved in their subject, precisely by virtue of that engagement"*.[3] The creative activity of designing is a deeply immersive, all absorbing process that includes subjective decision-making, intuition, emotion, sensitivity to aesthetics and consideration of values. Design research that is not informed by this will not be getting to its core or revealing its true potential. Furthermore, whereas the natural sciences study material phenomena and the world as it exists, the creative disciplines call upon the imagination to wrestle with and express different concerns and visualize alternative ways of knowing. In this way, design and the other creative arts complement the more objective analyses of the sciences – they seek to synthesize rather than analyze, and they involve human values, beliefs and ideals.

The practice of design requires and builds knowledge, know-how, experience and understanding. By drawing on the human imagination and struggling to find creative resolution, one encounters first-hand the occurrence of insight and synthesis. It is a process that by necessity involves the researcher. It is also unapologetically unsystematic. Systematic approaches are deliberately and rationally constrained by the frame of reference of the investigator or designer. By contrast, opening up one's view to many and varied experiences and encounters in galleries, museums, libraries and, most importantly, in the world itself 'allows in' the unexpected and the serendipitous, as well as outlooks and frames of reference different from one's own. This 'allowing in' is important for the creative process of designing, a process that involves the comprehensive and integrative modes of thinking associated with right-hemisphere brain functions. Designing involves a type of thinking or state of being that sees the big picture and makes connections, often challenging what we habitually take for granted. It is a type of thinking that is open to spontaneity, invention, discovery, unexpected juxtapositions and surprise.[4] In the discussions that follow, therefore, the concern is not with neutral conclusions but with understandings and insights arising from engagement in the dynamic, frustrating, creative and fascinating process of designing.

In earlier writings I introduced and developed an understanding of a *Quadruple Bottom Line for Sustainability* to inform our creative design endeavours.[5, 6] It comprises:

- **Practical Meaning** – providing for physical needs while ameliorating environmental impacts;
- **Social Meaning** – ethics, compassion, equity and justice;
- **Personal Meaning** – conscience, spiritual well-being, questions of ultimate concern; and
- **Economic Means** – financial viability, but not as an end in itself.

This differs from Elkington's *Triple Bottom Line*[7] in that the focus is on our understandings of meaning and meaningful actions. There is also the additional component of *Personal Meaning*, which recognizes the importance of the individual in achieving sustainable ways of living. To address this *Personal Meaning* element in a substantive manner we have to use a different kind of language. Rather than relying primarily on facts, analysis and information, or intellectual argument, rationalization and objectivity, we need to draw equally on the language of emotion, relationships, integration and composition. This involves intuition, subjectivity and the lived experience – the life-world or *Lebenswelt* – the world we share and live through in the present. This, too, is the language of creativity and the imagination.

Self-evidently, personal meaning has to be meaningful at the personal level; we have to engage, feel and experience a thing emotionally and aesthetically in ourselves. It has to touch us at a deeper level. So the question arises, how do we achieve this? Obviously not by restricting our inquiries and considerations to information and facts. First, we have to use more symbolic, evocative forms of expression that are capable of alluding to

5

those aspects of being human that lie beyond evidential confirmation but are, nonetheless, felt and known within oneself. Second, through the visual arts, we can create alternatives and envision different understandings and reveal different worlds. Through word and image we can engage with ideas in ways that transcend intellectual understandings and touch the heart. We appreciate creative works through the experiences they enable, which are aesthetic, emotional and intuitively felt. As Siegel has written, *"an embellished event can be closer to the truth than factual precision if its evocation is infused with intuitive wisdom"*.[8]

When we design we have to engage, and through this engagement the designer or practice-based researcher becomes involved, this is a necessary condition of doing design. Involvement means calling upon not just facts but also one's values, beliefs and aesthetic sensibilities, all of which are critically important. They are what make us human, they give our lives meaning and significance, they allow us to dream and offer us hope. However, these aspects of our humanity have been downplayed, sidelined and eroded in modern, economically developed societies. Today, this is being challenged. Grey, discussing Catholicism, suggests that today's older generation, emerging from more conservative, rigid times, have tended to espouse more liberal directions, a position that is in keeping with Enlightenment notions of progress and continual advancement. But, she says, *"the future is not where this older generation seems to think it is"*,[9] suggesting instead that many young people are rejecting such ideas and wanting a religious or spiritual identity that runs counter to evermore liberalization, novelty and transience, and is *"unashamedly traditional"*; one that demands discipline and high standards.[10] And it is certainly the case that the very traditional Latin Mass is today attracting younger congregations.[11] In a different arena, social anthropologist Scott Atran asks, *"What dreams may come from most current government policies that offer little beyond promises of comfort and security?"*.[12] He argues that today's violent extremism results from an erosion of meaningful values and beliefs. In an address to the UN Security Council he said his research indicates that, *"Violent extremism represents not the resurgence of traditional cultures, but their collapse, as young people unmoored from millennial traditions flail about in search of a social identity that gives personal significance and glory. This is the dark side of globalization. They radicalize to find a firm identity in a flattened world"*.[13] These developments, which characterize our time, can be understood as the after-effects of modernity with its focus on materialism, secularization,

6

liberalization, rampant consumption and a preoccupation with possessions. Modernity may have been able to offer physical comfort, better health and, perhaps, security, but it has failed to offer more substantive avenues to human meaning. Taylor has said that *"an essential condition of a life having meaning"* is that *"the repeatable cycles of life connect over time, and make a continuity"* and that the rejection of these ideas during the modern period has resulted in homogeneity and emptiness.[14] Some see a return to tradition as a route to deeper values and beliefs while others, as Atran's research indicates, take a very different route – searching for 'significance and glory' through fundamentalism and violence. While we might not be able to go back to some traditional way of living or believing, it is also clear that fundamentalism and violence offer no fruitful answers. But we can learn from the failings and the attributes of modernity and recognize that a rebalancing and enrichment are needed – in education, politics and enterprise. It is necessary to pay far greater attention to values, beliefs and deeper questions of human purpose; that is, the 'why' questions that have been so assiduously avoided as we advance our scientific and technological endeavours.

Here, the approach taken to design and design inquiry is concerned with word and image; left- and right-brain functions; the temporality of script and the immediacy of image. So let us consider for a moment the role of the word in creative practice. As we will see in Chapter 2, in the modern period, Western society saw a privileging of the word over the image, and an increasing emphasis on rational argument and intellectualized understandings of knowledge at the expense of more intuitive, experiential and tacit ways of knowing. In using words in my creative practice, therefore, the language I invoke is not restricted to the language of explanation and rationalization. It is also the language of indication and signification, pointing towards a direction of thought. This way of using words allows space for imagination and personal experience. Words become expressive elements in the creative act; through story and poetry they evoke ideas that transcend information and facts.

Image and object can play a similar role; they too can allude to deeper ideas. In many ways, creating designs, objects and images represents the flip side of much of what we tend to do, and often feel forced to do, within academia. By this I mean that designing involves important aspects – creativity, intuition, subjectivity – that do not fit comfortably into the evidence-based, measurable outcomes that have become bywords for our

7

overly narrow notions of legitimate knowledge. Design is not a wholly objective discipline. Designed things are visual expressions of values, their forms and images are visual statements; implicitly or explicitly they convey a position, as discussed in Chapter 3. Moreover, many of our responses to a form or an image lie beyond analytical dissection and rationalization. The focus is elsewhere, in the experience we have of the thing itself, which is holistic and instantaneous. The concerns here are attention, gaze, seeing, feeling, emotion, subjective experience and aesthetic experience.

The creative works included in the following chapters are not restricted to the creation and presentation of objects, but also include words in the form of descriptive accounts, stories, imagined futures and poetry, some by others, some from my own pen.

In Chapter 2, *A Narrowing*, we trace the long entrenchment of assumptions, conventions and outlooks that, over several centuries, resulted in a shift in worldview from traditional to late modern. This shift is not only associated with unprecedented environmental destruction but also with a narrower, shallower perspective, a loss of narrative unity, and a loss of meaning. The argument is made that, by focussing on rationalistic, techno-scientific solutions (such as eco-products, energy efficiencies and increased material intensities) design restricts its contribution to a variety of incremental changes that actually support the continuance of a fundamentally unsustainable system. Instead, design can widen its purview and be a catalyst for more substantive change by restoring a more balanced approach to the design of products in context and, in the process, contribute to a recovery of narrative unity and of meaning.

Chapter 3, *Counterpoints*, begins with a consideration of the continued effects of the modern worldview, which still dominates the economically developed Western nations. It then offers a series of design responses that contests this domination and points to deeper notions of human meaning, community and environmental care. These creative works express more intuitive, subjective ways of knowing. Together, the discussion and the designed objects offer a balanced approach that reveals the limitations of the late-modern worldview. It is argued that there is a need to develop a new outlook based on different assumptions and more profound ideas. The obstacles to such a development are discussed before considering opportunities for design in the cultivation of new understandings – not least by visualizing, through tangible symbolic artefacts, the inadequacies of current modes as well as new directions for positive change. Several examples of *counterpoint* explorations are presented, which indicate how design can be employed to challenge norms and manifest ethical considerations.

The discussion in Chapter 4, *The Shift*, looks at how design research can be taken in a direction that addresses critical concerns about material culture and waste in a more substantive manner. The process combines study, practice and reflection, and results in the interrelated outcomes of reasoned argument and reflective designs. Developing the arguments from the preceding chapters, a critique is made of modernist design and its links to mass production, globalization and consumerism. The inescapable connections to environmental harm and social injustice provide a case for context-based, distributed approaches suited to local needs and for a shift in values and priorities based on inner development and the examined life of the individual. Importantly, this takes the design agenda from one of gradual improvement within the current manufacturing context to one of fundamental, systemic change – from incremental design to holistic design.

In Chapter 5, *Creativity*, we consider the mindset and ways of working that are needed for such a fundamental change in outlook and approach; in particular, as the subtitle of this chapter indicates, the imperative of solitude. While group-based and solitary ways of working can both lead to original outputs, each will be quite different in terms of character and significance. Group work encourages rationalistic thinking modes, which tend to lead to pragmatic outputs and incremental improvements. Solitary ways of working are more suited to creativity, holistic ideas and synthesis. Here, the outcomes may be more visionary but will often be less practical. Hence, both ways are needed, but in recent times a strong bias towards group work has tended to undervalue these differences and obstruct forms of creative thinking that can offer more radical visions. Today, we have urgent issues to deal with so there is a need for just such radical visions, which can inspire and help foster more fundamental, systemic change.

Chapter 6, *The Mesh*, begins with a critique of modernity's unidirectional 'detached observer' view of reality, which is then contrasted with contemporary, co-evolutionary understandings of human activities. The chapter explores the positive contribution of these realizations, their implications for design, and the relationship of imaginative, intuitive ways of knowing to empathy, compassion and caring for others and the natural world. The significance of these understandings for the future of material goods is considered in terms of their design, their interpretation and their potential influence in contributing to positive change. Their relevance is considered also in regard to developing a more comprehensive philosophical outlook. Alongside these discussions, a series of artefacts has been created that alludes to aspects of human knowing that have become severely eroded during late modernity. Despite this erosion, and whatever form of expression they may take, the importance and value of the core ideas these artefacts represent will be critical to the development of more holistic understandings.

Chapter 7, *Rhythms*, looks more closely at ways of working and particularly at the connections between movement, making and meaning. There is much evidence to suggest that a strong relationship exists between traditional ways of making and using objects and environmental conservation, social cohesion and personal well-being. Traditional practices that involve repetitive physical routines can be calming and contemplative and can foster more holistic, integrated modes of thinking. These bring to the fore intuition and 'bigger than self' perspectives that are closely tied to values and questions of meaning; issues that are crucial to our understandings of contemporary design. This chapter demonstrates that engagement in traditional practices can play an important role in rebalancing our attitudes, cultivating more comprehensive understandings of ourselves, and providing a complement to the rationalized, instrumental approaches that dominate modern society. Four areas of contribution are identified: practical, symbolic, complementary and resilient.

Chapter 8, *Seeds*, draws together these various threads to show their interrelationships and to create an overall picture of the challenges facing design if it is to move in a direction that is more substantive, responsible and life enhancing. Many current approaches – grand schemes, ideologies and corporate agendas, including so-called *Corporate Social Responsibility* – are critiqued and shown to be not only wrong-headed but also often severely counterproductive. These obstacles to constructive change are often based in substantial vested interests. It is argued that positive, lasting change occurs through an emphasis on education, dialogue and people working towards the common good in their community and immediate environment, both of which they encounter on a daily basis and therefore know – not in the abstract but in fully rounded, concrete terms. Such change is urgently needed because current directions are jeopardizing the future prospects of humanity and feeding a growing sense of existential angst. On the positive side, it is clear that change is happening, new realizations are emerging and new approaches are developing. Design's contribution to this change is discussed in terms of the three exploratory strands introduced in Chapters 3, 6 and 7, and a fourth, introduced in this final chapter, which uses design to present vital but familiar things in new ways. This discussion leads into a new design agenda, its short-term implementation and its long-term implications and benefits.

11

2

A Narrowing loss of narrative unity and the nature of design change

now I saw, though too late, the folly of beginning
a work before we count the cost

Daniel Defoe

PROLOGUE: The Tell-Tale Notch

There is a narrow gap on the west coast of British Columbia where the Pacific becomes a rushing torrent twice a day. With the push and pull of the tides the ocean surges through this constriction, filling and draining the sheltered waters of a long, straggling inlet. It is a spectacular, unchanging routine.

To witness this remarkable sight one has to leave the tiny settlement of Egmont and follow a trail through the temperate rainforest. Here everything is submerged in a verdant dampness and the light is filtered and dimmed. The air is hushed by moss-covered trees draped in lichen and the forest floor is a criss-cross graveyard of fallen pine, spruce and fir. The pervading green is punctuated only by the bright whites and oranges of fungi that colonize the rotting trunks.

Continuing along the trail one begins to notice, interspersed with the slender trees, huge old stumps, ten feet tall and yards across at their base. These are the remains of first-growth cedar, some perhaps a thousand years old. From time to time one also notices, cut into their sides, a horizontal notch. It is a small thing, just a few inches across, yet it signifies a rupture – a violent shift in culture. This notch once held a board that supported a logger while he wielded an axe. And it was the resounding crack of the axe that broke the long-held silence of the forest.

Ecologist Aldo Leopold once described the axe as the taker.[1] It was wielded by a culture that saw nature primarily in terms of resources, and it decimated the first-growth forests of the west coast of North America. While this attitude was the result of a long transition that had been taking place in Europe over centuries, here it represented a sudden and aggressive break in the deep-rooted practices, beliefs and traditions of the native peoples. In effect, it was a forceful imposition of the modern worldview. This is the worldview that still shapes the nature of innovation and enterprise as well as broader societal directions, and it is in urgent need of revision.[2]

In precipitating positive change, design has the potential to make a valuable contribution, but we must bear in mind that the kind of contribution required goes far deeper than technological efficiencies or the creation of eco-gadgets. New attitudes and priorities are needed that are capable of embracing not just economic exigencies but also the various factors that constitute contemporary sustainability, including inner values and deeper understandings of human meaning. In this endeavour, thoughtful design can be both a catalyst for and an expression of transformation.

13

INTRODUCTION

In this chapter I consider the magnitude and nature of change required to address contemporary environmental and social concerns, and the role of design in contributing to such change. Current attitudes and societal norms are shown to be the result of long-established conventions and priorities. These are proving extremely resilient, despite the evident need for urgent reform. While not underestimating the scale of the task, the discipline of design – as an applied art that draws upon the human imagination and valorizes creativity – has the opportunity to play an important part in manifesting alternatives and tangibly demonstrating different priorities. In doing so, and if informed by philosophical, ethical and environmental considerations, it can make a constructive contribution to the nature, extent and pace of positive change.

The development of the modern sensibility began perhaps as early as the 1400s and continued undiminished well into the twentieth century. The long progression of discoveries and changing attitudes that occurred during this period yielded new outlooks and resulted in a *Weltanschauung* (worldview) that was quite different from that of the earlier, pre-modern era. Over time, new societal norms and conventions became consolidated and the modern worldview became deeply rooted and institutionalized.

As a consequence of this entrenchment, and despite many countervailing influences and accomplishments in recent decades, modernity's overarching assumptions and priorities remain largely unaffected and the direction of Western development continues apace. In the twenty-first century, for example, the perpetuation of exploitative, seriously harmful practices is justified primarily on economic grounds in the interest of maintaining competitiveness. This is exactly the same justification given for the perpetuation of similarly exploitative, seriously harmful practices in the seventeenth century. Then, these were slavery practices associated with empire and colonization, and politicians argued that any change would be economically ruinous and would allow other countries to benefit.[3, 4] Today, they are slave-like labour practices associated with international corporations,[5] as well as practices that cause environmental degradation. And politicians continue to make essentially the same argument; the British Chancellor of the Exchequer has said, *"We should not price British business out of the global economy. If we burden them with endless social and environmental burdens – however worthy in their own right – then not only will we not achieve those goals but the businesses will fail, jobs will be lost and our country will be poorer".*[6]

Perceptions that were centuries in the making, that are bolstered by convention and fortified by political, economic and educational policies, are unlikely to be transformed in just a few decades. However, it is these very attitudes and outlooks that are so strongly associated with the domination and exploitation of the natural environment and potentially hazardous effects on biodiversity and climate; with social injustices, division and disparity; and with a prevailing sense of unease and anxiety about the future. All these are part and parcel of contemporary notions of sustainability. Yet, even though the modern sensibility has been much debated and much criticized since the mid-twentieth century, its essential features persist, partly because of their long period of gestation and partly because no practical, desirable alternative has yet emerged. Despite this, the extent and speed of its deleterious effects suggest that, unlike the transition from the medieval to the modern, today we do not have centuries to develop a systemically different course. Therefore, it behoves us all, in whatever field we find ourselves – including

14

design – to consider how new, more fruitful directions may be nurtured and encouraged.

To better understand the nature of the modern sensibility, and thence the significance of the change that is needed, it becomes important to trace its development and establishment. Through such means we can recognize it for what it is, and how it differs from a sensibility that is in greater alignment with individual flourishing, social responsibility and environmental care. The implications of such change for design, briefly sketched here, will be the subject of later chapters, but it is clear that design change, along with broader societal change, is only likely to come about if current market-led, consumption-based directions are drastically altered. This will require far more effective and emphatic political leadership than has been evident of late among the liberal democratic governments of the Western nations. Such leadership will necessarily have to put far greater store in longer-term interests that serve the common good rather than short-term interests that serve electoral ambitions and myopic ideas about winning in an economic 'global race'.[7] A new sustainable realization is needed, and new kinds of material culture will have to be designed that help strengthen the common good of regions, nations and the global community. A critical ingredient of this will be ways of living that accord with human interests and aspirations while ensuring very significant reductions in overall levels of consumption.

15

THE EQUANIMITY OF WISDOM

There is evidence to suggest that in pre-modern times a fertile balance was achieved between rationalist–intellectual and imaginative–intuitive understandings of the world. As far back as ancient Greece, we see that advances in philosophy and the systemization of knowledge and laws occurred alongside advances in human imagination and unsurpassed achievements in the visual arts. Here, the former emphasizes intellectual, analytic thinking and requires us to become 'detached' and thus able to objectify the world around us, while the latter calls upon intuitive, synthetical thinking that mediates this objectification, allowing us to reconnect with other people and with nature. McGilchrist suggests that this demonstrates functions commonly associated with left- and right-brain hemispheres in somewhat balanced accord, and that expansion in human knowledge and understanding during this period involved *"moves in two diametrically opposed directions at once – towards greater abstraction from the world and, simultaneously, towards greater empathetic engagement with the world*".[8] He goes on to explain that if we pay attention to our real, engaged experiences, rather than abstract notions of the world, we encounter the coming together of these apparent opposites. Indeed, traditionally this reconciliation was considered to be the basis of wisdom. However, by the late medieval period, a decline in metaphoric and symbolic understandings meant that many traditional ideas and practices had become hollow and empty;[9] these developments are related also to a weakening of the Church, which had long provided a foundation for spiritual meaning and material stability. As a consequence, the period we can refer to as *early modern*, approximately from the beginning of the 1400s to the beginning of the 1700s, witnessed a host of very significant societal changes.

THE BIRTH OF THE MODERN

With its roots in southern Europe, the Renaissance (ca. 1400s–1600s) is characterized by a self-conscious development of individuality, and the emergence of individualism and the modern identity.[10] Renaissance education, known as *Humanism*, included study of ancient Latin texts, Greek philosophy, logic and the art of rhetoric, as well as mathematics, music, science and an interest in comprehending and mastering the natural world; all with the aim of fulfilling worldly ambitions. In its earlier years at least, it was also a period of revitalized interest in metaphor, symbolism and understandings associated with intuitive ways of knowing and the human imagination. Hence, an upswing in the arts, literature, creativity and culture occurred, along with a renewed emphasis on moral philosophy, reason, logic and, eventually, the emergence of secularism and a rationalism that was well suited to the pursuit of more pragmatic, worldly endeavours. It was, therefore, a time of tolerance, open-mindedness and broadening horizons.[11, 12, 13] A new interest in exploration and discovery led to the appearance of merchant adventurers, who expanded trade routes to the east and searched out new opportunities to the west and the recently discovered Americas. In turn, these developments in international trade and the ensuing growth in commerce spurred improvements in business practices, many of which were imported from other cultures; new accounting methods, for example, were learned from Arabia. The 'bill of exchange' became a new way of securing sales and merchants also became bankers.[14]

However, along with these many and diverse developments, from which was born a new confidence and sense of purpose, there emerged unfamiliar tensions and uncertainties. Through rapid global expansionism, Europeans were brought into contact with other civilizations, other ideas and other religions.[15] The advent of technologies such as the printing press enabled these new ideas and discoveries to be widely disseminated. As a result, belief in established understandings and assumptions became less assured, and this fostered a growing sense of anxiety and doubt.[16] These developments are also linked to discord within the Church and dissent against institutionalized religion which, in the early years of the sixteenth century, resulted in that violent rupture in the Western spiritual tradition known as the Reformation.

Hence, this was a period that saw major developments in culture, science and technology and a significant and enduring transformation in values, priorities and worldview. It gave rise to modern notions of individualism and progress, it emphasized the power of reason, and it established social and cultural institutions that continue to define much of the Western world today, including modern conceptions of democratic politics. Exploration, colonization and commerce created enormous wealth for some, and established new banking practices and increases in consumption. These innovations sowed the seeds of modern banking, heralded the beginnings of contemporary capitalism and established the pattern for consumer society. This period also seems to have given rise to a belief in European cultural superiority (see below), the impacts of which are still felt today.

17

A NARROWING

Whereas the Renaissance witnessed a renewed interest in the arts along with developments in philosophy and reason, the Reformation was a period characterized by a rejection of imagery, metaphor and symbolism.[17, 18] There was an insistence on the ostensible 'certainties' associated with rational argument, analysis and explication, all of which are associated with the intellect and predominantly left-hemisphere brain functions.[19] With its roots in northwestern Europe, the Reformation (ca. 1500s–1600s) was a time of dissent against the Catholic Church, its practices, priorities and failings. It is noticeable that the new approach to faith centred on language, words and liturgy and that the reformers encouraged a literal reading of scripture and frowned upon allegorical interpretations. The pulpit became a prominent feature of many Protestant churches, and clerical hierarchy and control were maintained through highly vocal practices that afforded a new authority to the sermon.[20] Religious imagery, which had been accessible to all, including the illiterate, and was therefore an egalitarian aid to faith, was destroyed or covered over, and contemplative traditions and more solitary, silent spiritual practices were looked upon with suspicion and generally disfavoured.[21, 22] Protestantism tended to stress the rationality of Christianity, in contrast to the Catholic tradition, which encompassed metaphor, symbolism and the mysteries.[23, 24] Also, and uniquely in the history of Christianity, Protestantism sanctified individualism.[25] Hence, these reforms can be seen as an attempt to align religion with a broader societal insistence on rationality, empiricism and individualism – changes that tended to prioritize words over imagery; explication over silence; rationalism over symbolism; literalism over metaphor; action over contemplation; evidence over imagination; facts over values; and individual rights and freedoms over responsibilities towards community, society and the common good. Rowson and McGilchrist suggest that this is a dominant theme in the development of Western culture, whereby "the abstract, instrumental, articulate and assured left hemisphere has gradually usurped the more contextual, humane, systemic, holistic but relatively tentative and inarticulate right hemisphere".[26] It is particularly ironic that these developments were supported by religious reform because Philo, writing in the first century CE, warned against these exact same issues in his interpretations of the Bible. Indeed, Philo's analyses of the Genesis story of Cain and Abel parallel Rowson and McGilchrist's discussion of left- and right-hemisphere brain functions. Philo, a Platonist, interprets the figure of Cain, who is vocal and articulate, as representing the world of the senses and human folly, and Abel, who remains silent, as representing higher understandings, goodness and truth. Hence, when Cain kills Abel, rationalism, empiricism and human error override the holistic, the imaginative and deeper understandings of truth.[27, 28, 29]

Following on the heels of the Reformation, the European Enlightenment (ca. 1600s–1700s) saw these ideas become further embedded. This was a period of growing confidence in dispassionate, instrumental reason and decline in traditional understandings and notions of the sacred. There was a retreat from the more holistic outlooks of earlier times with their complementary ways of knowing, that is, rationalist–intellectual *and* imaginative–intuitive. Many traditions, customs and sacred rituals that acknowledged this sense of interdependent completeness were prohibited. There was a new optimism and a new sense of capacity, power and invulnerability in humanity's ability to determine right action through reason alone, and to order and shape the future by controlling both the material environment and the structures of society.[30, 31] It was a period that sought certainty through a rejection of all those aspects of our humanness that are ambiguous, mysterious or imaginative. Under the scrutiny of this rationalistic eye, ritual, ceremony, imagery and silence, which can all be rich in implicit and metaphorical meanings but do not seek to explain, came to be seen as impenetrable and absurd. Metaphor ceased to be regarded as integral to the conveyance of meaning, and the profundity of allegorical imagery was replaced by mere signs, superficial indicators of verbal meanings, but, in themselves, no longer embodiments of depth and meaningfulness. As a consequence, meaning became independent of form, which McGilchrist identifies as *"one of the most damaging legacies"* of this stage of Western development.[32] A new authority was granted to scientific and analytical methods, utilitarianism, materialism, secularism and the ideology of individualism. These are all elements of the era we refer to as *modernity*. Legitimate knowledge was to be grounded in provable facts and theoretical principles supported by scientific evidence. Predictably, this had the effect of undermining the import of the human imagination, intuitive apprehension and the contemplative path, all of which had been part of religious and spiritual practices and of notions of human wisdom for centuries.

There were some, of course, such as the poet William Blake, who opposed this attempt to discover the rights and responsibilities of humankind and the meaning and purpose of creation purely in terms of reason, regarding such a project as *"an impious denial of the sacred truth of the imagination"*.[33] Nonetheless, the ideas and proscriptions of this Age of Reason took hold and resulted in a narrower view of reality. It is this narrowed view of intellectual thinking, occidental rationalism and progressive technological means, but with little idea of ends, that is concomitant with what Weber referred to as the disenchantment of the modern world.[34]

In the same years that Blake was penning his poetry, Captain James Cook was sailing the world on his voyages of discovery. In March 1778, he anchored his ships *Resolution* and *Discovery* in the sheltered waters of Nootka Sound on the west coast of Vancouver Island. His journal of this interlude in his voyage north is notable both for what it says and how it says it. It is a systematic, rather meticulous inventory and classification of the land, its resources and its people. He lists the trees and their types, the animals, birds, fish, and minerals. There is a methodical itemization of the trade goods of local inhabitants, the various animal skins, fabrics and other materials, as well as the things they value most from the ships' stocks. He describes the size, shape and colour of the people themselves, their dress,

19

their jewellery and body decorations, their houses, furniture, weapons, arts, musical instruments, modes of transport, tools, social structure and language.[35] In other words, Cook's journal is written from a thoroughly modern perspective. It is an objective, evidence-based accounting, devoid of sentiment and reflection. The facts are laid out along with references to the monetary value of certain items and a keen awareness of their potential importance in commerce. It is a description that reveals a resolutely instrumental mindset about natural environments and other peoples. It is a mindset that was evident a little over a hundred years later when the loggers arrived to notch and fell the first-growth temperate rainforests. It is a mindset that persists to the present day, where the utilitarian and monetary value of 'resources' remains paramount.

In their style and tone, travel writings from non-modern, non-Western authors often exhibit a markedly different perspective. The eleventh-century *Record of Stone Bell Mountain* by Chinese author Su Shi, for instance, is no inventory of purely factual information. It weaves together description of place, imaginings, fears and follies. As the author seeks the truth behind the legend of Stone Bell Mountain, he reflects on human naivety and foolishness, how we decide what is true, and the obstacles to finding truth.[36] It is a piece of writing that is at once factual, philosophical, moral and reflective. As such it offers a far broader and deeper perspective on being human than the bare, utilitarian facts that preoccupy the modern eye.

These changing perceptions and priorities in Western society established the basis for advancement in scientific knowledge and discovery; the striving for objectivity; and the developments in technology, industry, production and growth that arose during the eighteenth and nineteenth centuries. The Industrial Revolution completely transformed ways of living and society as a whole. The transition from dispersed, rural craft-style production to factory production saw the rise of industrial capitalism along with massive urbanization. With expanding applications of mechanized production, this pattern continued into the twentieth century. Industry was gearing up for the mass production of identical, efficiently processed consumer products; this would eventually lead to the mass consumption of products and the attendant mass disposal of millions upon millions of tonnes of consumer waste. At the same time, influential voices in society were calling for an abandonment of the past and of traditional sources of knowledge and wisdom.[37, 38]

As in previous times, prominent figures from the arts, including Kafka, Huxley and Waugh, were expressing a deep sense of disquiet and regret at the loss of a critical part of our humanity.[39] However, the predominant view is evident in the following extract from a book for schoolchildren from 1945, when confidence in a future shaped by advances in science and technology was at a high point. *Miracles of Invention and Discovery* is introduced as follows:

> In the space around this world exist myriads of invisible waves carrying speech and music from one end of the globe to the other at the velocity of light. By means of comparatively thin wires, gigantic power is distributed from mighty generating stations to thousands of industrial plants. Glittering metal monsters bearing freight and passengers speed through the skies defying nature's law of gravity.
>
> These are just a few of the miracles that have been discovered and invented by man in his endless battles against time and the elements.[40]

This aggressive language of defiance and combat against nature's laws and the natural environment exposes an attitude that lies at the heart of today's environmental crisis and contemporary debates about sustainability. It is an attitude that endures to the present, emboldened by new advances in biosciences and digital technologies. It is revealed in the way in which today's scientific endeavours are supported largely on instrumental grounds rather than on the intrinsic value of science.[41, 42] It is an instrumental intent still permeated by the language of control and exploitation of nature, rather than by terms reflective of a more sensitive, symbiotic relationship. For instance, an eminent molecular scientist recently encouraged an audience of schoolchildren to consider a career in science by saying, *"Scientists are trying to find out enough about how bacteria work to be able to cleverly manipulate their behaviour … if you like the idea that you will be the first one to ever think about something on Earth and that you might actually change Earth by doing that, you should be a scientist".*[42] It is important to bear in mind, too, that the change enabled by scientific research, even with the best intentions of scientists, is developed and steered within a dominant milieu in which specialized knowledge is employed to win competitive advantage, maximize efficiencies and boost short-term financial gains. Within the corporate milieu the primary goal is neither social good nor environmental care but quarterly earnings.[43]

21

INDIVIDUALISM, SUPERIORITY AND MEANINGLESSNESS

Perhaps the most significant development of modernity has been the notion of individualism.[44] The systems and institutions that arose during this period of human history were designed to favour, protect and support the rights and privileges of the individual over common or collective interests. Both the free-market economy and political systems based on liberal democracy support individualism; indeed, individualism and contemporary models of democracy are intimately linked.[45] As we have seen, these developments occurred during a time of growing interest in the intellectual power of reason and legitimate knowledge was increasingly being linked to the methods and findings of science.[46, 47] While these reforms offered new possibilities for individual and political freedom, enterprise and wealth creation, they were also dogged by signs of dissonance and instability. There was an increasing sense of alienation, isolation and meaninglessness, which was associated with a denial of transcendence.[48, 49]

In addition, all these developments were bound up with empire, the foisting of Western ideas on other cultures and the positional superiority that accompanied European hegemony,[50, 51, 52] and they were followed by an enduring legacy of exploitation.[53, 54] Furthermore, the rise of individualism and self-interest, along with a philosophical outlook of materialism and the associated desacralization and disenchantment of the world,[55] removed any moral or spiritual barriers to the exploitation and eventual destruction of vast expanses of the natural environment. We would be remiss, therefore, to consider the achievements of modernity without also recognizing its severe and lasting impacts.

Significantly, many of these occurrences were based in abstraction and reductionism, and this inclination meant that the role and contribution of other ways of knowing became less important. These include intuition, creativity, tacit knowledge and more holistic understandings that depend on direct experience.[56] Critically, a recognition of the importance of both these ways of encountering the world, which are divergent but complementary, yields a far more comprehensive and empathetic outlook.

Thus, the modern sensibility, despite its many, many achievements and benefits, actually represents a profound contraction or disambiguation in understandings – a narrowing of outlook that prioritizes certain aspects of the human condition to the detriment of others.[57, 58] And it is this constricted, partial view that is inextricably linked not only to enormous social and environmental impacts but also to the deep sense of meaninglessness and ennui that has always shadowed this period in human development.

POWER, CAPITALISM AND BUREAUCRACY

Accompanying modernity's philosophical, scientific and technological developments was a will to power that became manifested in the form of capitalism and was attended by a rise in bureaucracies.[59] Traditional understandings that recognized cycles and repetitions, offered continuity and change, and possessed both instrumental and intrinsic value became less important. They either faded away or took on new guises to fit within the predominant, more pragmatic, especially market-led, rationale.

These attitudes and understandings still prevail in our political, educational, and public and private sector organizations. Their bureaucratic tendencies and narrow economic priorities are illustrated in some disturbing approaches to environmental issues. For example, much effort is currently being put into the measurement, quantification and monetization of nature. Under the auspices of so called ecosystem services, the aim is to allocate a financial value to streams, wetlands, species and even to the aesthetic and spiritual value of natural places and vistas.[60, 61] This reliance on numbers gives the approach an appearance of neutrality and objectivity which, in reality, masks a gross oversimplification that is anything but objective. Costs and prices are selectively allocated and transient social artefacts are based on subjective decision-making. Consequently, these attempts to use bureaucratic, market-led modes where other, broader forms of governance are needed have *"led to a dangerous collusion between entrenched financial and corporate interests, on the one hand, and entire natural ecosystems, on the other"*.[62] The result is that we allocate a price to that which is priceless, and nature becomes just another commodity.

While giving precedence to such methods may be misguided, they do illustrate the sheer power and persistence of the unmodulated rationalistic outlook. By maintaining this outlook, we compromise our thinking and our ability to tackle the critical issues of our time. It leads to deeply distorted ideas about knowledge, the world and the nature of the human condition and it is leading us down a path of worsening social inequity and remorseless environmental destruction.

On occasions, however, we do see encouraging exceptions to this general path – realizations that complementary ways of encountering the world are needed. One example comes from the field of medicine, where a

23

professor of cardiovascular research at UCL and Yale launched a poetry competition for his students because he feared they were becoming too narrowly focussed and *"intellectually brutalized"*.[63]

EMBEDDED UNSUSTAINABILITY

From the foregoing we see that the political and corporate agendas of contemporary Western societies, which are firmly established in a growth-based capitalist system, are deeply rooted in historical events and fuelled by scientific progress and technological advancement. It is a system driven by product innovation and production that is heavily – many would say ruinously – dependent on natural resources, energy use and ever-expanding markets. On the grounds of delivering increased consumer choice, it promotes overproduction, and, consequently, massive waste is an inherent part of its constitution. As markets and choices expand and as product disposal and replacement cycles become ever more rapid – a condition vigorously encouraged by advertising – demands on the earth's materials, energy resources and natural ecologies escalate. This upward trend shows no signs of abatement despite higher energy efficiencies and improved material intensities.[64, 65, 66]

24

It is a system that also has severely damaging social consequences. First, the competitive individualism it promotes through production of status-oriented 'positional goods' is insidiously divisive.[67] Second, because of its links to an increased sense of dissatisfaction, stress and depression, the multiplication of choices can be detrimental to individual welfare.[68] Third, disparities between wages have increased enormously over the last few decades,[69, 70, 71] whereas research suggests that greater equality is the route to a society improving *everyone's* quality of life, including the most well-off, and is a necessary facet of a sustainable economic system.[72] Hence, rather than being a benefit to society, this kind of consumer capitalism is, in reality, highly damaging. The social good is not served by maximizing the personal wealth of the few while continually sowing seeds of envy and discontent.

Finally, and with disturbing parallels to the colonialism of former times, today's emphasis on globalization, free trade and the export of Western-style democracy and consumer culture to other societies is a form of cultural imperialism that is innately inequitable – the essential premise being that the forms of governance, society, economics, culture and thinking developed and maintained among Western nations are incontrovertibly correct and need to be adopted by all other nations, irrespective of their own particular traditions, cultures or points of view.[73] However, as Said has pointed out, there is *"a profound difference between the will to understand [other peoples] for purposes of co-existence and humanistic enlargement of horizons, and the will to dominate for the purposes of control and external dominion"*,[74] whether that be for political control, for resources, or for expansion of markets. Nevertheless, by invitation, persuasion or other means, the lifestyles and consumer cultures that became common in the 'developed' nations of Europe, North America, Japan and Australasia over the course of the twentieth century are, in the twenty-first, being adopted globally. Roughly half the world's 'consumer class' is now located in the 'developing' world.[75] This, despite the fact that these forms of consumer capitalism and the lifestyles they engender are proving to be entirely antithetical to contemporary notions of sustainability.

Notwithstanding their widespread adoption and seeming intractability, these perspectives, priorities and systems have all been created by people. They are also relatively recent. There have been, and in some parts of the world still are, ways of living that are very different from those we consider normal. Those of us who live in the West have little justification to deem it our right to enlighten those living in other nations or to cause them – through imposition, punitive sanctions, coercion or seduction – to adopt our ways of civil order, economic growth and consumer culture, along with their inevitable social and environmental repercussions. Rather than constantly seeking to expand our markets and global influence, we have the opportunity to learn from those who retain less destructive, more socially cohesive ways of living. And, importantly, we have the potential to change – to listen, learn and do things differently in order to curtail the rapacious destruction of nature and the promulgation of a form of individualism that is both divisive and increasingly perfunctory and aimless. Historian Eamon Duffy has characterized contemporary Western society as being dominated by a system in which people are dehumanized and isolated, and that has promoted an idea of freedom as unrestricted individualism. This has resulted in the depletion of collective understandings along with the common language that enables such understandings to blossom. Related to this, he argues that Western society's emphasis on the acquisition of more and more knowledge will never allow us to appreciate the goodness of reality and our place in it.[76] To have such an appreciation, fidelity to the heritage of human wisdom is required; a heritage of insight and understanding that spans history and draws from all civilizations. In Western society, after years of

25

conscientiously rejecting the past as 'old hat' and looking only to the future, such an appreciation demands a new sense of humility. It also means reversing worrying trends of political interference in education curricula in which preferential support is given to those subjects deemed to be useful to the economy, and where support is withdrawn from other critical areas.[77, 78] It is only through a more comprehensive education that, as a society, we can gain a sense of the importance of this heritage of wisdom, which, in turn, provides a basis for commitment to broader considerations and deeper values.

BEYOND INDIVIDUALISM AND THE INADEQUACY OF PROGRESS

It is evidently the case that knowledge arising from investigation and experiment, rational analysis, theory development and explication can accrue over time. And it follows that human understanding based on such knowledge is able to progress. Also, from the foregoing, it is clear that this form of knowledge became increasingly privileged during the modern period and, to a large extent, this tendency continues to the present day. As a result, other kinds of knowledge have become devalued and less prominent in the centre ground of public discourse. These other kinds of knowledge, which would seem important to modulating human behaviour and achieving a more balanced worldview, are not and can never be cumulative in society as a whole, and they stand outside the overly narrow interpretation of progress described above. These are the kinds of knowledge that are located in and have to be learned by each individual in his or her journey through life. Furthermore, and even though the meaning-seeking, spiritual apprehension seems to be common to us all and a feature of our humanness,[79, 80] many of these other kinds of knowledge are neither transferable nor shareable.[81] They are subjective, experiential, intuitive and tacit. They relate to the ways in which we encounter and interpret the world around us, to the ways in which we learn to behave within our physical and social environments. These ways of knowing are holistic rather than reductionist, they are concerned with subjective experiences rather than objective facts and they enable us to synthesize the bigger picture rather than analyze its particulars. They are associated with knowledge and understandings in context, with spiritual well-being and inner values, and the development of character, conscience and notions of what is right and good. It is these kinds of knowledge that can inform our judgements and temper what we are *capable* of doing by giving due consideration to what we *ought* to be doing. However, as MacIntyre has explained, these traditional ways of knowing are dependent on two essential concepts, *narrative unity* and *practice*. *Narrative unity* pertains to the individual person, the subject of a narrative that begins at birth and continues until death. It is this narrative unity that allows a person to be accountable for all the activities, decisions and experiences that make up his or her life story. It is tied to unity of character and hence to one's sense of personal identity.[82] It is also the case that a person is not only accountable for their own life but because lives are interwoven one can ask of, and be expected to be accountable to, others; hence individual narratives are interrelated and interdependent. This effectively counters the ideology of individualism, which has become such a prominent feature of contemporary society, but it does not compromise the importance of personal character and individuality. Rather it recognizes the relationship between individual persons, community and society as a whole.

The unity of an individual life is the unity of the narrative embodied by that life, and this is intimately related to notions of virtue and practice. It raises questions about how best to live out that unity, about how one *should* live. *Practice* in this context refers to activities and decisions that are sustained by a disposition of virtue, which helps us negotiate a path in life that strives to avoid harmful and immoderate or selfish behaviours. In turn, such practice increases our self-discipline, self-knowledge and understandings of the good.[83]

The period of modernity tended to erode these holistic, unified notions of a human life. Areas of knowledge became divided into specialized silos – pure sciences, applied sciences, social sciences, fine arts and applied arts. Similarly, an individual's life became divided into discrete segments, each characterized by its own distinct qualities, norms and modes of behaviour – work, leisure, public life, private life, childhood, adolescence, old age.

A consequence of these moves towards compartmentalization is that the narrative unity of an individual's life becomes lost and with it our notions of personal identity, character, conscience, duty and accountability.[84] This lack of accountability is reflected in globalized practices where the division of labour fragments human activities, thereby preventing holistic understandings of actions and their consequences and effectively permitting the avoidance of responsibility.[85]

Thus, historical developments in how we think about ourselves and our world and the loss of narrative unity and associated practices have all contributed to our contemporary worldview.

27

DESIGN AND THE NATURE OF CHANGE

The narrowed worldview of modernity/late modernity is still a relatively recent phenomenon, one that was preceded, as we have seen, by more holistic outlooks in which beliefs and ritual played a prominent role in influencing behaviours.[86] With particular relevance to design, it is only with the enormous expansions of mass production and mass consumption since the mid-twentieth century that the tangible consequences of this constricted view have become widely recognized in terms of their maturation, magnitude and severity. In this period, not only has production efficiency based on a strict economic logic become paramount but theoretical ideas have also played an increasingly important role;[87] and theories are a form of rationalized abstraction that concern general rules – they do not deal with concrete realities in context.

Design, however, is an applied discipline that does deal with concrete realities and if it is to deal with these in context, it will need to move away from its allegiance to corporate agendas aimed at generalized mass production for global distribution. Approaches are required that are far more sensitive to individual needs, social and cultural diversity, the qualities of locale and the interrelated effects of material consumption. Furthermore, our ability to sympathetically elucidate design in context is dependent on the fact that, in purpose and practice, design is a discipline that is integrative. It brings together and seeks to synthesize rationality, efficiency and instrumental value with imagination, inspiration and intrinsic value. It makes use of data, reasoned argument and expert knowledge but also draws on experience, aesthetic sensitivity and tacit knowledge. By attempting to reconcile and harmonize these complementarities within a particular context, design can contribute to a sense of narrative unity. Connections are created between human needs and tasks, materials, place, knowledge and skills, effects and implications. In this way, our activities become contextualized, comprehended and, over time, adjusted in order to be in accord with individual needs, social and cultural conditions, and the characteristics of place. All these things help build a more profound sense of meaningfulness, and they are the very things that have to be restored if we are to effectively address the burgeoning challenges of sustainability.

There are strong parallels here between an argument for the importance of localized design and making and Duffy's discussion about the value of folk traditions in religion. At first glance, local practices can seem narrow and parochial, and they tend to be governed by rules of behaviour and expectations that may seem onerous and overly restrictive to the modern eye. Yet, folk traditions and, similarly, localized design and making practices can bear fruit that is critical for the appreciation and stewardship of nature, for collective understandings and community cohesion and, at a personal level, for a more profound sense of purpose and meaning. Their very rootedness in the earthy realities of life gives them a truth untainted by marketing hyperbole and glitzy facade. Being localized, their implications and repercussions are more fully known and, consequently, responsibilities can be properly acknowledged and borne. In the case of localized design and making, such traditions are not subject to the compartmentalizing of tasks, the dissipating of accountability or the externalizing of production costs, such as pollution, health care and social deprivation, that otherwise could have a negative effect on the corporate bottom line. In addition, localized, collective practices embedded in community represent a strong counterpoint to contemporary individualism. They are less dependent on the points of view or feelings of the individual, but are instead grounded in historical precedent and collective understandings, and it is these very attributes that help contextualize the lives of individuals and in the process offer a sense of integrity, dignity, continuity and meaning.[88] Hence, such practices help restore a sense of narrative unity to our lives.[89]

29

CONCLUSIONS

I worry that a very narrow perspective on what
it means to be a human being is the only view
that has any currency at the moment

Sarah Teather[90]

Present concerns about social inequity, environmental degradation and the loss of a sense of meaning are inextricably linked to the conventions, doctrines and societal norms that took hold during the period of modernity. Of these, the ideology of individualism, which perhaps reached its culmination during the 1980s with the so-called free market policies of Reagan and Thatcher,[91, 92] can be seen as the central accomplishment of this phase in the evolution of Western thought.[93] It is apparent, too, that concerns about sustainability will not be addressed effectively or extensively by simply continuing in the same vein, perhaps with incremental adjustments here and there. The growth-oriented, consumption-based economic system that has come to dominate modern societies is inherently socially divisive, excessively dependent on natural resource use and waste production, and intimately bound up with a loss of meaning. In this light, ecosystem service models that attempt to monetize and marketize nature are a continuation of the prevailing thinking. Similarly, rationalized, 'objective' numerical approaches, such as product life-cycle assessment, not only tend to mask the subjectivity of the decision-making involved, but also fix our attention on incremental improvements to an inherently problematic system.[94] Again, the established instrumental focus of design as a 'problem-solving' activity that leads to improved technological solutions represents a continuation of the same kind of thinking, rather than any innovative shift in thinking.[95]

To address the challenges wrought by this overly narrow outlook, which Nagel argues *"is ripe for replacement"*,[96] we first have to consider a restoration of ways in which ethics and self-transcendence (bigger-than-self) values and priorities can become integrated in our business practices. It becomes necessary to recognize that the dominance of reductionist, evidence-based research and rational argument can bring us only so far[97] and that decision-making has to take into consideration not just what is most efficient and financially profitable within the boundaries of the law but also questions of what is meaningful, right and good. This amounts to a recognition of the importance of complementarities and a restoration of the balance they imply.

Design can contribute to this change by developing creative works that imbue our visual and material culture and our day-to-day activities with something of those ways of knowing that have become progressively devalued and neglected in recent times – the tacit, the intuitive, the meaningful and the profound. Among the various professions involved in the creation and production of our material things, it is the designer who has the wherewithal and the responsibility to visually express imaginative, constructive ways forward. If sensitively considered in relation to context, the designer's contribution can play an important role in restoring complementarities and narrative unity and repositioning outlooks and attitudes. Such design work will stand in contrast to predominant norms – implicitly asking us to reflect on these differences, the values they represent and their relationship to self, others and the world.

3
Counterpoints restoring balance through design

on the contrary, it will do very well.

Jane Austen

INTRODUCTION

The basic rules of optics tell us that, when we look at the world through a microscope or a telescope, the greater the magnification, the smaller our field of view. The more we seek to know about the details, the more difficult it is to discern how they connect up and the less understanding we have about their value and meaning in the bigger scheme of things.

In recent times, we have placed great emphasis on the acquisition of detailed facts about the visible, physical world. This has led to major advances in knowledge, especially in the natural sciences, which has been used to develop extraordinary material capabilities and benefits. It is also true that these things have been achieved at great cost to people and planet. At the same time, less attention has been paid to the bigger scheme of things – to questions about where we are heading and what it is all for. We seem to have become so mired in facts and information that we can no longer see the wood for the trees. But we should not think that clear-cutting the forest will improve our vision. A better plan would be to step back and look at our activities from a different angle – an angle that may yield broader meanings.

While we may not be able to focus on detailed facts and broader meanings simultaneously, when put together they allow us to gain a far more balanced view of our activities, our world and ourselves. With mounting social inequity and environmental problems, it is imperative that we learn to see our endeavours, our notions of progress and our approaches to technology and consumption from a different perspective. In this, design has the potential to make a thoughtful and imaginative contribution by creatively challenging established norms and visualizing more considered and considerate ways forward; ways that synthesize longer-term, bigger-picture questions about values and purpose with detailed attention to utility, context and people.

Critical to this discussion is the recognition that any attempts to address the social and environmental problems of our times in a significant and lasting manner will depend first and foremost, not on physical changes, technological innovation and the implementation of specific measures, but on a changed philosophical outlook or reconstituted worldview. It is, therefore, pointless to go about implementing concrete changes without first considering this core outlook.[1] For example, if our view is such that we see practical endeavours as a route to continual progress, then we will especially value knowledge acquisition, innovation, new activities and material improvements. On the other hand, if we hold that progress is about seeking deeper understandings of human purpose and ultimate meaning, then inner development, reflection and material simplicity will be valued. There may be many shades of grey between these two poles, but the important point is that our philosophical outlook determines how we make judgements about our activities, their purpose and their merit. Therefore, at a time when so many of our endeavours are closely linked to social and environmental damage, we should look first at ourselves and our ingrained beliefs and assumptions.

This discussion begins by examining the priorities of the worldview that predominates among contemporary, economically developed countries. It is shown that the emphasis on rationalism and evidence-based, accountable facts, the growth in bureaucracies, and a bolstering of individualism, as established in Chapter 2, go hand in hand with a decline in empathy, ethical behaviour, social obligation and environmental care. The argument is made that to deal effectively with the negative consequences of this worldview it is necessary to develop a new kind of normal, one that recognizes more profound notions of meaningfulness. These ideas are associated with creativity, the human imagination, the synthesis of the rational with the intuitive, and the development of a more comprehensive sense of narrative unity. For these very reasons, design, both as process and outcome, is an appropriate means of contributing to positive change. Through design, we can both visualize the limitations of our current modes and demonstrate creative possibilities based on new understandings. Design is considered here in terms of the effects of its outcomes – the designed artefact, its production, its use and its presence in the world. In working towards positive change, the role of the designed artefact is discussed in relation to several design approaches: incremental improvements to products within the current production system; grassroots development of alternative approaches; objects that provide a focus for contemplation and deeper understandings; counterpoints that critique current norms by expressing a contrasting position; and holistic approaches to design, called here *rhythmical objects*, that encapsulate practices and values conducive to contemplation and systemic change. In this chapter, several examples of counterpoint objects are presented that demonstrate how design can be employed to challenge norms and manifest ethical considerations. Further variants that address the loss of avenues to meaning and re-seeing the familiar are included respectively in Chapters 6 and 8. Rhythmical objects are discussed in Chapter 7.

33

THE CRUX OF THE PROBLEM

All around the globe roads are jammed, airports are at capacity, construction and concrete relentlessly consume natural environments, and a continuous stream of information clamours for our attention, persuading us that we need a new product or service. Meanwhile, escalating emissions and growing socioeconomic disparities bear witness to the fact that the world is too busy, too ambivalent or simply too enamoured with its own immediate preoccupations for any substantial commitment to environmental stewardship and the common good. Indeed, there is a woeful irony and an inherent inconsistency in politicians signing up to environmental targets and standards while simultaneously striving for more innovation, more production, more consumption, more exports and more growth. This fundamental contradiction has resulted in years of evasion and obfuscation, in commitments without conviction,[2] a decline in business ethics,[3] a reduction in empathy,[4] false expectations and a gnawing sense that today's harried preoccupations are stealing the future.[5] We have created a way of life in which sufficiency has no merit – a way of life without silence, foresight, reflection or wisdom. It is self-evident that a wise society does not knowingly destroy the very ecosystems on which it depends for survival. A wise society does not create social divisions so egregious that the result is ubiquitous despair, discord and conflict. A wise society does not permit the spending of billions each year sowing the seeds of dissatisfaction among its citizens to encourage them to buy products they do not need and that the planet cannot afford. The pity is that, in the process, a Paradise Lost has been conjured from our downward glance; the so-called developed societies have, in the words of Milton, "ransacked the centre, and with impious hands / Rifled the bowels of their mother Earth / For treasures better hid".[6]

As I discussed in the previous chapter, the dominance of individualism, materialism and rationalism in Western society, and their global repercussions lie at the heart of today's increasingly grave condition. The advances in science, technology and industry that led to rapid urbanization naturally caused drastic reductions in rural populations.[7] This social transformation created a physical distancing from natural cycles, seasonal rhythms and shared understandings of the natural world. And shifting priorities and roles, the division of knowledge into narrow specialisms, and the resulting, severely atrophied view of the world eroded both narrative unity and individual accountability.

This focus on specialized knowledge and the ability to manipulate and control the physical world is part of a dominant culture of instrumental rationality. In this culture, pragmatic problem solving is pursued for profit, which means that scientific discoveries are rapidly transformed into technological applications. Such applications are the drivers of mass production, mass consumerism and economic growth. It should also be appreciated that science, quite naturally, expands the kinds of knowledge that fall within its own sphere of inquiry. Moreover, these areas of knowledge and their significant contribution and value tend to be viewed within a materialistic perspective rather than within a broader compass that embraces ethics, human values and ends.[8]

Such knowledge and its acquisition can be articulated, explained and demonstrated. In contrast, intuition and inner values are concerned with matters that are intangible and often inexpressible in words; attempts at description or explanation tend to be less definitive and more hesitant.[9]

Thus, the logic and lucidity of reason combined with the weight of verifiable data have had the effect of overshadowing and devaluing the significance of intuitive ways of knowing and in the process our understandings have become more limited. As a consequence, science's idea of its own importance has tended to become inflated[10] and other areas of human understanding, critical to individual well-being and social welfare, have become diminished.

These relatively recent developments go against centuries of teachings that regarded the types of useful or pragmatic knowledge that modern society holds so dear as relatively insignificant compared to the kinds of inner knowledge on which questions of meaning, values and human purpose depend.[11, 12] Deeper understandings, which transcend purely rational explanation, arise from a combination of study, practice and reflection, and they are intimately linked to more holistic apprehensions of reality and a sense of unity or wholeness.[13, 14, 15] Specialization based on abstraction and rational analysis tends to obscure this more holistic view. Connections and interactions among different aspects of human activity, and their cumulative effects on people, society and the natural environment, become opaque to us, and, in so doing, their implications go unheeded.

These conditions have contributed to a decline in a sense of meaningfulness in our endeavours,[16] and a loss of social continuity and cohesion – for example, growth in consumerism is linked to a weakening of community life.[17] In recent times, immoral and even criminal behaviours among those in prominent positions are one symptom of this deficiency in narrative unity and the associated sense of responsibility on which an ethics of virtue, social justice and communal trust depend. Such behaviours have occurred across a wide spectrum of society and include self-enriching and illegal practices among bankers;[18, 19] expenses scandals among politicians;[20] sexual abuse of minors by priests and media personalities;[21, 22] and unlawful phone hacking by journalists, linked with police corruption.[23] These, together with revelations of secretive citizen surveillance practices on a global scale by government agencies,[24] tend to undermine confidence and trust in the traditional 'pillars of society'. Such examples indicate that the extraordinary advances we have made in science and technology have not been attended by a corresponding progression in moral character and, at the risk of sounding quixotically old-fashioned, in leading what we might refer to as a virtuous and upright life in which a developed sense of goodness, right action and justice permeates all aspects of our activities.

Rationalistic, instrumental endeavours that rely on analytical and accountable approaches may be rich in data and detail, but they tend to lack bigger-picture perspectives and a unifying sense of purpose, and they are closely associated with the rise of individualism. In turn, because of its promotion of self-enhancement values and individual rights over self-transcendence values and the common good, individualism is associated with a rise in social inequity and with the objectification and rapacious exploitation of the natural environment.[25] In the latter case, the destruction continues to grow despite decades of environmentalism and widespread awareness of the impacts; annual climate-changing emissions from human activities are still increasing at alarming rates.[26] The rise of individualism means that care for the commons – the atmosphere, oceans, fresh water systems, forests, biodiversity, public space – is in free fall.

This individualistic, instrumental view of reality, with its depreciation of communal goods and its prioritization of the market, also results in enormous socioeconomic inequities both within the economically developed countries themselves and between the richer West and the so-called undeveloped or developing nations.[27, 28, 29] And, as we have seen, contemporary, secular democracy and individualism go together. In the period of colonialism people who for millennia had lived in harmony with natural systems became subjugated and exploited and had their lands taken from them. In post-colonial times, many of the same attitudes prevail with a host of countries being deemed by Western powers to be in need of development. Young and others have made the point that these countries have gone from being colonies of Western powers, to independence, to 'in dependence'. Through organizations like the World Bank, the International Monetary Fund and the World Trade Organization – all of which are dominated by the Western powers – these 'dependent' nations become cripplingly indebted and exploited for their labour and their resources. And those who attempt to oppose this subjugation often feel the full wrath of Western displeasure through punitive sanctions or military force, until such time as compliance is achieved.[30, 31] This domination is further reinforced by the Internet. The vast majority of information available on the Web, via sources such as Google and Wikipedia, is produced and controlled by the richer nations – predominantly those of Europe and North America. It is often thought that a lack of connectivity is the main obstacle to the democratization of information, but the problem is larger and more complex. Lack of representation and participation in contributing to the information that is available is related to social disparities, economic inequalities, regulation, infrastructure and politics. This raises real concerns that the worldview and areas of knowledge that dominate Europe and North

America become reinforced by the Internet, and that other worldviews, perspectives and ways of knowing become drowned out.[32] An additional consideration here is that the kinds of knowledge and information that can be conveyed via the Internet are those that can be described effectively through words, i.e. explanatory and factual knowledge that provide details and specificities about discrete topics – the very kinds of knowledge that have been prioritized in the West since the Enlightenment. Consequently, by their absence, there is a danger that forms of knowledge that lie beyond words, that are tacit, and are known through the human imagination and through practice and experience become even further devalued and marginalized because of their inability to be effectively conveyed by such media. In turn, as Internet penetration continues to increase around the world, cultures that have traditionally maintained more holistic and balanced worldviews, and have valued more intuitive, tacit ways of knowing based on direct experience, are having their perspectives narrowed. With greater access to online information and advertising, the ideas and priorities of the rich Global North become increasingly influential. Research at the Oxford Internet Institute into the availability of recorded knowledge on the Web reveals patterns of widening inequality, increasing informational poverty and deep structural biases, including gender biases;[33] in effect, this state of affairs amounts to a kind of informational imperialism.

37

TOWARDS A NEW NORMAL

Even though empiricism, reason and rational argument were afforded a privileged position during modernity,[34] a position largely maintained in the present period of late-modernity, their limitations in answering deeper questions about values and purpose have been recognized for millennia.[35] The early Christian theologian Augustine of Hippo warned against reducing our understandings to prosaic, factual levels of interpretation where we take metaphor and figurative expression in a literal sense and seek explanation rather than meaning. We are capable of deeper understandings that lie beyond words – understandings that can be known to oneself and perceived in some sense by others.[36] Rationality, positive knowledge, and empirical evidence about the material world are certainly vital aspects of human knowledge and understanding; they are necessary and important but they are not sufficient. Embracing the intellectual *and* the intuitive, the objective *and* the subjective recognizes the importance of the whole person, in the fullness of their being.

Significantly, too, rational argument contains no criterion for truth; equal conviction can be elicited on both sides of a debate. Rational argument may allow us to see an issue from different perspectives, which can help clarify our views, but discursive thought *per se* does not provide a benchmark for determining what is right and true. Similarly, scientific accomplishments and discoveries that expand our understandings of the world and the universe can fill us with awe and inspire us, but judgements of value do not rest on existential facts. The worth of such information can be appraised one way or another, according to one's a priori viewpoint.[37] We can also turn to human history for precedents and insights, but what we make of the historical evidence will very much depend on the philosophical views we are holding when we set about our enquiries.[38] Authoritative texts such as scripture are, in themselves, also inadequate. We can certainly view such texts favourably if they represent an authentic account of the inner experience, despite any errors and discrepancies they may contain.[39] However, we must also bear in mind that their use of language is often figurative and they require careful interpretation. They frequently contain passages that are, ostensibly, contradictory and it is perfectly possible to elicit equally compelling but conflicting interpretations from the same passages;[40] and, importantly, any interpretation we make will be coloured by our own pre-existing philosophical outlook.

Whether we turn to worldly facts and explanations, rational argument, history or authoritative texts, ultimately it is not through these external things that we find meaning and a sense of purpose and value in our lives. Questions about existential knowledge have to be addressed via suprarational means[41] and, naturally, to do this we have to consider the person, the individual subject in the world. Human beings have ideas and experiences that have no objective existence and cannot be explained rationally or even fully expressed. Rather, it is through the imagination that we are able to find meaning, value and purpose – be this through engagement in the arts or through religious practice. This is a world not of observable facts but of first-person experiences and relationships. It is the living, contingent world of 'I' in the world, of self-awareness, being and belonging, I–You encounters, intentions and accountability, virtue and vice, which is quite different from the world as described by the systematic explanations of science. Indeed, it is a world that is incommensurable with science because it involves subjective knowledge and experiences and concepts of personhood that do not figure in the kinds of explanations provided by science. This is the life-world that presupposes and emerges from physical reality.[42] Observable facts will never provide us with an adequate means for grasping what a symphony or a poem is about.[43] We can read explanations and arguments about the significance of a Pollock painting, and we can study and analyze its individual drips as much as we like, but we must stand back and experience it as a whole if we are to appreciate it as a work of art for ourselves. For many kinds of human expression – be they through words, music, art or religion – their form and content must resonate with the human imagination and take us on journeys of the mind. Only then can we 'see' their power and significance; that is, when we connect them to what is fundamental to our own inner being.

The ideology of individualism is also related to our notions of the 'outer', the 'inner' and the holistic. While individuality is an important facet of our being, we are also members of family groups, social groups and communities and we have a moral duty to consider others as well as ourselves. In the context of developing new, substantive directions that are capable of coming to grips with the critical social and environmental challenges of our time, as well as notions of personal meaning and individual fulfilment, it becomes necessary to look again at this ideology, particularly its rather extreme late-modern form. It is an ideology that assigns ethical pre-eminence to the values, interests and rights of the individual, over and above collective interests and the common good. Being a product of modernity, it is also bound up with rationalism, materialism and an idea of the person as an objective observer of the world 'out there'. While this view is important, it is not the whole picture. Another understanding sees the individual as part of the world. These notions of *detached observer* and *person within the world* are complementary; both views contribute to our understandings of reality. The first focusses on the details while the second allows an integrated awareness of the whole. But it is the first, with its ability for reasoned argument, explanation and analysis that has come to dominate Western society, with a corresponding devaluing of the experiential, imaginative and implicit kinds of knowledge that allow for the more synthetical view of the *person within the world*, which forms the basis of empathy.[44]

Many of the deficits of consumer society can be linked to this emphasis on 'detached' notions of individualism within a culture of instrumental reason. There is a strong relationship between these priorities and the objectification and domination of other peoples and the natural environment. Not only does instrumental reason have nothing to say about the ends to

39

which it is applied or about a sense of deeper human purpose[45] but also specialist arguments can serve to effectively block the more profound and, arguably today, more critical 'larger' perspective.[46] This narrow view of reality is associated with a strident techno-scientific optimism that, in turn, has generated an unprecedented dependency on sophisticated, sometimes worryingly intrusive, technologies. The effects of this ideology are far-reaching and they tend to further bolster individualism. Our production and use of millions upon millions of electronic devices, along with our seemingly endless desire for the very latest models, are stoked by a consumer capitalist system that constantly promotes self-interest and self-centred, immoderate behaviours that effectively reify individualism. Moreover, use of these screen-based gadgets distances us physically and mentally from each other and from direct experience of the natural world – offering only filtered, meagre glimpses of a richer reality. Drawing on the work of Lyotard, Sim contends that these developments in techno-science and corporate capitalism are wholly unconducive to the rhythms and patterns of human life because they create externally driven directives related to power, control and the demand for efficiency.[47]

40　　A more integrated outlook would seek to reconcile those aspects of ourselves related to *detached observer* with those of *person within the world.* This is critical to our understandings of sustainable futures because those who consider themselves part of a greater whole are in a better position to recognize their interdependencies and their responsibilities towards community, society and the natural environment. Compassionate concern for others and the world is not at odds with an individual sense of self. Indeed, it is strongly connected to the development of inner values and spiritual well-being.[48] Hence, a tempering of individualism is not a rejection of the importance of the individual, nor is it a rejection of the individual contribution, including individual creativity. In fact, there is a vital need for greater attention to individual creativity and the conditions that foster it. A retreat from immoderate, self-centred individualism can yield a view of individuality that fosters integration, synthesis and self-transcendence values. In turn, the cultivation of self-transcendence values accords with a more holistic outlook and the common good.

Problems arise when narrow ways of thinking and limited aspects of human knowledge come to be regarded as the *only* ways of encountering the world – to the exclusion of others. When this happens, they become intransigent ideologies. One example is religious dogmatism, which was prevalent in the West in pre-modern times and is still evident in many places today. In the economically developed world the dominant ideologies take a secular form – materialism, rationalism and individualism all play a major role, pervading everything from politics to business to education. And despite longstanding criticisms from many quarters,[49, 50] these severely limited doctrines continue to restrict our outlooks and our perceptions of reality, and they are taking us down a dangerous path. Science and technology are held in great esteem, and imaginative, mythic forms of thought have come to be regarded as largely irrelevant to modern society. This is not only unparalleled in human history but it is also a category mistake to think of poetry, myth, spirituality and religion in terms of logical argument and factual information, and on that basis dismiss them as inferior or peripheral to the main business of society. Many aspects of human thought and experience that draw on the imagination help align us psychologically or spiritually with ethical behaviour and long-established notions of virtue, compassion and reciprocity.[51] Such thinking allows us to transcend the prosaic realm of objective facts to attain a more integrated, unified appreciation of existence. It is this so-called perennial philosophy that provides a basis for our notions of goodness and right action.[52] All these aspects of life are indiscernible to the observations of science and are quite different from the kinds of knowledge that science can provide. They are not fully expressible or explainable through language, but can be known – at least to some extent – internally, tacitly and experientially. These critically important but rather inscrutable facets of human knowledge have tended to become devalued as contemporary culture has become increasingly preoccupied with material benefits and technological potential.

41

Hence, while explicit, codified forms of knowledge can contribute to our understandings, they are not the whole story. We also need to synthesize these discrete aspects of knowledge into a coherent whole – and this requires personal commitment, discipline and work. Integrative ways of knowing are critically related to sense-making, meaning-making and inner values. Importantly, they are rooted in the subject, in direct experience, and tacit rather than explicit knowledge. It is this synthesis that allows us to see the bigger picture along with and through the practical aspects of day-to-day living. Our responses to these deeper, but indefinable questions find expression in the arts and in symbolism. These represent an equally valid but quite different kind of knowledge from the facts, figures, data and descriptions about the world that emerge from science. They are related to silence and contemplation, and affirmed by intuitive apprehensions of reality.

And they are the basis for attaining profound understandings of what we hold to be true.[53, 54] Eagleton refers to these deeper ways of knowing as the 'eloquent silence' at the heart of the subject, which is always prior to the human-made phenomenal world of objects and reasons.[55] To know that acts such as slavery are wrong requires a prior belief in its injustice.[56] Subsequently, one may attempt to defend this position through argument, empirical evidence or external authority, but whether by reason, evidence or dogma, such means can elicit equal conviction on both sides of the debate.

Intuition (inner perception) and intellect (capacity for rational thought) are complementary and interrelated. Through the fusion of the holistic and imaginative with the particular and the rational we are able to look back, learn and build meaning from the past as we explore new possibilities and look to the future. Together they offer a broader and deeper picture of reality than the reductionist outlook that has dominated Western development for so long. An outlook that values these more profound understandings allows us to draw upon the heritage of human wisdom to inform inner values; imaginative, intuitive ways of knowing put us "*in the correct spiritual or psychological posture for right action*".[57] This not only contributes to a sense of meaningfulness in our endeavours but also enables us to envision new possibilities in art, science and technology. If our views are informed by historical precedents and notions of goodness, truth and right action, we will be in a far better position to create a meaningful vision of the future.[58] Holistic, integrative understandings are critical ingredients of human flourishing, ethical behaviour and environmental stewardship.[59] Accordingly, they are deeply connected not only to the welfare of the individual but also to the collective good.

The worldview that has dominated the richer nations, especially Northern Europe and North America, in recent centuries has resulted in a prejudicial and manifestly destructive one-sidedness in perspectives and endeavours. It has fostered social atomization through its emphasis on individualism and consumer capitalism, the latter fomenting division through its constant promotion of competitive social positioning. It has also created a distorted version of democracy, one that upholds the interests and rights of the individual over and above the common good. Even though today democracy, individualism and rational instrumentalism tend to be regarded as inseparable, classical notions of democracy were strongly tied to spiritual sensibilities, which stem from our suprarational, imaginative side. Duty and self-sacrifice for the collective good were afforded the highest respect. They were regarded as essential complements to individual interests and important facets of individual growth and wisdom. Ever since the revival of interest in classical Greece during the Renaissance, and the development of individualism and political thought during the Enlightenment, Athens has been viewed as the birthplace, and the Parthenon the symbol, of democracy. Yet, in many ways this is a superimposed identity, forged to reflect ourselves and our own priorities and values; this is an example of the point made earlier that everything we learn from our experiences of the world depends on and is moulded by the a priori philosophical outlook we bring to those experiences. The Parthenon was primarily a sacred temple and classical Greek democracy was inseparable from broader facets of human apprehension – the spiritual sense, religious beliefs, myths, rituals, links to the past, cultural memory, place, and self-sacrifice for the common good.[60] In contrast, modern neoliberal democracy has largely set aside these important meaning-seeking aspects of the human condition that are critical to deeper notions of goodness, right action and moderation. This deficit has yielded a version of democracy that, to all intents and purposes, licenses and endorses a ruinous form of free-market economics. Democratic governance and oversight for the good of society as a whole has been eclipsed by an excessively powerful form of globalized corporate capitalism that operates across and between national laws and regulations and lacks any reasonable notions of restraint.

43

Within this market-oriented version of democracy, imaginative expressions of human knowledge are shaped to serve corporate priorities and, in the process, they become distorted and degraded. Even though the arts have always been strongly associated with the perennial search for human meaning and happiness, they tend only to be relevant to the corporate world of consumer capitalism in as much as they can be used and exploited psychologically for purposes of profit generation. Sadly, the applied art of design has long been associated with such exploitation. This is especially egregious when the creative gift and subjective, imaginative ways of knowing are used to nurture envy, dissatisfaction and unhappiness.

Design practice combines periods of exploration and working with materials and processes, with periods of deep absorption and reflection. It is in this intense process of thought and action that imaginative insights arise and disparate facets become integrated into a coherent whole. This spontaneous synthesis, a critical ingredient of the creative process, transcends rational, linear, methodical ways of thinking. These creative aspects of design, given their links to deeper notions of human understanding, ought not to be usurped in order to merely serve economic ends and corporate self-interest. Their close relationship to ethics and self-transcendence values suggests that they ought to be directed towards furthering not just individual interests but also the common good. In this, the creative skills and visualization capabilities of design can be employed to give actuality to more comprehensive, equitable and imaginative directions.

OBSTACLES TO THE DEVELOPMENT OF A NEW NORMAL

From the foregoing it is clear that contemporary society privileges cognitive knowledge, explication and intellectual capabilities that are useful for problem solving and developing practical applications. But the emphasis on material benefits and financial concerns serves to continually reinforce self-interest and individualism. Accordingly, many of the priorities of contemporary 'developed' societies can be seen as self-reifying barriers to positive change. They include:

Rationalism and Materialism: These confine human thought to a cage of factual information and discursive abstraction. The resulting outlook fails to raise the mind's eye high enough to recognize the importance of tacit knowledge and the kinds of insight that have traditionally been conveyed through allegory, metaphor and symbolism. Consequently, our ability to apprehend the beauty, splendour and inherent goodness of mundane reality becomes eclipsed by the urge to exploit it for material and economic gain. Rationalistic arguments and evidence-based decision-making dominate government agendas and modern bureaucracies. Undue weight is placed on the physical and the factual, even though these are wholly inadequate when it comes to ideas about values and virtue. Despite their cladding of logic, these approaches mask a predisposition that cleaves to what is possible over what is meaningful. This has given rise to the disturbing trend of adding more and more layers of bureaucracy to every walk of life in the form of regulation, measurement and administration. Such so-called evidence reveals a way of thinking that is so prosaic it is stultifying. It supports no larger vision than a continuation of materialistic forms of progress and growth for their own sake amid a distorted notion of accountability. Nonetheless, and despite vast increases in information, there is no clear idea of ultimate concern and relatively little heed is given to the social and environmental devastation it is leaving in its wake.

44

Specialization: The highly specialized scientific and technological fields generated by these priorities are becoming barriers to gaining a more holistic, integrated overview of the state and purpose of humankind.[61] This is not to say that notions of ethics and goodness have disappeared, and it is important not to overstate the case. However, with increasing specialization, more profound questions about motive and meaning go unasked – they simply do not feature in the workaday agendas of many business leaders, politicians or researchers. An holistic, coherent view of the world becomes obscured by a focus on narrow particulars. With increased specialization there is a concentration on expert knowledge, information gathering and information technologies, rather than on expertise and wisdom, respectively understood as knowledge coupled with skill and knowledge coupled with right judgement.[62] This is why holistic, integrated understandings of virtue within a unified narrative have become unravelled in modern 'developed' societies.

Non-holistic Interpretations: Bearing in mind the insufficiency of specialization, together with the earlier discussion of *the outer*, *the inner* and *the holistic*, serious questions arise about the adequacy of modern technological forms of communication and the behaviours they enable. Texts, emails, form filling and videoconferencing are all based on partial forms of interpretation. They all substitute, but in a deficient manner, for proximity, presence and the fullness of communicating mutually as people. As a result, nonverbal, empathetic, intuitively perceived aspects of our humanness become obscured and go unrecognized. In so doing, society and we as individual members of it become diminished, and, to an extent, brutalized by the austere logic of explication, rationalism and abstraction.

45

Business Practices: Examples of highly questionable and unconscionable business practices are many. A few of the more flagrant include: *Harmful Products:* The manufacture and marketing of products to young people that are known to be addictive and, in some cases, carcinogenic,[63, 64] and the marketing of all kinds of products, including high sugar-content foods, to children. *Financial Practices:* Highly speculative 'casino' banking practices[65] that put ordinary people's savings at risk to gain high profits and bonuses for those involved, and companies that offer short-term loans at exorbitant interest rates and then use bullying tactics on the vulnerable to recover debts.[66] *Patented Seeds:* The development of genetically modified, patented seeds, and control over seed supplies by international corporations have been linked to the development of agricultural monocultures that are highly susceptible to disease, pests and drought, and to the indebtedness, despair and suicides of hundreds of thousands of farmers.[67, 68, 69] *Arms Trading:* the continued development, trade and use of the most abhorrent kinds of weapons, which go far beyond any justification based on national defence.

All these practices detrimentally affect our capacity for virtue and love, including our respect and care for the natural environment.[70] They fly in the face of substantive notions of ethics that were developed over centuries within the Western tradition, from Aristotle to Aquinas. Virtue ethics include the individual virtues of prudence and magnanimity as well as social virtues, such as solidarity and justice, and their enactment is dependent on their habituation through the development of moral character.[71, 72] Yet these business practices have become normalized within contemporary Western society. All are symptomatic of a culture oriented towards maximization of profits, for which innovation and new products are seen as critical. As Fulcher has pointed out, "*It is not the nature of the activity itself that matters but the possibility of making profit out of it*".[73] The activity can be selling cigarettes, gambling with other people's money, controlling seed stocks, producing landmines, or launching an endless stream of 'improved' devices onto the market. The purpose is profit – sought via an assiduously focused, amoral (and often immoral) system that appears to be inherently incompatible with a culture of care, responsibility and stewardship. It is certainly incompatible with higher notions of human potential.

Educational Bias: These outlooks and approaches have led to preferential support in education for pragmatic endeavours linked to the economy. This includes political interference in public education to give precedence to those subjects considered useful to economic growth, and where support is withdrawn from other areas.[74, 75] Policy and enormous amounts of public funding are directed towards training, impact and the short-term utilitarian needs of private sector business and industry. Education in the more rounded sense, which includes the arts, philosophy and ethics, and the world's heritage of spiritual teachings, has waned. Accordingly, rationalism, empiricism, instrumentalism and a constricted, lacklustre worldview become self-reinforcing. Teachers become 'service providers', students become 'customers', administration rises – form filling, target setting, assessment and reporting. The education process becomes results oriented, with imaginative, inspiring teaching and learning being achieved in spite of the system rather than being encouraged and facilitated by it.

Culture of Acquisitiveness: The present consumer capitalist system of techno-scientific optimism supports a corporate agenda that creates doubts, dissatisfactions and wants by focussing on our weaknesses and our vanities. When the means of doing this is via personal communication devices that effectively separate, isolate and target individuals with intrusive advertising, we have created a system and conditions that hinder discernment and are incompatible with peace of mind. These kinds of distracting, frenetic environments may support economic growth but they are impediments to thinking and to achieving a state of tranquillity – thought being essentially a quiet 'inner' affair. It is undoubtedly the case that the powerful, which today take the form of major global corporations, tend to monopolize noise.[76] One way of challenging this predominant but damaging ideology is to endorse silence.[77] Hence, a critical factor in achieving a more balanced, integrated outlook will be the development of a culture that sees value in contemplation, inner silence and deeper values, and this, in turn, requires the development of conditions that are conducive to such priorities.

Disposable Culture: The widespread production and use of disposable products, from plastic water bottles and fast-food wrappers to the agricultural application of polyethylene crop covers and bale wraps, offers clear evidence of short-term convenience and profits trumping longer-term responsibilities and a duty of care. When such waste is burned, either because of inadequate recycling options or because it is cheaper to do so, it becomes a leading source of air pollutants.[78] Plastic trash and other discarded waste make our towns, countryside and shorelines unsightly and are a physical manifestation of negligence and indifference. Disposable plastics are turning our oceans into 'plastic soups' and are having devastating effects on sea life.[79, 80] Tens of thousands of marine animals – seabirds, seals, turtles and whales – die each year from consuming or becoming entangled in plastic waste. Smaller marine creatures concentrate toxic chemicals in their bodies by ingesting plastic particles,[81] a process known as *bioaccumulation*, and, due to prey–predator relationships, this leads to *biomagnification*, whereby animals higher up the food chain accumulate elevated toxin concentrations.[82, 83] For people, these toxins are associated with a variety of medical problems, and their ingestion is especially dangerous for at-risk groups, such as pregnant women and the developing foetus, small children and the elderly.[84]

Environmental Degradation: Ever more roads, airports, railways, construction, consumption and industrial-scale 'monoculture' farming inevitably results in habitat depletion, air pollution, water contamination and increases in noise, all of which adversely affect quality of life and jeopardize physical and psychological health. A degraded environment inhibits a state of silence – both outer, worldly silence and inner peace. In turn, this negatively affects our consideration of others, and the cultivation of a reasonable and humane outlook.[85, 86]

Even though these contemporary inclinations would have us think otherwise, more profound understandings of reality and our place in it are dependent neither on the acquisition of things nor on the acquisition of facts and data. This is to look at deeper values and meaningfulness from the wrong angle entirely. Instead, it is a matter of trust.[87] As the eleventh-century Anselm of Canterbury said, one should not seek to understand in order to believe, but one must believe in order to understand.[88] The heritage of human wisdom, which spans human history and emerges from all civilizations,[89] tells us that this is a question of intuitive apprehension and inner conscience over external authority. And while we are more than capable of drawing on and thriving from understandings based in intuition, imagination and the spiritual sense, we must bear in mind that when these are placed under the scrutiny of the rationalistic eye they become divested of their potency and their merit. The very process of seeking to analyze and explain denies their very nature and renders them barren and worthless.[90]

If we are to develop different attitudes, behaviours and work practices, these entrenched perspectives represent a very considerable hurdle. Piketty, in his comprehensive study of modern capitalism, has concluded that the market economy based on private property, if left to its own devices, drastically increases the wealth of the wealthy and reduces the incomes of everyone else, creating massive inequalities, potentially destabilizing democracies and threatening the principles of social justice on which they are built. He suggests that the long-term impacts are *"potentially terrifying"*.[91] The path down which consumer capitalism is taking us is based, essentially, on self-interest and greed, which are often tainted with corruption.[92, 93] All of this contravenes the wisdoms of the ages – from the

48

Abrahamic traditions, which speak of the relationship between wealth and ruthlessness, and the need for moderation, to Socrates' moderate city,[94] to the Middle Way of Buddhism. These traditions, set aside by the 'developed' nations only relatively recently, have been replaced by the ubiquitous mantras of consumerism. The unrelenting artifice of advertising fills our lives with noise – both visual and aural – constantly trying to stimulate our senses by generating false excitement and nurturing self-interest, competitive individualism and societal atomization. This not only goes against any comprehensive understanding of wisdom but actively works against the establishment of conditions conducive to its flowering.

And yet, despite these fundamental defects, these perspectives and approaches dominate contemporary society and they are proliferating and becoming ever more embedded around the world. As Said has emphasized, the endurance and tenacity of these approaches is more understandable when we recognize that within their narrow, highly selective fields of vision, they are highly productive.[95] This has enabled them to continue, despite their wider and increasingly serious repercussions.

THE OBLIGATIONS OF DESIGN

49

A new path for design is needed that values a much broader outlook and is capable of reassessing, and potentially reinterpreting and restoring, many things that were cast aside in our headlong rush to progress – craft, connection to the earth, and design's relationship to community and locale. We must integrate these with the benefits of technology in a manner that decreases resource use, pollution and waste, and nurtures ways of being that support social justice, environmental care and personal meaningfulness. There is a need to explore ways forward that reverses the onus – away from escalating product development for an already saturated market to one that restricts the build-up of clutter in our lives. While this may be alien to contemporary ways of thinking, it correlates with wisdom traditions that warn against immoderate wealth and power; it also correlates with contemporary ideas about sustainability. Such a direction demands a reassessment of priorities, a reconsideration of how ethical principles and deeper values can become a more substantive aspect of design education and design practice, and a consideration of what difference such principles and values might make to design outcomes. It asks us to consider again the baseless notion of finding happiness and fulfilment through more and more things, over and above those required for basic needs and reasonable levels of comfort. It asks us to learn to see disposable packaging and the design and production of limited-use, irreparable products as unacceptable in an advanced society. And, given the magnitude of their negative effects, it asks us to revise our notions of 'innovation' and 'progress'. Taken together, these represent a very significant shift in our thinking and practices that moves us away from an economy based on consumption, new product development and the continual creation of dissatisfaction through increasingly pervasive marketing techniques.[96]

If design is to contribute to such substantive change, it has to honour and judiciously employ the creative gift that it is called upon to realize through form. Through creativity and the human imagination we are able to articulate that which remains silent within us, that which lies beyond rational explanation. Creativity and imagination are not only critical to the arts and our experiences of beauty but also to our sense of the transcendent and to meanings that concurrently exist both *extra* and *intra* to materiality; meanings that lie beyond the mundane confines of materialism. With this in mind, we can consider the effects and impacts of design from several interrelated perspectives, including the designed artefact, its production, its use and its presence in the world:

50

Designed Artefact: The direct contributions of the designed thing itself. These include instrumental benefits and aesthetics but can also include symbolic meanings. All these are inherent to and expressed through the tangible, visible thing.

Production: The indirect contributions and/or losses associated with the artefact's production and eventual demise. These can include manufacturing jobs and wealth generation along with socially exploitative practices and environmental degradation. There are also the cumulative effects of producing, and eventually discarding, many millions of different kinds of products. In a globalized production system, these are often invisible to us but they are, nevertheless, identifiable as benefits or detriments.

Use: The use of designed products can either contribute to or detract from a culture of thoughtfulness and care that enhances individual and social flourishing and community relations. These may be less tangible, less immediately discernible, and more difficult to prove or measure, but, nevertheless, they are important to the collective good and to a sense of well-being. Although largely invisible, they can be known intuitively, in our dealings with others and in our sense of neighbourliness and common purpose. There are also the hidden costs of use in terms of energy consumption and emissions, which cumulatively are substantial.

Artefact Presence: The outcomes of design, in their lasting presence, can have either positive or negative effects on our understandings about what is worthwhile, and on our comfort levels. When a product is designed, produced and becomes present in our society it implicitly conveys ideas about priorities and values. It becomes a tangible manifestation of particular values. And its presence will have an effect on us, on our priorities and values. If our endeavours are conceived and directed in ways that uphold common values and interests they will tend to enhance our own personal sense of belonging, identity and well-being, all of which help impart a deeper sense of meaning to our lives. While these considerations may lie beyond the realms of evidential proof, they are knowable internally, through subjective experiences and silent reflection. Their promise is dependent on goodwill and trust, and the belief that being fully alive ultimately requires us to rise above rational self-interest and the utilitarian but prosaic benefits offered by contemporary forms of neoliberal democracy and corporate capitalism.

51

It follows that, within the current, globalized manufacturing system, design endeavours that attempt to make immediate, practical changes and improvements are unlikely to have any substantial or lasting positive effect. This is because any such design will still have to conform to the values of the corporate system of which it is a part, and it is these values that lie at the heart of the problem. Corporate capitalism prioritizes short-term financial gains over social and environmental concerns, and its continual manufacture of material wants is the means of ensuring these gains. A design process that strives to embody more profound considerations will not fit with this system. It will not conform to the methods, aesthetic conventions or market-oriented expectations that have driven commercial design practice and mass production for many years. Entirely different approaches are needed – approaches that derive not only from the particularities of context (socio-cultural needs, place and environmental care) but also, and more importantly, from a different place within ourselves. Self-enhancement values, selfishness, social status, ambition and short-term priorities have to give way to self-transcendence values, compassion, humility, trust and longer-term contributions. The manifestation of such values through design, in the qualities of our material productions, will express and help feed more fundamental change. Through its presence in the world, such design will implicitly convey ideas about deeper priorities and values.

As it probes new directions and explores new conceptions of material culture, this type of design will need to be open, adaptable and much more locally based. Somewhat inevitably, therefore, in the face of globalized corporate interests and enormous social and environmental problems, such small-scale endeavours may appear to be ineffectual and futile. However, if informed, considered and pursued with conviction, these kinds of design developments can be a basis for change and a vanguard of hope. Change has to begin somewhere and in design it begins with the values, priorities and intentions of each individual designer.

We can now consider some potential routes for the development of more responsible, meaningful design endeavours:

Incremental Design: Yields somewhat less destructive, incrementally improved versions of existing products in ways that fit within the prevailing corporate-led, growth-based economic model. Some might see this as a pragmatic way forward that, while not perfect, is better than nothing. However, such approaches tend to be counterproductive because they give the impression of change but do not represent a significant, long-term strategy – the overall, intensely destructive direction remains unchanged. In essence, this kind of incremental 'sticking plaster' design is a form of eco-modernism[97] and as such it is unable to address the fundamental, systemic changes needed today.[98] Understandably, perhaps, it tends to be the preferred route of most corporate and political leaders because it does not challenge the existing system. Many so-called 'green' products, as well as products that replace existing technologies with 'eco' technologies, fall into this category.

Grassroots Design: Refers to bottom-up approaches that are not only in accord with environmental and social responsibilities but are also meaningful at a personal level with respect to one's beliefs, ethical position and conscience. It requires and helps cultivate a more localized production model – one that builds deeper awareness of the benefits, repercussions and true costs of producing and using material goods and associated services. This kind of design, which is inseparable from the making process, can contribute to the building of community, the restoration and care of local ecologies, and a personal sense of identity and narrative unity. Traditionally, craft sits in this category. Such grassroots endeavours can be achieved by professional designer-makers[99] and by nonprofessionals working individually or in collectives, with or without the input of skilled designers.[100, 101]

Contemplative Design: Focuses on nonutilitarian, symbolic objects whose presence serves to remind us of the need for inner work. In this sense, they can be regarded as spiritually useful objects; they provide a focus for contemplation and attention to inner values and deeper meaning. This type of design suggests a direction that goes beyond thinking of products primarily in terms of outer, practical utility. By acknowledging the importance of deeper human needs, *contemplative design* can contribute to the development of a more balanced outlook and a more beneficent worldview. Examples include devotional artefacts, which today we tend to regard either as art or as kitsch, but when approached from the inner perspective, are actually aids to contemplation and inner development.[102]

Counterpoint Design: Buchanan has said that "*if technology is in some fundamental sense concerned with the probable rather than the necessary – with contingencies of practical use and action, rather than the certainties of scientific principle – then it becomes rhetorical in a startling fashion*".[103] When we move from the investigation and comprehension of scientific facts and principles about the natural world of phenomena to employing these facts and principles for human utility through the development of technologies, we are implicitly saying that these applications and these technologies are of value. Hence, design is tacitly values-laden. It asserts and endorses a position and, for that very reason, it is rhetorical; as Buchanan goes on to say, "*technology is fundamentally concerned with a form of persuasion*".[104] Descriptions and explanations of such design work will, naturally, attempt to justify the arguments around which the design is based and so they, too, will declare a position and will be rhetorical. Moreover, when that design work and those arguments declare a position that contrasts with and challenges established norms and current directions, it will be inherently polemical. Even though this can be problematic from an objective, academic perspective nonetheless subjectivity, the tacit expression of values and the assertion of a position are fundamental to both technological development and the discipline of design and are, therefore,

53

critical characteristics of design practice. By the same token, they are critical characteristics of practice-based design research within academia. This cannot be helped and should not be avoided. On the contrary, it should be embraced because it is an essential characteristic of the discipline. Significantly too, the inclusion and assertion of values are crucial aspects of being fully human and essential requirements for moving away from our current, inherently destructive modes of living towards more sustainable renditions of material culture.

Whereas mainstream commercial design implicitly reinforces the norms and expectations of the market-oriented system of which it is a part, counterpoint design is used here to raise questions about that system by expressing an opposite position. In the context of design research and discipline development, this should not pose a problem, as long as that position is properly declared and made fully transparent. The focus of practice-based design research should be on the consistency of the arguments and the success of their transmutation into form, not the fact that design and its associated arguments are values-laden because, as we have seen, this is an integral and essential ingredient of the discipline.

54

In this type of design work, through the creative design process, a general, abstract issue such as 'existential malaise' or 'instrumental rationality' is transformed into the particular and expressed in concrete terms via tangible objects or arrangements. In the process, taken-for-granted issues are made real – their transmutation into physicality yielding specific and potentially powerful statements that enable the familiar to be seen anew. Rather than attempting to analyze, explain and lay out the various points in a logical, linear order, these kinds of objects synthesize ideas into an integrated composition that is perceived almost instantaneously. Such objects provide a focus for the viewer to reflect on common assumptions and conventions and to see them again for the first time. Hence, *counterpoint design* can be understood as a particular variant of *contemplative design*. It employs allegory and symbolism along with the techniques of visualization, and it may use irony, humour, surprise or pathos to deal with abstract ideas and experiential concerns. It is complementary to discursive forms of expression and thus it can be appropriately accompanied by written commentary or annotation.

Rhythmical Objects: *Rhythmical objects* integrate aspects of *grassroots*, *contemplative* and *counterpoint design*. In their presence, modes of making and the activities they enable, these artefacts cultivate practices conducive to mutually reinforcing relationships between contemplative inner modes of being and outer physical actions. On the one hand, they become tangible symbols of more moderate, more judicious pathways and, on the other, their production and use promote skill building, attentiveness and reflection. Like the many community-based social innovations that have arisen in recent years, these objects, created for local use from locally available materials, can become unassuming indicators of transition – the outer symbols of a different philosophical outlook, which is the necessary precursor to more fundamental, systemic change.

Through the development of a range of propositional objects, I have previously explored *grassroots design* in relation to sustainability,[105] as well as *contemplative design*, and made an initial foray into *counterpoint design*;[106] some of these earlier studies are shown in Figure 3.1.

This present discussion further develops *counterpoint* examples along with brief written accounts and evocative texts. Through this means, the intuitive and creative is balanced by the rational and explanatory – thus combining complementary traits of the human condition, often associated with right- and left-brain functions. Variants of this approach are included in Chapter 6, as *Vestiges of Grace*, and Chapter 8, as *Seeds of Change*. *Rhythmical objects* are discussed in Chapter 7.

COUNTERPOINTS

A number of interconnected issues associated with the predominant philosophical outlook of late-modernity are presented here in the form of *counterpoints*. Each of these artefacts makes a visual, oppositional statement about a particular contemporary issue related to this outlook. These tangible expressions of ideas are developed through the creative, intuitive design process. In presenting these artefacts, a photograph of each is shown along with a title, an evocative descriptor and/or a brief statement about the philosophical position or stance behind its creation. This dual visual-textual mode of presentation acknowledges the importance and complementarity of the intuitive and rational aspects of our nature. Whereas the meaning of explanatory texts can be clear and precise, objects and images are less categorical. They are open to different interpretations; any particular understanding will depend on the object itself and the perspective of the observer. So while not wishing to hinder multiple readings, the respective texts, whether evocative or explanatory, help avoid any

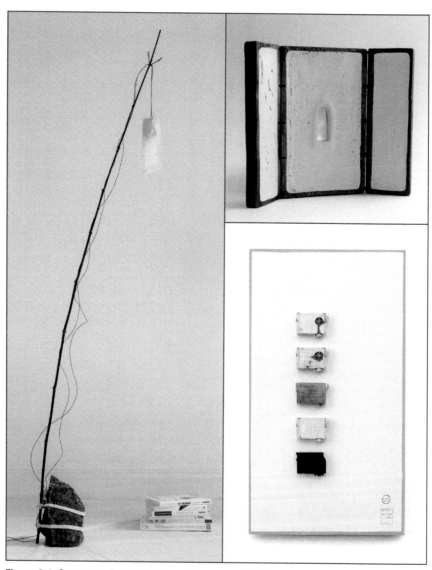

Figure 3.1 Grassroots, Contemplative and Counterpoint Design

Left: *Bamboo and Stone I* – floor lamp; mass-produced parts and unprocessed local materials.[107]
Top Right: *Oriel Triptych* – a trans-religious contemplative object. Bottom Right: *Land* – disposable ink cartridges that end up in landfill.[108]

misinterpretation of intent. When complemented by an explanation of the basis and intentions being explored and brief statements or intimations about the individual pieces, a series of designed artefacts such as these constitutes a type of discipline-appropriate primary data within a practice-based design research programme. Gaver has referred to this an 'annotated portfolio', of which he says, "*However valuable generalised theories may be, their role is limited to inspiration and annotation. It is the artefacts we create that are the definite facts of research through design*".[109] This is one way of valuing exploratory design work and recognizing its crucial role in advancing ideas and knowledge within and beyond design research agendas.

Examples of such explorations from my own practice are shown in Figures 3.2–3.16. These pieces bring together a number of themes and elements, and all are accompanied by words. Five of the pieces, *Beyond Words* (Fig. 3.4), *Water* (Fig. 3.6), *Neophobias* (Figs. 3.12 and 3.13), *Confesión* (Fig. 3.14), and *Finale* (Fig. 3.16) actually incorporate text as an important design element. The series *With Hidden Silence: Relic, Dominion, Nature* (Figs. 3.9, 3.10 and 3.11) employs mystery and 'not knowing' as a basis of object value. These pieces explore alternatives to modernity's quest for certainty and implicitly ask the viewer to consider broader understandings of human knowledge – including intuitively apprehended but indeterminate ways of knowing and understandings of truth. In this way, the series represents an attempt to find synthesis and reconciliation between, on the one hand, intuitive intimations, concrete expression, application and specificity, represented by the image, and on the other, intellectual certainties, abstraction, theories and generalities, represented by the word. These two quite different, but complementary, sides of our nature are expressed in the form of tangible objects in, respectively, *Human Rites* (Fig. 3.15) and *Finale* (Fig. 3.16). Both of these objects deal with death. Discussing traditional understandings of love and truth, Shortt says, "*Our obliviousness to these points, especially in the developed world, feeds a reluctance to think about the inevitability of death*".[110] But as he goes on to say, by facing up to this reality "*we come to negotiate our lives with greater wisdom: to unpeel ourselves from selfish desires*".[111] These two pieces bring such concerns to the fore and make them visible, but where the former emphasizes the age-old cultural need for ritual and ceremony to mark the passing of a human life, the latter expresses the end of life and the cessation of pain in more logical, instrumental terms. The articulation of such ideas through tangible objects allows them to seen as 'real', rather than remaining as abstract notions. This 'making visible' is a key contribution of design – ideas become visualized and concrete. In this case, both objects can be understood as visual metaphors that represent the two sides of our being that have to find harmony and integration if we are to develop a more comprehensive, inclusive idea of design.

57

These various objects, when taken together, can be understood as expressions of unease, physical manifestations of things felt. They offer a focus for reflection, quietude and stillness, and stand in contrast to the one-sidedness of words alone, noise, and explanation. Being visualizations rather than reasoned justifications, they touch aspects of human understanding that may be tacitly understood but cannot be fully described or expressed. Nevertheless, through their presence they offer insights and perspectives, reveal relationships, and invite pause. Further details about the origins of *Confesión*, Fig. 3.14, and the English version, are included in Appendix 1.

As we have seen, the history of the modern era and, hence, of the development of the contemporary condition, is one in which silence, imagery, contemplation and many aspects of human understanding that emerge from attention to the inner life became devalued and sidelined. It is an outlook that still pervades political, corporate and educational agendas. These *counterpoint* objects offer a fitting way of highlighting and contesting the deficiencies of this outlook. They are an attempt to offer some respite – some space for silence and reflection.

58

Words and imagery represent different ways of knowing and appreciating the world. The first demands literacy and is limited by language. The second is available to all, irrespective of learning and mother tongue, and for this reason it is more egalitarian, equitable, and universal. Imagery presents a synthesis of ideas and meanings and a focus for silent acts of contemplation – a route into the imagination and those deeper facets of our humanity that are so vital for cooperative, conciliatory and desirable ways of living. In this, we can learn much from traditions in which contemplation, solitude and silence remain valued ingredients of deeper paths to wisdom and well-being. These are the issues that design has the means and opportunity to address and bring forth today. Design can raise awareness by offering alternative perspectives on material culture. And it can create propositions for an alternative path – one rooted in place, holistic in vision and meaningful in its presence.

Silence is a potent alternative to reasoned argument. Sometimes it is the only appropriate response to the unanswerable dilemmas generated by reason's abstracted rigour. It is through silence that we can appreciate that which surpasses explication and proof – that which lies beyond words, but is knowable in ways that are immediate, subjective and incontestable. Silence is a critical ingredient of deeper ways of knowing but it is increasingly rare in today's society where we are often hard put to be free of intrusions and cravings. We have nothing to fear from silence but we have much to fear from its absence because a world without silence, reflection and a quiet mind is a world without wisdom.

CONCLUSIONS

We have seen in this chapter that the discipline of design can contribute to positive change by adopting various courses of action. *Incremental* improvements that are compatible with current manufacturing and economic requirements may be an appealing option but such approaches serve to reinforce rather than contest our current, unsustainable system. Hence, this is an inadequate response, which is why I have referred to it as a 'sticking plaster' solution. *Counterpoints* recognize that designers, in applying their creative skills, can develop artefacts that synthesize critical issues into tangible aesthetic statements. These can be a potent way of addressing contemporary concerns in nonverbal formats. Their power lies in the aesthetic experience, rather than rational argument or empirical evidence. Essentially, these kinds of objects are physical encapsulations and symbolic representations of critical concerns. They complement and add to rational argument and empirical evidence, and, in doing so, they contribute to a more holistic understanding of contemporary problems and dilemmas. Clearly, if we are to develop more balanced outlooks, intuitive and tacit ways of knowing will need to be ascribed far greater value and it is here that design can make a substantive contribution. A further route is through what I have referred to as *rhythmical objects*, which, on the face of it, may appear more practical (see Chapter 7). However, as with *counterpoint design*, their real value lies in their symbolic role. Such approaches result in objects that lend themselves to multiple interpretations and adaptations – to suit different situations, conditions and contexts. Hence, they can be regarded as allegorical objects; their outer forms and literal meanings are symbols of deeper moral or spiritual ideas.

Design can play its part within a much larger spectrum of change. In this, our current economic system, which is locked into unsustainable growth, is in need of urgent and substantive reform. Obviously, a growth-based system that is dependent on ever increasing production, energy use and waste cannot continue *ad infinitum* New outlooks are needed that foster more benign ways forward; in this endeavour, education will be the most important ingredient. The kinds of design explorations discussed here can be routes for educating by design. Likewise, they are routes that can inform design education itself because the discipline of design also has to develop new ways of thinking about the nature of material culture, its origins, its use, its meaning, and its ultimate demise. While acknowledging the critical need for economic reform, design can make creative contributions towards positive change. Through visualization and tangible form it can access and address those deeper aspects of our being that are intangible – the ethical, the spiritual, the meaningful and the intuitively felt. The invisibility and shadowy presence of these critical facets of our nature mean they cannot be pointed to or proved but they can be recognized and recreated through the imagination. It is through such means that we can, perhaps, extend our field of view, find a path out of the trees so that we may once more perceive the wood, and thus help restore balance through the contributions of design.

COUNTERPOINTS

arguments in form

Figure 3.2

Last Supper – *take this and divide it among you*

Contemporary consumption is untempered by ideas of sufficiency and balance; in today's growth-based economy there is no such thing as enough. With globalization, tasks are separated, knowledge is dispersed and understanding is obscured. With no overview there is no oversight, and responsibility is avoided. *Last Supper* is a physical expression of immoderate depletion.

Materials: *northwest coast pebbles and sand, fir, autumn leaves*

Figure 3.3

Mayday – *an international distress signal*

The limits of reason were reached long ago. Decades of environmentalism, scientific observations and evidence-based research that make the case for substantial change have not dinted progress, growth and destruction. Here, the rational, written word remains unread in unopened bottles. There is a need to conjure the imagination; to appeal to the heart. *Mayday* is a wordless plea from that which cannot cry.

Materials: *unread messages, old bottles, paper, string, wax, new life*

Figure 3.4

Beyond Words – *an aid to silent reflection*

The tacit, the intuitive and the self-transcending represent another kind of knowing. Modern times have given precedence to words over imagery, explication over silence, rationalism over symbolism, and action over contemplation. In pursuit of certainty, individualism has been sanctified and religion intellectualized.[112] A narrower, rationalistic identity has been imposed on age-old understandings that, in former times, were more generous and more holistic. *Beyond Words* honours intuitive perception, silent reflection, the ineffable.

Materials: *1747 leather-bound edition of* The Book of Common Prayer of the Church of England *tied and sealed with hemp and bandaged in linen*

Figure 3.5

Oedipus Eyeglasses – *accessory for an existential crime*

When Oedipus realizes that he has married his own mother, he puts out his eyes. It is the price for committing an existential crime, for polluting something that, thereafter, can never be restored. We too are committing an existential crime – violating nature to such a degree that our very survival is threatened. Existential crimes are attended by self-blindness. "*We put out our eyes, and then insist that the sun is a fiction of the poets*".[113] Not recommended for those with vision.

Materials: *reading glasses, Cumbrian blackthorn*

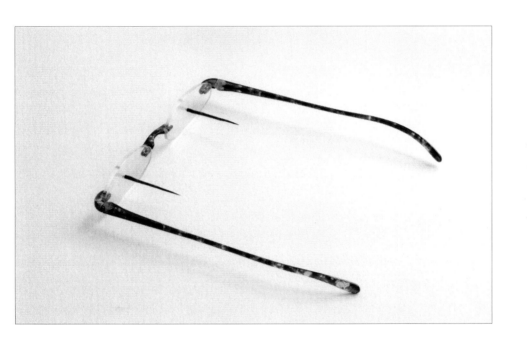

Figure 3.6

Water – *a modern history*

silent	spring
acid	rain
three mile	island
torrey	canyon
conflict	mineral
fracking	well
commodification	contamination

Materials: *bottled water, bespoke labels*

Figure 3.7

Shackles – *connected 24/7*

In pocket or purse, wherever we go, whatever we do, we are connected to other places, other people and other concerns. Unpredictable, uncontrolled and intrusive, the addiction-like use patterns create a form of digital slavery. On a mountain, on a beach, we are shackled. In the process, we relinquish solitude and quietness of mind and implicate ourselves in the disappearance of peace.

Materials: *mountain boots, beach sandals, chain*

Figure 3.8

Concept – *complete protection from handheld relationships*

Physical separation, social fragmentation and partial, susceptible, screen-based views of reality offer only impoverished encounters. Isolated from the fullness of life and robbed of vitality, there ensues a deterioration of meaningful relationships, intimacy and empathy; a disinterest in anything not online.[114] *Concept* – the responsible option for communication planning.

Materials: *phone, condom*

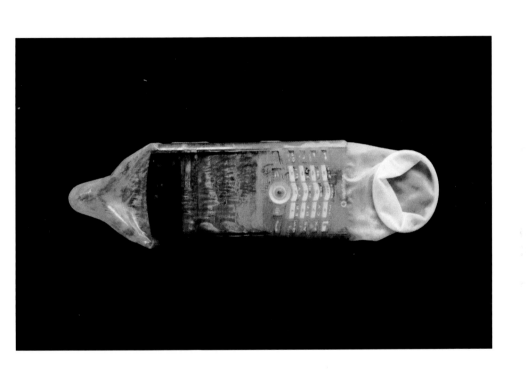

Figure 3.9

With Hidden Silence – *the value of doubt*

Inspired by a long line of enclosed objects from Duchamp's *With Hidden Noise* (1916) and Man Ray's *L'Enigme d'Isidore Ducasse* (1920) to the more recent wrapped works of Christo and Jean-Claude, each of these pieces contains an unspecified item. In contrast to modernity's drive for certainty and its increasing abstraction,[115] here value lies in substantiality and the aesthetics of uncertainty. In knowing, the riddle is solved, the aesthetics are destroyed, the value is lost. In not knowing, the object remains – alive, dynamic, purposeful.

I   *Relic*

fragment in hidebound box

Figure 3.10

With Hidden Silence – *the value of doubt*

II   *Dominion*

conformity in felt wrap

Figure 3.11

With Hidden Silence – *the value of doubt*

III   *Nature*
petrified in fleece

Figure 3.12

Neophobias - *commodified cures for the ailments of consumerism*

An endless spiral of distraction overpowers the senses, planting doubts, cultivating fears. Deeper values fade from view, leaving only disquiet and unease. The inner is quashed by the outer. This cabinet of commodified cures for the ailments sown by consumerism reveals the paradox of market-led 'solutions'. Our anxieties become corporate revenue opportunities.[116] Resting on a deficient philosophy of materialism, the time is ripe for these damaging ideas to be consigned to the past; to be regarded as destructive, misconceived and antiquated.

Materials: *reused wood, reused jars, 'cures'*

Neophobias – *commodified cures for the ailments of consumerism*

Detail – six 'cures' for potential ailments arising from consumerism: indifference, inattentiveness, and a sense of superficiality, inadequacy, inferiority and irrelevance. Other ailments in the cabinet include: banality, indecisiveness, obscurity, timidity, awkwardness and incompetence.

Materials: *reused wood, reused jars, 'cures'*

Figure 3.14

Confesión – *relic from a future past*

Who can imagine
the unimaginable? The act
of self-inflicted desolation.
A lost humanity.

Relic from a future past
etched on iron. A remnant
of despair. A testament
of loss.

Materials: *mixed media on recovered metal sheet*

Confesión: No estoy ni seguro de por qué estamos hablando de esto, es como si ya no fuese nuevo ni raro. Por supuesto no lo hemos hecho siempre. Hubo un tiempo, antes de que yo naciera, en el que había otras cosas. Quizá las personas más maduras todavía se acuerdan de cuando eran muy jóvenes, de cuando había fincas ganaderas, árboles frutales y cosas así, y algunos incluso dicen recordar una época en la que las cosas que vivían en el agua se agarraban y se utilizaban como comida. La gente solía comerlas. ¿Puedes imaginar comer cualquier cosa que salga de esta inmundicia? Pero eso pasaba hace mucho tiempo. Yo nunca he visto tal cosa con mis propios ojos. Algunos dicen que todavía se pueden encontrar lugares pero yo nunca los he visto y tampoco he encontrado a alguien que los conozca. Todo lo que sé es que hacemos hoy en día. Naturalmente hay cosas que no puedes hacer, hay reglas. No es que puedes hacer todo lo que quieras. Hay leyes. Antes la gente encontraba cosas viejas en las playas, en los hoyos y las podía quemar para cocinar, pero ahora todo eso ya no se hace, ya no puedes encontrar cosas así. Hoy solamente se sala y se mantiene seca y después de un rato ya no está mal. Evidentemente hay todo un proceso antes de que sea salada: se sacrifica y se corta en tiras. Lo hacen allá en el cañón, fuera de la vista. La gente no quiere ver todo lo que pasa allí. Yo no podría hacer ese trabajo, allí abajo, en los sombras y con el frío. Por eso trabajan allá, porque el frío minimiza el olor. Y el ruido, todas aquellas mujeres, todo el día ¿Pero tienes que vivir, no? Hombre, yo no podría hacer ese trabajo, de ninguna manera. Sé que puede parecer raro si lo digo, pues siempre ha sido así desde que tengo memoria, pero sigue sin gustarme, no creo que sea lo que tendríamos que hacer, sabes. Tiene buen sabor, sobre todo la más seca cuanto más la dejas madurar más se pone, y sabe muy rica. Hay diferentes nombres para los diferentes tipos, hay toda una variedad. La parte vieja, esa que fue ahumada, se supone que es la mejor, aunque está muy cara, __ __ __ no la pueden __ ya no queda nada por quemar.

Figure 3.15

Human Rites – *shrouded by materialism*

Winding weeds
Embrace the illusory
Delusory
Disinfected shell.

Death, fundamental
to life is yet despised
by the modern mind
and sullied by its
sanitized commodification.
A life loved dispatched
without caress and smell
of decaying intimacy.
In celebrating the life,
the silence is filled,
the heart spurned.
Away!

Let me mourn,
let me grieve
I am become
this severing wound.

A life expired,
stirring the breath of
our enfolding mortality,
demands its due.

Materials: *earth-coloured calico, handcarved bone bodkin, hemp cord, dried plants*

Figure 3.16

Finale – *premedicated death*

The banality of choice over the counter to the other side.
An unbearable decision, a painful burden on a society
where the self-administered last hurrah becomes
a duty of care towards the ebb and flow of a
bloodied vein that slowly, and slower,
irreversibly slows, and slackens
and imperceptibly weakens
and finally lets
go.

Materials: *0.5 mm hypodermic needle, 5.0 ml syringe, pre-injection swab, 10.0 ml sterilized vial, card packaging*

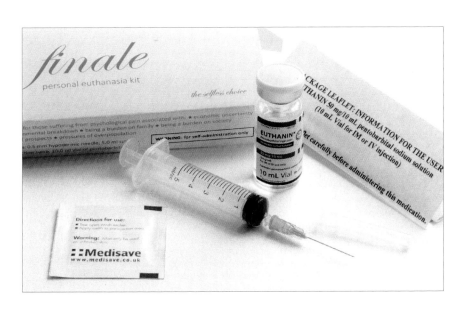

4
The Shift
an inward path to
holistic design

Your means are very slender, and your waste is great

William Shakespeare

INTRODUCTION

In this chapter I describe the context, outcomes and insights of exploratory, practice-based design research conducted over a prolonged period. The research focuses on how contemporary concerns about personal meaning, social equity and environmental care disturb our assumptions and understandings of design, which can lead to new ways of thinking about how we create our material culture. The combination of study, practice and reflection results in the interrelated outcomes of reasoned arguments and designed objects. By reflecting on the work that has emerged, new insights can be drawn that reveal both the journey taken and, more importantly and only in retrospect, the discoveries made as the process unfolded and evolved. This reflection on the longitudinal progression of discovery by design enables first-hand experience to contribute to the task of developing a more meaningful and more socially and environmentally sustaining conception of material culture.

The discussion begins with a consideration of design as it emerged during the twentieth century and its ties to mass production, globalization and consumerism. Because these developments are inescapably linked to unprecedented environmental and social harm, the agenda of design research is developed from one of gradual improvement within the current manufacturing context to one of fundamental, systemic change; that is, from incremental design to holistic design. The critical role of design practice and the importance of creative thinking, intuition and subjectivity in the development of these findings are described and explained.

PERPETUATING THE PROBLEM

Today, we continue to design and manufacture products that are useful, attractive and affordable. In doing so, we are perpetuating and, indeed, expanding the mass-production system that arose in the twentieth century during the period known as Modernism; a period characterized by cultural and artistic responses to modernity and the industrialization of society. This system of production has been very successful in generating wealth, raising material standards of living for many and creating jobs; in the process it has also raised our material expectations.

Modernism's influence continues to dominate design, as is evident in the minimalist products of some of the world's most successful companies – Apple in the United States, IKEA in Sweden, and Braun in Germany. These products, which express the culture of the Bauhaus and Modernism's ethos of *less is more*,[1] have strong appeal through a combination of instrumental and socio-positional value coupled with affordability. Within our consumption-based, globalized economic system, this kind of design and production has proved to be highly exploitative of people and nature. Corporations constantly seek out cheaper labour markets, resulting in low wages, poor-quality jobs,[2] reductions in employee benefits, debilitation of unions,[3] and a downward spiral of working conditions, often in the world's poorest countries. In recent years, these activities have been frequently linked to child labour and other exploitative practices.[4,5,6] In regard to the natural environment, rising emissions[7] and rapid loss of habitats and species[8] make it all too evident that industry responses to the environmental repercussions of its activities have been grossly inadequate. In addition, through globalization and free-trade agreements, corporations exploit trans-border loopholes to avoid tax,[9] resulting in fewer revenues for public services, including the clean-up of waste and pollution, and a deterioration of the commons.

93

Within this system, waste can be understood not just in terms of landfill, pollution and emissions but also in terms of the socially damaging effects, including the waste of human talent, potential and opportunity. So while there may be benefits, there are also very significant deficits; perhaps above all, it is a highly competitive system that takes advantage of, rather than adequately providing for, those most in need of support.

Contemporary design is part of this system, and as such it contributes to an industry that seeks continual expansion and growth. This is achieved by saturating the market with products and employing a multi-billion-dollar advertising sector to persuade us all to consume more and more things, most of which can't be repaired, have fragile finishes, and are rapidly superseded. Electronic devices become technologically outdated within months and subsequent product releases, with slightly more advanced applications, are given an updated outer form that provides an external sign of internal change. This new appearance serves as an indicator to others that the owner is technologically up to date, which in today's society, and fomented by marketing, confers a certain prestige. Such tactics consciously combine technological and psychological obsolescence to drive sales, inevitably escalating waste. Consequently, the lifespans of most electronic devices are extremely short – as little as two years for many computers and mobile phones.[10] Even though the activities they make possible can have inherent value, such as a video conversation with a loved one living abroad, the value of these devices is primarily instrumental in nature. They are essentially functional tools that are readily discarded and replaced. Products that employ more stable technologies – kitchen appliances and handheld products such as hairdryers and power tools – could potentially last many years, but, due to modern modes of design and manufacture, they too are frequently unable to be repaired and thus virtually disposable. Again, this helps drive sales and escalate waste. Even basic objects like chairs, tables and cabinets, when mass-produced from low-grade materials, will wear badly, be difficult to maintain and have only a short useful life.

These approaches have become the norm in contemporary society because they reduce costs, increase profits and keep us buying. It has led to a fetishizing of superficial choice[11] and, inevitably, to overproduction. It is a system based on deregulated, free-market fundamentalism, and it primarily serves corporate interests and the wealthy few.[12] Former chief scientist at Unilever, Peter Lillford, has said, *"Everybody thinks that waste reduction is, in principle, a good idea but the industry doesn't want to sell less stuff. Waste, in principle, is good business".* [13]

In recent decades the discipline of design has been making some attempts to address environmental issues in the field of consumer products. Typically, it has adopted such measures as reducing materials use and energy consumption, improving efficiencies, specifying nontoxic materials, and adopting reuse and recycling. As discussed in the previous chapter, this eco-modernist type of design helps create greener, slightly less damaging products, but the consumption-based system in which it exists is not changed to any significant degree. And it does not affect the pervasive outlook that the good life rests on material acquisition.

To unmake waste we must unmake the outlooks, values and priorities that lead to waste. There is undoubtedly a need to consider more profound notions of meaning, but our busy world of never-off communications and passive entertainments tends to eliminate time for the inner life. Our technological prowess has seemingly entranced us and created a dizzying overconfidence in our own capabilities – capabilities that are focussed firmly on material benefits and sense-based experiences. Yet, as we produce increasing numbers of gadgets and leave in our wake a decimated world of squalor and pollution, we seldom stop to ask why. In her book, *New Maladies of the Soul*, Professor Julia Kristeva conjures a vivid image of where this all tends to lead:

95

> *I am picturing a sprawling metropolis with glass and steel buildings that reach to the sky, reflect it, reflect each other, and reflect you – a city filled with people steeped in their own image who rush about with overdone make-up on and who are cloaked in gold, pearls, and fine leather, while in the next street over, heaps of filth abound and drugs accompany the sleep or the fury of the social outcasts.*
>
> *This city could be New York: it could be any future metropolis, even your own.*
>
> *What might one do in such a city? Nothing but buy and sell goods and images, which amounts to the same thing, since they both are dull shallow symbols. Those who can or wish to preserve a lifestyle that downplays opulence as well as misery will need to create a space for an "inner zone" – a secret garden, an intimate quarter... .* [14]

THE TRAJECTORY OF CURRENT DEVELOPMENTS

Scientific knowledge is always moving forward, and when this knowledge is applied to serve human needs it can yield many benefits. But the fact that the knowledge on which they are based is always advancing inevitably means that the resultant applications, technologies and products are in a persistent state of becoming obsolete. In our current production model this is manifested as redundancy and waste. Furthermore, the demand for growth means that new products constantly have to be developed and so the *rate* of product obsolescence also increases. Hence, soaring levels of waste, pollution and emissions are not simply unfortunate side effects that can be rectified through further technological advances – they are fundamental to the system itself. Despite this, technological advancement continues to preoccupy manufacturing industries because, in our consumption-based economy, it is this that provides competitive advantage. 'Greener' products such as electric cars, solar-powered devices and energy-efficient appliances may offer some improvements but they do not get to the heart of the matter. They have little impact on the overall detriments of consumption and their presence serves to maintain rather than contest the current system. Far more substantial change than this is needed – change that leads to fewer products, less consumption, greater restrictions on advertising and reduced dependency on energy-hungry gadgets.[15, 16]

The goals and priorities of corporate and political leaders are, however, often antithetical if not hostile to such change, despite the fact that the vast majority of climate scientists maintain that major reductions in energy use and successive emissions cuts of around 10 per cent per year over coming decades are needed to avoid dangerous levels of warming.[17] Clearly, a system that depends on ever-growing markets for short-lived technological products will be a system that relentlessly escalates environmental harm and unsustainable lifestyles; and, indeed, this is exactly what is happening. The International Resource Panel of the United Nations Environmental Programme (UNEP), while noting that *"technological solutions have substantial potential to prevent harm to humans and ecosystems"*, explains that, over the last century, driven by *"scientific and technological advances, the extraction of construction materials grew by a factor of 34, ores and minerals by a factor of 27, fossil fuels by a factor of 12, and biomass by a factor of 3.6 ... This expansion of consumption was not equitably distributed, and it had profound environmental impacts. Over-exploitation, climate change, pollution, land-use change, and loss of biodiversity rose toward to [sic] top of the list of major international concerns".* The report also notes that substantial reductions will only be forthcoming with *"radical technological and system change".*[18]

THE DIGITAL IMPETUS

The rapid worldwide adoption of digital products indicates that their benefits are clearly regarded as outweighing their costs, at least in the short term. The technologies on which they depend are on course to yield a host of increasingly sophisticated products and applications that will offer new capabilities in many aspects of life – communications, gaming, shopping and healthcare, as well as interconnected objects, systems and services. The magnitude of investment in this area, its vast potential, and its rapid pace of development mean that these technologies will continue to be highly dynamic and transient for the foreseeable future.

While digital services can provide a wide array of benefits, there is no doubt that they are accompanied by many drawbacks, all of which receive far less attention. In the free-market capitalist system we look to opportunities for growth in an imbalanced, if not blinkered, manner. We can think, for example, of small towns welcoming 'big box' retailers to set up their stores on out-of-town sites, with the promise of local jobs and increased choice, only to find that they result in net reductions in employment and overall retail earnings,[19] increased infrastructure costs and congestion, and the decline of town centres.[20] Similarly, major disadvantages accompany digital developments. These include the costs of societal atomization and the loss of privacy associated with data tracking, as well as the personal and social effects of stress and anxiety that attend disruptive technological change, as occurred in earlier times, during the transition to the modern era. There are also the environmental costs; over the next few years, the global production of e-waste is set to rise by some 33 per cent.[21] This will be accompanied by further resource extraction and product production as well as increasing levels of data storage and associated energy use and emissions. Moreover, the effects of digital products and services are self-reinforcing because the data tracking and targeted marketing they enable are used to constantly encourage further consumption. For all their sophistication, therefore, current forms of digital products and services actually represent more of the same – more consumption, more waste and more social division – rather than any significantly new direction.

DESIGN FOR RADICAL CHANGE

In design, we can make inroads into eradicating waste by imagining and helping to develop forms of material culture that do not conform to this dominant milieu. Tinkering with and attempting to adapt the present system is likely to have little effect because continual growth tied to rising consumption simply cannot be sustained on a finite planet. More radical approaches are needed – the creation of ways of living that are environmentally responsible, socially equitable and personally fulfilling requires systemic change.[22] Such an enormous task is, of course, easier said than done. There is much vested interest in the current system – in our institutions and corporations – that serves to obstruct positive change, hinder reasonable and responsible dialogue and muddy the debate. A recent study found that millions of dollars of so-called 'dark money' linked to major charitable foundations and 'big oil' are being channelled toward climate change denial.[23] In 2016, The Rockefeller Family Fund, which was founded on the oil industry, announced its intention to divest from fossil fuels, in doing so it also stated on its website:

> We would be remiss if we failed to focus on what we believe to be the morally reprehensible conduct on the part of ExxonMobil. Evidence appears to suggest that the company worked since the 1980s to confuse the public about climate change's march, while simultaneously spending millions to fortify its own infrastructure against climate change's destructive consequences and track new exploration opportunities as the Arctic's ice receded.[24]

In developing new directions for design that are representative of different priorities, we must consider those ways of knowing that have been undervalued in recent times. Non-modern worldviews are generally able to transcend the mundane world of materialism and reach beyond the five senses and scientific knowledge of the external world to include the inner person and the imagination. In this regard, it is significant to note that *"there are no worlds that are not imaginary, no conceptual fixes on the environment that do not somewhere require the projection of a context that is not available to us in its entirety"*.[25] This more inclusive worldview, which places value on the subjective and inner development, enabled pre-modern cultures to live in closer harmony with the natural world, and gave rise to some of our most creative and profound works of literature, poetry and art. Today, it can provide a new basis for design.

Throughout human history, serious consideration has always been given to finding balance between outer actions and inner reflection. A different perspective and new priorities emerge when both are allowed to flourish. We can, at once, consider the future while also living more fully in the present. As American writer Henry Miller says,

> Seeking intuitively, one's destination is never in a beyond of time and space but always here and now. If we are always arriving and departing, it is also true that we are eternally anchored. One's destination is never a place but rather a new way of looking at things.[26]

It is this inner life beyond the senses and the intellect that yields a quality of perception and a subtlety of distinctions and meanings[27] far more profound than those offered by the captivating narrative of consumerism. To restore balance, it becomes necessary to reconsider the place and role of these deeper aspects of our nature. These ways of knowing are quite different from the kinds of progressive, transient knowledge that drives techno-scientific advancement and, as Miller says, they impart a sense of stability in a changing world. They are explored and comprehended through philosophical deliberation, self-examination and inner evolution and, for many, through belief systems and spiritual or religious practices; and we should not forget that the scientific enterprise itself is also a kind of a belief system.[28, 29] Significantly for this present discussion, these meaning-seeking ways of knowing are also realized and expressed through creative endeavours and the arts.

99

The arts are not primarily grounded in knowledge of material phenomena but in culture, imagination and the human inclination for creative expression. The arts are judged in terms of their quality, not their empirical accuracy or correctness; we speak of artistic excellence and originality or artistic vacuity and incompetence. Undoubtedly, too, there is a temporal aspect to such judgements – it is often the case that the passage of time is needed for the significance of an artwork to be fully appreciated. The best of the arts resonates with that which is permanent in us, that which is tacitly understood but may lie beyond explicit description. In doing so, artworks can become enduring contributions to human civilization – always relevant, always new. The poetry of Homer, the plays of Sophocles, the music of Hildegard of Bingen, the novels of the Brontës, and the images of Andrei Rublev and Matisse – all speak to us across the centuries – still fresh, still affecting, still meaningful; as the novelist Graham Greene wrote, "Ideas never changed, the world never moved: it lay there always, the ravaged and disputed territory between two eternities".[30]

Hence, in contrast to the evolving and therefore transient nature of scientific endeavours, the arts are concerned with meanings and essential human truths; they do not progress in the same way, and the best of them are timeless. Scientific knowledge and the accumulating technological capabilities that proceed from it allow us to achieve practical tasks in highly sophisticated ways. But where science seeks to explain and describe, art is concerned with meanings and values, and the outcomes primarily address questions of understanding. As we saw in Chapter 3, these two views of the world are largely incommensurable, pointing to what Scruton refers to as *cognitive dualism*[31] – two views coexisting within the same material environment but seeing it and interpreting it in different ways. We can experience the world in a direct way, where we are connected to the reality of existence in its complex, dynamic and ever-changing state and where we feel part of the whole. We can also experience the world in a manner that is more detached – we abstract ourselves from the world and *"'experience' our experience"* in a way that is simpler and in some respects clearer. In this abstracted mode we delineate, categorize and create a world that is more understandable and more easily controlled and made useful to our needs.[32] Importantly, the meaning-making preoccupations of the arts, and the values and priorities they engender, are located in and emerge from the more direct, living world of human experiences: our relationships with others – family, community and society, and our relationships with the natural world. These are subjective, particularized, located experiences, not objective, values-free facts about material phenomena and causes. As Ward says, *"Meaning and understanding are, for human beings, existential; they concern our very living and ability to live. Life is 'the bearer of meaning', Ricoeur tells us. We dwell in life-worlds that language generates"*.[33]

Design is not only a kind of language, a mode of expressing ourselves, it also straddles these two views of the world – but the designer has neither the specialized knowledge and capability of the scientist and technologist nor the creative freedom of the artist. The designer is a generalist and synthesizer who strives to find resolutions that effectively integrate the *what* and *how* questions of functional design with the *why* questions of meaning making and aesthetic expression. Restoring balance in design implies moving design agendas beyond the priorities and aesthetic conventions of Modernism to embrace this richer world of meaning and permanence in a manner that is consistent with critical contemporary concerns. A design approach that emerges from solitude, contemplation and creative insight takes design beyond a consequentialist morality to an interiorized, principled notion of ethical behaviour and decision-making. Even though our material productions are based largely on the findings and applications of science, these crucial, values-based aspects of design fall outside its jurisdiction and expertise. As discussed earlier, our material productions and the manner in which they are designed and presented imply a notion of the good life, and notions of the good life are shaped by our values and concepts such as justice, right thinking, right action, duty and virtue, all of which transcend science and descriptions of the physical world.[34]

Through our forms of expression, whether in words, images or objects, we declare our views and our values and, in doing so, we assert a position with respect to others and the world. These relationships between the individual 'I' and other people and the world in general form the basis of human meaning and of meaningful actions. These relationships form our sense of identity, our moral behaviour and the nature of our contribution to human culture. It is for these very reasons that design is quite different from the sciences and should not attempt to adopt their methods and processes, even though it often relies on the findings of science in its work. The methods and processes of science are simply inappropriate within the design sphere, they employ a different language and seek different kinds of outcomes. Design, and indeed any creative act that invokes the imagination, includes the language of the subject, the 'I', and the 'I's intentions, reasons and choices. This is the 'I' of personhood, which is emergent – a continual becoming and negotiation in relation to others and the world. When 'I', as the creator of a piece, attempt to express through design what I mean, and when I consider how I feel about its success in achieving my intentions, I am dealing with notions of self, the subject, in relation to the object. I am saying something in a manner that recognizes social and moral values, norms and understandings, and I am declaring a position through this particular form of expression. This position may be in accord with the mainstream direction of commercial design or it may challenge it – either way, it will involve subjective decisions and value judgements. It may recognize others as subjects too, or merely as objects – consumers, units of consumption. Whatever position is adopted, through creative practice the designer is expressing certain values and implicitly saying 'I am accountable for this expression, this state of affairs' – for saying something *in this particular way*.

101

THINGS THAT ENDURE

G. K. Chesterton argued that traditional fairy tales and legends are timeless because they are products both of the human imagination and of many people in a particular locale.[35] Fairy tales, folk tales and mythical stories tell of the human condition itself and they are inherently democratic. They embody values and meanings that are common to everyone, to our shared humanity, and this is why they are so enduring. *The Tales of a Thousand and One Nights*, the legends of King Arthur and the stories collected by the Brothers Grimm continue to speak to generation after generation and, as they move through time, they become imaginatively embellished by the storyteller, allowing them to remain relevant to new audiences.[36] Such stories, originating from ordinary people, have a social value. They express the culture that arises organically from the experiences of people in a particular place, and the sharing of this culture through common forms of expression helps build community coherence. These grassroots, imaginative forms of expression are living artefacts because they continue to be changed and adapted in ways that are natural and familiar.[37] Their value lies both in the collective and the individual – in common sources and shared understandings as well as in the expertise of the individual storyteller, who brings them alive through creative interpretations that are responsive to context. By comparison, modern novels are the product of one mind and the vast majority are quickly forgotten.

These points can be applied just as well to the artefacts of our material culture. Contemporary mass-produced material goods are prosaically functional and are driven by innovation and newness. If they have symbolic value it is created in a top-down manner by marketing departments and linked to status, social positioning and division. And for the most part this is a material culture that is quickly outdated, discarded and forgotten.

Accompanying, but in stark contrast to, globalization, corporate ascendancy and developments in the digital, there has been a growing interest in place-based initiatives and areas of endeavour that are either unable to be digitized or at least less concerned with technological solutions and international markets. These include a growing interest in local products and foods, as well as social innovations that support localism and self-determination,[38] alternative economies,[39, 40] slow design,[41] and renewed interest in craft objects, locally made products and material artefacts that are culturally significant.[42, 43] Turner Prize–winning artist Grayson Perry has said that he wages war on 'global culture', arguing that trying to appeal to everyone leads to blandness. He creates work that emerges from a particular place and culture – work that may well be, and evidently is, valued elsewhere.[44] Similarly, the music of Estonian composer Arvo Pärt has universal appeal but it is firmly grounded in a very specific tradition, that of Orthodox Christianity.[45] All these examples allow the grain and texture of real world encounters to be more fully experienced, enhancing interpersonal connections and understandings, building and binding community, and contributing to a sense of meaning, belonging and identity.

As with stories, artefacts that emerge from a particular place can embody common meanings and address the human condition in ways that are both located and democratic. In doing so, they contribute to a common ground and a common good that serve to connect and unite people. And over time, locally produced artefacts can be adapted and imaginatively embellished by the designer to meet new conditions and needs, thereby offering both continuity and change. Quite humble artefacts, if made from quality materials, can often be enduring and useful over many generations, becoming more beautiful with age. These may include local housing forms, furniture, textiles, sacred objects, jewellery, household goods and tools. In order to address today's social and environmental challenges, new ways forward will have to give far greater consideration to these kinds of approaches – to localizing our economies and to place-based initiatives that are community focussed. Such a transition requires radical systemic change and imaginative, egalitarian visions. Clearly we cannot continue with the current consumption-based system because it is rapidly depleting the natural environment and the manner in which it serves corporate agendas is socially destructive. Moreover, vested interests make it unlikely that it can be effectively adapted.[46]

A more distributed, grassroots approach can allow a wide variety of initiatives to arise that take into account local knowledge, skills, needs and conditions – and here there is potential for design to make a thoughtful and sensitive contribution. The resultant artefacts, and the materials, processes and meanings they embody, can serve to reflect and reinforce values, beliefs, customs and more enduring aspects of human culture. Such artefacts would not only be functional and useful but also tangible representations of more considerate and responsive attitudes. They would then be contributing not to a destructive spiral of production, disposal and waste but to the development of a meaningful and lasting social and material culture. In this context, objects become far more than formal expressions of function, and far less than premeditated expressions of status based on consumption. Through their modes of making and their essential character

103

as things, they can be representative of deeper understandings of what it is to be human and symbolic of values that accord with communal coherence and social justice, individual flourishing, and environmental care. These kinds of objects can be enduring because their value lies not just in what they allow us to do but also in what they mean, and that meaning emerges from place, people and, potentially, from values that tend to virtue.

It follows that, in the activity of designing, we have to be conscious of what values are being adhered to and expressed through design. We have to ask ourselves if these values align with a culture of care and consideration for others and the natural environment, or if they spread envy, greed and social status. The designer has to consider these questions in the round, in terms of the intended purpose of the artefact as well as its making, use and after-use. These are complex issues requiring judgement in relation to context and contemporary concerns. The benefit of any specific contribution will not be fixed, but will be relative to the circumstances of a particular time and place. Notably, too, this raises questions about our ability – as designers, producers, and as a society – to address such context-sensitive questions within a fast-changing globalized production system.

104 OUTLOOK SHIFT – TOWARDS A MORE MEANINGFUL MATERIAL CULTURE

At the beginning of this chapter I suggested that to unmake waste we have to unmake the outlooks, values and priorities that lead to waste. The development of more egalitarian, grassroots approaches would go some way to achieving this because it allows our endeavours to respond more effectively to context and helps foster an economy of localized production and service along with communal interdependencies, care for others, and greater environmental awareness. However, while our outlook is to some extent shaped by society it is also shaped by our inner values, which are nurtured through more introspective modes of being. By giving due regard to inner development, we begin to see our actions in a new light and, over time, we may cultivate a different outlook, deeper values and redirected priorities. While each of us has the opportunity to do this, those in the creative arts are also able to show, in the form of tangible artefacts, what difference this might mean for our actions in the world. By demonstrating this difference through design we move from generalities and abstractions to concrete examples, which can be reflected upon and discussed. In adopting such a route, designers can bring critique to the broader philosophical issues and normative assumptions that underlie current approaches. This can then inform their creative work, and the resulting designs will help raise awareness and contribute to a broader shift in perspectives.

This brings us to the practice-based components of design research, which necessarily include subjective elements, as discussed earlier. Various interrelated strands emerging from an extended period of practice-based design research are summarized below. These were developed in an organic manner and, as is to be expected in any emergent, creative process, the paths taken vary from the methodical to the serendipitous. In this particular, personal example of practice-based research, and recognizing that there are many overlaps and iterations, the process can be broadly categorized as developing in the following phases:

Incremental Design: Functional designs that incorporate one or more common elements of environmental care such as reduce, reuse and recycle. Creative outcomes include practical objects such as chairs, cabinets, lamps, music equipment and telephones. All employ reused or recycled materials and local skills and therefore, to a greater of lesser extent, adhere to notions of 'grassroots design', which was one of the approaches to design change introduced in the previous chapter.

105

Design for Inner Reflection: Designs for focussed attention – for dedicating time to reflection, and inner development. The presence of such objects in our lives also serves as a reminder of the importance of the inner life, which is so easily forgotten in today's busy daily routines. Design outcomes include objects that offer a tangible focus for single-pointed attention and contemplation – these include specifically designed objects as well as objects that are simply selected elements from the natural environment. These, therefore, can be understood as forms of 'contemplative design'.

Critiques of Consumerism: The methods of design are used here not to create functional objects but to address ideas about the nature of our material culture in the context of contemporary challenges and issues. In this regard, scientific evidence, rational argument and logical explanation are all important but they represent a purely intellectual understanding of the issues. This type of knowledge alone has proven woefully inadequate in stimulating timely and substantive change. Design has the capacity to express ideas in another way – visually and experientially through objects. In doing so, issues of concern are communicated via an holistic aesthetic experience; they are not conveyed sequentially, explicitly or intellectually but instantaneously and tacitly. Such objects, which are impressionistic and whose meanings are declarative and interpretative but less definitive than text-based accounts, can stimulate thought and invite reflection. They exist in the natural world of the senses, but their meanings can transcend the physical and point to a deeper, psychological interpretation. In this way, creative design can build on but reach beyond the findings of science. This is a necessary and important step, because we can have all the facts but, to make a difference, the issues have to touch us personally, on an individual level. Creative, imaginative design speaks not only to the rational, objective side of us but also to our intuitive, subjective side and, crucially, it is through this deeper, values-based understanding that such ideas start to take root and thence begin to change one's perspective, attitudes and actions.[47, 48] Going beyond rational argument, objects can offer a form of critique that touches the emotions as well as the intellect; the heart as well as the head. More specifically, design can be used to express and reflect back to us counterpoints to societal norms, especially critiques of consumer goods and consumerism and the broader issues they raise about growth, energy use, inconsequential choice, waste and the pervasive culture of dissatisfaction created by the advertising sector. These objects straddle 'contemplative design' and 'counterpoints'.

Critiques of the Dominant Worldview: Employing similar means, but extending and broadening the sphere of consideration beyond consumerism *per se*, design can be employed to constructively critique the dominant worldview; a worldview that still largely represents the values of modernity, even as it is being adapted to include late-modern or after-modern sensibilities. Essentially, this design work constitutes a critique of modernity and its enduring legacy, it includes objects that make visible and implicitly question these unsustainable outlooks, values and priorities. The aesthetics of a designed object, too often regarded merely as applied facade or superficial style, actually contribute to the experiential world of meanings and constitute an important and revealing aspect of an object. Essentially, the aesthetics are an expression of the values of those who created it. An object's aesthetics, therefore, express and reflect much about who we are and what we hold dear. These objects can be understood as 'counterpoints'.

Holistic Design: Emerging from attention to these inner aspects of our personhood and the consequent shift in outlook, our design work can begin to embody deeper values and new attitudes. Transcending intellectual knowledge through aesthetic and emotional experiences, design can take into account the personal, social and environmental effects – positive and negative – of object manufacture, use, maintenance and disposal. Perhaps especially through localization and place-based initiatives, design can make positive and appropriate contributions to change. Through such means, it can be part of a broad movement that, as we have seen, is already happening around the world where people are taking greater responsibility for their material culture, their food production and energy supplies, away from globalized, corporate agendas. Local approaches are small-scale, flexible, adaptive and can be represented by various sectors – for profit and non-profit as well as voluntary and amateur. In this way they can contribute to an economy of responsible production and service rather than an economy of consumption and disposal. Local-scale design, as we have seen, can be expressive of context-specific interests and values. Such artefacts, therefore, will contribute to a sense of identity and community, thereby helping to restore many of those things that have been lost in globalized forms of consumer capitalism.

107

This design work includes functional objects whose making and/or use help cultivate inner development. The practices enabled by these objects are often characterized by repetitions and silence, allowing the mind to wander and de-focus, which is a necessary condition for the imagination, synthetical insight and creativity to flourish.[49, 50] Examples include activities such as knitting, spinning, and whittling; these will be discussed in greater depth in Chapter 7. These practices address both the outer person of actions in the world and the inner person of reflection and imagination. More broadly, holistic design refers to integrative design work that strives to bring together all the above categories by addressing utility, localization, values and meaning, and empathy with nature. In this way, outer, worldly benefits become integrated with what are traditionally regarded as deeper, inner or higher considerations. With this synthesis, we shift from objects of primarily instrumental value, which are so easily discarded and replaced as needs and technologies change, to objects whose perceived value lies not just in their functionality but also in their inherent qualities as things – their history, aesthetics, and their enduring meanings, as embodied in their materials, making, use, and cultural or personal symbolism. Here, design outcomes include enabling artefacts, which in their use provide opportunities for quiet contemplation, and integrative artefacts; both embody deeper values and enduring meanings.

We see from the above sequence of discovery and development that the creative endeavour begins with outer considerations, under the heading *Incremental Design*, which address practical, worldly concerns such as functionality, place, materials, processes, reuse, and environment. This is where each individual is bound to begin, in the outer world of sense-based understandings. However, by questioning current directions and our own assumptions, the work increasingly becomes informed by deeper considerations about values and priorities. Through study, creativity and reflection, we start to see consumerism and the worldview of which it is a part in a new light. Insights and realizations develop through dedication to inner understanding – the examined life. This leads to a shift in outlook, new priorities, and a more comprehensive interpretation of material culture; that is, *holistic design*. Examples from these design phases from *incremental design* to *holistic design* are shown in Figure 4.1.

In addition, it is important to recognize that, through inner development, the basis of the design work changes over time; in effect, there is a reversal in the ordering. Beginning in the sense-based world of practical applications, the work increasingly encompasses substantive values and matters of deeper concern; here the movement is from *outer to inner*. Eventually, this inward journey can lead to a shift in outlook, which reshapes the values and priorities we bring to our design endeavours; the movement here is from *inner to outer*. *Outer* and *inner* are related, but there are no direct connections. The natural world of physical matter is separate from and dissimilar to the inner world of reflection and deeper notions of personhood. As Scruton says, *"The human world, ordered by first-person awareness, emerges from the order of nature, while remaining incommensurable with it"*.[51] Even so, the inward path, and its attendant shift in outlook, does affect the nature of our actions in the world, including the ways in which we do design. Indeed, the practice of design itself can be a way of pursuing inner growth and understanding. Design combines knowledge development through study, object creation, and reflection. It is exactly this combination of thinking, doing, and contemplation that helps foster greater understanding, insight and a fundamental shift in outlook.[52] The personal journey from outer to inner via design practice is shown in Figure 4.2, using specific design examples.

108

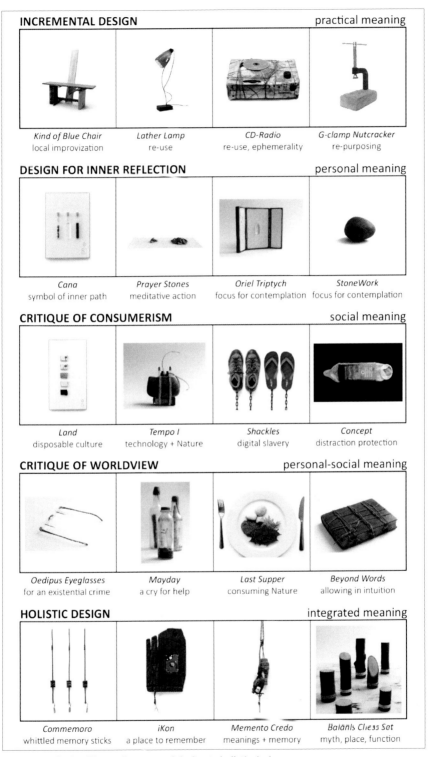

INCREMENTAL DESIGN — practical meaning

Kind of Blue Chair	*Lather Lamp*	*CD-Radio*	*G-clamp Nutcracker*
local improvization	re-use	re-use, ephemerality	re-purposing

DESIGN FOR INNER REFLECTION — personal meaning

Cana	*Prayer Stones*	*Oriel Triptych*	*StoneWork*
symbol of inner path	meditative action	focus for contemplation	focus for contemplation

CRITIQUE OF CONSUMERISM — social meaning

Land	*Tempo I*	*Shackles*	*Concept*
disposable culture	technology + Nature	digital slavery	distraction protection

CRITIQUE OF WORLDVIEW — personal-social meaning

Oedipus Eyeglasses	*Mayday*	*Last Supper*	*Beyond Words*
for an existential crime	a cry for help	consuming Nature	allowing in intuition

HOLISTIC DESIGN — integrated meaning

Commemoro	*iKon*	*Memento Credo*	*Balanis Chess Set*
whittled memory sticks	a place to remember	meanings + memory	myth, place, function

Figure 4.1 Design Phases: incremental design to holistic design

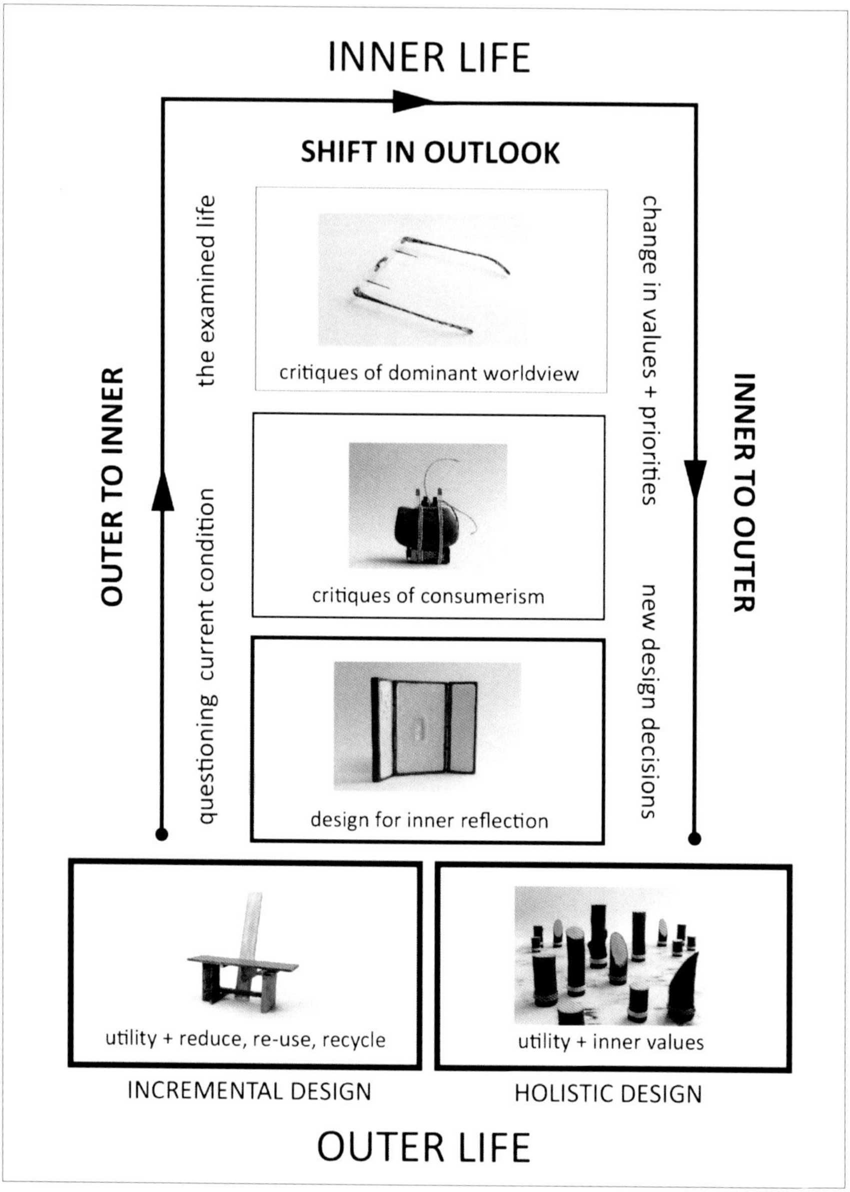

Figure 4.2 Personal Journey: from outer to inner via design practice

A more generalized version indicating the basis and comprehensive nature of the shift from *Incremental Design* to *Holistic Design* is offered in Figure 4.3.

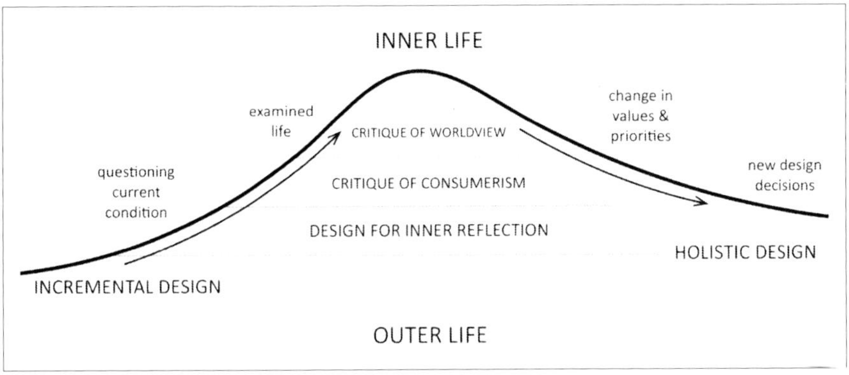

Figure 4.3   Design Shift: from incremental design to holistic design

HOLISTIC DESIGN, FAMILIAR BEAUTY AND ENDURING MEANING

As we have discussed, many contemporary mass-produced products are highly susceptible to technological and psychological obsolescence. By contrast, repairable products based on stable technologies and good quality materials can last many years. The creation of more enduring forms of material culture has both environmental and social benefits. In general, longer lasting products are less environmentally harmful. Energy-consuming products may be the exception to this,[53] but even here, upgrade is often preferable to complete replacement. As we move from machines and devices that are in a state of relatively rapid advancement to products based on more stable, low or no technologies, our material culture takes on a different aspect, becoming valued in ways that transcend mere function. Because they last, we become accustomed to their presence. If they are created in a manner that is sensitive to their context of use, unpretentious and of good quality materials, they can be seen as both fitting and beautiful even as, or indeed because, they acquire the signs and scars of age. The importance of localization and context-appropriate design is tied to this. As John Ruskin pointed out in his discussion of the Westmorland Cottage, however beautiful in itself, an object still has to be suited to and in harmony with the spirit of the place in which it exists, without which it *"excites no sympathy"* and *"would be dead"*. Its beauty, he argues, emerges from its fit within its context, its use of the natural materials available within that place and its modest aspect.[54] Similarly, Perry has said, *"one of the biggest aspects of beauty is familiarity"*.[55] We can see that this familiar beauty engenders a sense of belonging amongst one's surroundings, which is further strengthened by the shared human experiences enabled by things

111

that last. It is here, amid these common experiences that affections, obligations and a sense of responsibility towards each other and the place itself – natural and human-made – can develop. It is here, in the living world of experiences and activities, that substantive values and enduring meanings connect with enduring objects. And, of course, this living world of experiences and activities is facilitated in part by 'fitting' material things.

It becomes evident that the value of an object resides partly in itself as a thing of beauty that is appreciated as such; partly in its instrumental role as a thing that allows us to achieve something else; partly in its role in enabling specific human experiences that are of inherent value; and partly in its role in contributing to an enduring and hence familiar material world that helps foster common understandings. These interrelated factors surpass the stringent primacy of instrumental value and profit margins to also recognize critically important relationships that involve deeper human values within the social and environmental context. By acknowledging the importance of all these roles, we arrive at a far more comprehensive interpretation of design – one that strives to create objects that are, at once, functionally relevant, spiritually enriching, socially reifying and environmentally responsible.

112 CONCLUSIONS

We see that many of the negative effects of contemporary products, such as e-waste, emissions, landfill and pollutants, lie in the particularities of their material thingness, in the ways they are designed and produced. There are also the poor employment conditions in their manufacture, privacy issues, addictive use behaviours, and targeted marketing based on data mining. In today's globalized corporate milieu, an object's particularities are determined largely by factors related to competition within a globalized, growth-based economic system. To remedy these environmental and social effects will require substantial shifts in policy, binding international agreements and regulation, and far greater efforts in terms of corporate ethics and responsibility. From this larger perspective, the contributions of the individual designer may be relatively small but nevertheless they can be constructive and influential because the designer is able to visualize and hence 'make real' new, more positive directions. However, to achieve meaningful and significant change, the designer will have to develop imaginative and innovative directions that are reflective of quite different priorities and radically new understandings.

Transient technological products can hold significant value, but this value lies in the functions or opportunities they allow, not in their material thingness. This is actually the case for many products whether or not they incorporate the latest technologies, are physically transient, or are more enduring. Values and meanings are found through their use – the functional capabilities, practices and customs they enable. These experiences and activities are dependent on and presuppose the product's material thingness. We can conclude from the arguments presented here that some other form of material thingness is urgently required – one that results from a far broader, more comprehensive understanding of design. An understanding that rejects built-in obsolescence and the aesthetics of seduction and, instead, leads to functional products that embody deeper human values. An understanding that recognizes spiritual as well as utilitarian needs and pays far greater attention to social obligations and environmental responsibilities.

Such a direction is not just a matter of outer actions, policy changes and more information. To unmake waste we have to unmake ourselves, our worldview, and the assumptions, values and priorities that lead to such debilitating levels of waste, environmental destruction and social disparity. To do this, we must recognize the importance of the subjective, the intuitive and the emotional self. And we must acknowledge the critical importance of the inner path and the examined life in developing a different outlook, deeper values, and more responsible and, ultimately, more fulfilling priorities. This discussion represents one perspective, one personal journal and one interpretation of what this inner path might mean for design.

5
Creavity and the imperative of solitude

*A creative act unavoidably
bares a part of the soul*

SOLITUDE, GROUPS AND CREATIVITY

Since the advent of Internet-based communications, much attention has been given to the so-called wisdom of crowds. Co-creation and participatory approaches are often used, as one might expect, in community-based initiatives, social innovation and service design, but they are increasingly common, too, in academic research. In their funding calls, research councils frequently stipulate the use of collaborative processes, networking and multidisciplinary participation. Such initiatives can be very positive and empowering and there is little doubt that they can lead to constructive change that reaches beyond more traditional, more narrowly focussed 'siloed' disciplines. However, when it comes to creativity and the development of more visionary or inspiring ideas and ground-breaking innovation, there is much evidence to suggest that solitude is a critically important factor.

Henry Miller wrote, *"Artists never thrive in colonies... . What the budding artist needs is the privilege of wrestling with his problems in solitude"*.[1] Similarly, Steve Wozniak, cofounder of Apple Computer, says that creative work is best done alone, where the process can be fully controlled. He warns against trying to do creative work in a team or by committee.[2] This sentiment is echoed by film director Mike Figgis: *"Film-makers cannot flourish and grow unless you give them room to do so. And creativity cannot exist in a system of committees".*[3] These insights from exceptionally creative people are reinforced by the findings of psychology; Feist says, *"To be creative requires solitude – the capacity to be alone".*[4] The critic Robert Hughes has explained the relationship between solitude and the creation of meaningful outcomes:

> *The basic project of art is always to make the world whole and comprehensible ... not through argument but through feeling, and then to close the gap between you and everything that is not you, and in this way pass from feeling to meaning. It's not something that committees can do. It's not a task achieved by groups or by movements. It's done by individuals, each person mediating in some way between a sense of history and an experience of the world.*[5]

Yet, we know that many creative projects – in art, design, architecture, filmmaking – require the creative contributions of many people and cannot be accomplished alone. In this discussion, I would like to consider these questions of solitude and collaboration, and their relationship to creativity, in order to better understand why solitude seems to be such a critical ingredient of the creative endeavour; what happens in groups that appears to hinder creativity; how group work and solitude can come together and the appropriate roles of each; and why getting the balance right matters, especially in the context of contemporary design and its attempts to address the many, often conflicting, issues raised by sustainability.

COLLABORATION, GROUP PROCESSES AND CREATIVITY

Human beings are social animals. We choose to live, work and spend our leisure time with others. We value being a part of a community – whether it is the community in which we live or the professional community of our colleagues at work. We create online communities of sorts through social media, and we seek to be with others when we play sports, practise a religion, or spend time in a city park. We often feel more comfortable when we do things with or alongside other people. But we are also individuals and there are times when we prefer to be alone – so we can get our thoughts in order, have time for reflection, or concentrate on a particular activity free from distractions. When it comes to creativity, however, many practitioners and academics suggest that collective ways of working are unconducive to creative thinking. Indeed, it seems that creative insight and the all-important creative synthesis phase are hampered by the conditions generated by collaborative processes. A closer examination of group-working processes reveals a variety of factors that, together, serve to hinder creativity.

Computer scientist, author and composer Jaron Lanier argues that collective decision-making can be useful when: the collective does not define the question;[6] the 'answers' can be evaluated simply, e.g. as a single number;[7] the collective is guided by individuals who ensure quality control of the information informing the collective;[8, 9] and incremental improvement is sought; collective decision-making in practice being a conservative force and less suited to radical creativity and innovation.[10]

Norman and Verganti's work adds weight to the idea that Human Centred Design (HCD) approaches such as co-design, participatory design and collaboration are suited to incremental but not substantive or radical change. Incremental improvement is not a highly creative form of change; Norman and Verganti refer to it as 'hill climbing'. They say, *"Incremental innovation tries to reach the highest point on the current hill. Radical innovation seeks the highest hill"*.[11] Human-centred design approaches, in which progress is continually discussed and feedback sought from stakeholders, help guarantee continual improvement. But it is precisely this guarantee that differentiates it from more radically creative approaches. In fact, Donald Norman *"was unable to find any example of radical innovation"* that emerged from a Human Centred Design process.[12] In addition, Lanier's point about the need for an individual to guide the group and ensure quality control of information finds support from the field of applied social psychology. Coutts and Gruman emphasize the importance of strong directive leadership by an individual when engaging in group work.[13] If we do not take these factors into account then collective decisions can be much worse than those made by individuals.[14, 15]

Significantly, these necessary conditions for effective collective decision-making can never be wholly satisfied in creative fields such as the applied arts, including design. Creative 'answers' cannot be reduced to a simple numerical value. One creative proposition will always be more or less appropriate or more or less successful than another; creative 'answers' are always a matter of judgement.

COLLABORATIVE PRACTICES INCOMPATIBLE WITH CREATIVITY

Collaborative practices, group-based processes and workshops tend to follow pre-planned methods and typically result in outputs such as strategies, frameworks, guidelines, and toolkits. Such processes demand activity and busyness and they can be very productive. However, productivity is not the same thing as creativity and in many respects these processes are incompatible with creativity:

1. Methodical approaches: The use of pre-established methods can present an obstacle to creativity. The word 'method' stems from the Latin *methodus*, which means following a rational procedure or a way of doing something, especially according to a defined or regular plan.[16] As such, their use in projects that require creativity and imagination, which are so often fuelled by serendipity, intuition and non-systematic practices, is questionable. Creative thinking does not follow a rational methodical plan and therefore it is unlikely to flourish when constricted by the orderly, time-dependent approaches of a typical workshop. Also, systematic research – such as collecting information from literature or gathering and analyzing ethnographic data – may be useful in other aspects of a project, but they are not a critical part of the creative design process and an over-emphasis on such processes and such information can serve to inhibit creativity. Zeckhauser points out that more information does not necessarily *"lead to creative decisions and creative ways forward"*.[17] Acquiring data is not the same thing as being creative. More data can inform what we may wish to do – for example, acquiring information about what attributes a new product or building may require – so talking with people can provide the necessary background for developing the design brief. But this is not creativity, this is information.

2. Unreflective environments: While face-to-face interactions may be important for building effective working relationships, numerous studies have shown that busy, talkative environments and group-based working conditions can compromise creativity.[18, 19, 20]

3. Lack of creative expertise: Collaborative workshops can be useful for gathering perspectives, generating ideas and collecting specialist information. However, workshops and other group-based methods typically involve people from a variety of fields and participants generally do not have knowledge, skills and experience in applied creative practice. As will become apparent, this expertise is essential to all practice-based disciplines.

4. Designer as facilitator: Because they generally involve participants from a diversity of fields, group-based activities and workshops require effective facilitation and designers often take on this role; a role for which they may not be especially qualified. With respect to creativity, this kind of facilitated process is problematic for two main reasons. First, when in the role of facilitator, the designer is no longer engaging in the immersive, creative process, or making use of his or her design expertise. The facilitator is meant to adopt a neutral position and manages the progress of the group as they address their given tasks and achieve the stated objectives of the event. Second, it is a process that usually involves a great deal of talking, note-taking, questioning, judging, and analyzing; often there is much use of Post-it notes, diagrams and mapping. All these activities call upon rational argument and the kinds of logical, conceptual thinking associated with the left cerebral hemisphere.[21] When engaging in this kind of thinking, we tend to look at the individual parts, analyze the details, and seek explanations. It is suited to linear, systematic processes, the scientific method and evidence-based research. This way of tackling a problem is useful for developing incremental changes and improvements but is less suited to the more radical, creative solutions that emerge (unsystematically) from a more holistic view. Additionally, in the context of a workshop or other group process, participants are required to make their thoughts explicit and this can actually be counterproductive to creativity.[22] Ezio Manzini, an expert in social innovation projects and participatory methods, has criticized this kind of design by facilitation, or Post-it design as he calls it. He recognizes that these approaches frequently lack creativity and result in banal outcomes. Notably, he argues that design is a specific culture and design experts are needed for their creativity. A process that involves contributions by nondesigners, he says, should include nonsystematic approaches that allow for dialogue and meditation as well as the designer's creativity and culture, which he describes as *"their ability to conceive large scenarios and/or original design proposals"*.[23] This view is entirely in agreement with those of Miller, Wozniak, Figgis and Lanier.

In line with Manzini's observations, various researchers have shown that collective processes are often afflicted by so called groupthink, which is a byword for flawed decision-making. According to Coutts and Gruman, it is the result of several factors including pressure to reach agreement among the group; a tendency for effective decisions to be overridden by the need to agree; and a tendency not to engage in a thorough consideration of all the relevant information.[24] Zeckhauser describes a similar process, suggesting that group processes are afflicted by biases and behavioural inclinations that

118

reinforce why an idea will work and why an idea makes sense.[25] As a consequence, group processes tend to suppress new ideas and new ways of looking at an issue and when they aggregate people's views, which they commonly do, much information becomes discarded.

There are many examples from history which demonstrate that collective decision-making and groupthink can lead to aberrant behaviours, poor outcomes and even widespread panic. The disastrous 1961 *Bay of Pigs* invasion of Cuba and the 2002 WorldCom fraud, at the time the largest fraud in US history, have both been attributed to groupthink.[26] Other examples that belie the so called 'wisdom of crowds' include the mass hysteria that gripped Europe and North America in the seventeenth century where thousands were tried for witchcraft;[27] the so-called *Tulip Mania* in The Netherlands of the 1630s where, before the crash, one tulip bulb held the same value as a luxurious Amsterdam house;[28] the overreaction in 1950s America, spurred by McCarthyism, to the suspected presence of Communists;[29] and the widespread alarm and havoc surrounding what became known as the Y2K millennium bug in computers. With respect to creative endeavours, Michael Arrington says, *"When too many people have product input, you've got lots of features but no soul"*.[30] An example of this is the 1967 film *Casino Royale* starring David Niven – generally regarded as the worst Bond film ever made. Critical reviews highlight its lack of unifying vision: *"a conglomeration of frenzied situations ... lacking discipline and cohesion"* [31] and *"the result is totally unfocused"*.[32] These criticisms are hardly surprising when we learn that this film had a total of five directors.[33]

119

Collaborative Practices in the Design Process and Accountability: From the foregoing, it seems that while participatory, group-based and collaborative approaches may not be effective in generating ground-breaking innovation or radically creative solutions, they do have an important role to play within the overall design process. In the earlier pre-design stages, they can be usefully employed to identify needs, garner ideas, views and expert opinions, and draw on specialist knowledge in order to more fully understand the issues and to inform the development of a comprehensive design brief that has clear, well-informed objectives and design criteria. They can also be used effectively in later, post-design stages in suggesting potential improvements and polishing and refining a design outcome through incremental improvements based on user feedback. But if we adopt collective approaches to generate the creative solutions themselves, not only does creativity become compromised, potentially resulting in banality, but effectively we also disperse and thus relinquish responsibility and accountability for our design decisions and actions. Outcomes that are the product of everyone become the responsibility of no one. And if we widen our perspective, to include the larger system of globalized production in which contemporary design exists, we see that it is this very distribution of decisions, tasks and roles throughout the various arenas of production, distribution and waste creation that is allowing us to abnegate responsibility for the social and environmental repercussions of our collective actions.

SOLITUDE AND CREATIVITY

In contrast to the certitude that accompanies systematic methods and incremental change, there is no guarantee with creativity. The creative process involves risk taking – one never knows if it will lead anywhere fruitful. Creativity is concerned with exploring, experimenting and probing new possibilities. It is not about familiarity and feeling comfortable; doing what we have done before is not creative. The use of systematic methods in the creative design process, including in design education, is in many ways entirely antithetical to the serendipitous, unpredictable nature of creative idea generation.[34] What matters for creativity and innovation is *"a sense of focus, a mind in effective concentration, and an adventurous individual imagination that is distinct from the crowd"*.[35] The creative designing process is an immersive, often intuitive, and all-absorbing but unsystematic integration of thinking, doing and reflecting. It is fostered by engaging in creative practice itself, developing one's knowledge and ability and gaining experience. In other words, it involves developing a *design expertise*, which can be understood as an integration of theoretical knowledge, practical skills, tacit knowledge and experience. Its development can take years of studio practice and experience. Like other practice-based endeavours – learning to be a musician, an athlete, a pilot or painter – such expertise is hard won and it includes much non-explicit, embodied knowledge. In the creative process of designing, this expertise includes visualization skills, aesthetic acuity and sensitivity, and the ability to creatively synthesize complex often competing ideas and priorities into a coherent and particularized whole. This represents the designer's expertise, which is called upon to develop and express oneself creatively. It does not guarantee creative outcomes, but it does enable them to emerge.

Synthetical, reflective modes of thinking that are so closely associated with creativity and spontaneous insight are entirely different from the rational, methodical processes found in the typical group workshop. The heart of creativity, which is associated with meaning seeking and holistic understandings, is primarily a highly concentrated solitary endeavour that is inarticulate, non-rational, and oblivious to the passing of time.[36] For these very reasons, it is easily sidelined in time-dependent, group-based activities that rely on people speaking up and explaining their thoughts.

Conditions for Creativity and the Importance of Solitude: An extensive body of research indicates that intuition, imagination, holistic awareness and the 'Ah-ha' moment of creative synthesis *"is associated with activation in the right hemisphere"* of the brain.[37, 38] These less explicit ways of thinking, which can yield creative insights not only in the arts but also in mathematics and the sciences, are enhanced by certain conditions that include ceasing from talking, a calm and quiet environment free from distractions, and being physically comfortable and mentally tranquil.[39, 40, 41] When working on creative ideas, problem solving and activities that require deliberation and reflection, key factors are visual and auditory privacy, and personal space where the individual can control levels of heating, lighting and air quality, and arrange furniture to create an environment conducive to their way of working.[42, 43] This helps explain why many creative people such as writers, composers, artists and designers often prefer to work at home.[44]

121

It becomes evident that there are strong links between purposeful silence, solitude and creativity. The reflective, creative process does not talk or explain, but it sees relationships, integrates and perceives meaning; it is a mode of thinking that artists call *in the flow* and athletes refer to as *in the zone*. It is worth noting too that creative insight often occurs when we look away – when we temporarily emerge from our absorption and are not directly focussed on the problem. It is just these periods of rest from the task in hand that are conducive to creativity. In academia, this is precisely what is recognized in the tradition of the sabbatical, which, as MacCulloch has pointed out, has long been regarded as *"a vital part of the creative process rather than simply an end to it"*.[45] From this it is apparent that creative synthesis cannot be pre-planned. It is both spontaneous and serendipitous, occurring at times when one may be thinking about something else entirely, or not thinking about anything in particular, or driving on an open road, or jogging, or in that half-awake state first thing in the morning. At such times, when we are not talking or distracted or aware of time passing, we experience a shift in consciousness – into the right-hemisphere mode that is linked to creative thinking.[46] I include a brief personal reflection on this process as Appendix 2.

The Individual Nature of Creativity and Why It Matters: The act of designing is an act of human intentionality that leads to a creative outcome. In this, it is quite different from the physical sciences, which seek to objectively acquire and analyze information about natural phenomena. The physical sciences examine phenomena that exist or have existed and they make predictions based on this empirical evidence. As such they limit their inquiries to questions about how the world works and about what factors account for particular phenomena. Consequently, they can be pursued in a largely objective manner, without the beliefs and values of the investigator entering the picture; findings are expected to be repeatable, whoever carries out the study.

In contrast, design is concerned not with examining existing phenomena but with creating that which does not yet exist and this involves subjective decision-making. The design process often entails hundreds of first-person decisions and it is from these that the originality of the designer emerges. Normally, we do not want or expect the outcome to be repeatable by another designer; indeed, if it were it would likely be regarded as unoriginal and an infringement of intellectual property rights. Also, because design decision-making involves subjectivity, it is not values-free. For this reason, as with other creative arts, the discipline of design has to deal with values-based questions of 'why'. Therefore, design has a responsibility to consider the ethical implications of its decisions and actions. In taking on the task of creating something new, the designer becomes accountable for bringing about a future state of affairs that conforms to their design intention.[47] And while many different people may have a role in the production process, it is the designer who is the principal actor in conceptualizing, creatively envisioning and defining this particular state of affairs. Therefore, to a significant degree, it is the designer who is both responsible and accountable not only for characterizing the nature of that state of affairs but also, it would seem, for its implications and consequences. This is an onerous responsibility. According to The Ecodesign Directive of the European Commission, *"More than 80% of the environmental impact of a product is determined at the design stage"*.[48]

INDIVIDUALS AND SOCIAL BEINGS

To be clear, the foregoing discussion is not intended to suggest that creative endeavours can or should result solely from the efforts of solitary, nay isolated, individuals; we are both individuals *and* social beings. At times we seek solitude and reflection. At other times we seek the company or expertise of others. Naturally too, our creative endeavours will be informed, influenced and enabled by such interactions. We do not develop creative ideas in a bubble, exclusively from our own resources: *'No man is an island, entire of itself; every man is a piece of the continent, a part of the main'*.[49] However, while it is important to acknowledge the contribution of others, it is also important to recognize that solitude and interior reflection, which tend to be undervalued in contemporary society, are essential for the specific, highly focussed creative act. As the artist Marcel Duchamp made clear, in the creative act, we go *"from intention to realization through a chain of totally subjective reactions"*.[50] Duchamp describes the creative act as a function of the individual, the subject. It is just this kind of individual, focussed, synthesizing creative act – with its *"efforts, pains, satisfaction, refusals, decisions, which also cannot and must not be fully self-conscious, at least on the esthetic plane"* [51] – that is so critical for envisioning radical change and systemic shift. And it is just such radical change and system shift that many see as necessary conditions for sustainable futures.[52]

123

These features of creative disciplines like design – intentionality, subjectivity and values-laden – are entirely in accord with Buchanan's assertion that design is a form of 'demonstrative rhetoric', which also infers a values-based stance.[53] And because design decisions are made by the individual designer during the creative designing process, it is here at the individual level where accountability rests. Today, because of large scale production for international markets, our design decisions can have global impacts so it is especially important to acknowledge this first person locus of responsibility and accountability. In addition, interior reflection, which is an inherent part of the solitary approaches to design described here, helps shift the ethical emphasis from one of incremental improvement of existing designs to an interiorized causative notion of ethical behaviour and design decision-making. In today's context of *design for sustainability,* this means that an intention to reduce the negative consequences of design is replaced by a creative process that is based in virtue ethics from the outset. In other words, we shift the aim from 'less bad' design to 'good' design, from improvement to aspiration.

Visionary, Inspiring and Innovative Creativity by Individual Designers:
Ground-breaking designs by individual designers not only say something new
in the context of their times, the best of them allow us to see things in a
fresh light and in doing so they contribute to society and to the development
of the discipline itself. While such designs often involve the expertise of
others in bringing them to reality they are, nevertheless, the result of a single
creative vision and strong creative leadership. There are many examples to
choose from – such as Eileen Gray's chrome and glass *E1027 Sidetable*,
1927; Alvar Aalto's bent plywood *Paimio Armchair*, 1930; Frank Gehry's
Guggenheim Museum in Bilbao, Spain, 1997; the electrical products
produced since the 1950s by the German company Braun under the "less,
but better" design leadership of Dieter Rams;[54] and the late-twentieth/early
twenty-first-century fashion designs of Vivienne Westwood. We can also
include more idiosyncratic and more experimental contributions such as
Jurgen Bey's *Tree Trunk Bench*, 1999, which comprises a very large log
fitted with three traditional chair backs cast in bronze; Thomas Thwaites'
Toaster Project, 2010, which presents the process of designing an electric
toaster from scratch; and Andrea Branzi's *Grandi Legni* series, 2009–2010 – a
collection of large interior structures that reach beyond modernity to include
references to magic, myth, history, technology and deeper aspects of the
human condition.

124

SOLITUDE AND COLLABORATION IN REALIZING CREATIVE PROJECTS

Drawing on both analytical, left-hemisphere and synthetical, right-hemisphere
thinking, we benefit from each of their complementary strengths. When kept
in balance, they foster a sense of completeness. When they become
separated, there follows a feeling of emptiness and meaninglessness.[55] And
yet, *"the story of the Western world is one of increasing left-hemisphere
domination"*.[56] Solitude, silence and periods of reflection are not valued in
modern society. We are expected to be constantly busy, connected, and
achieving in order to demonstrate our social worth. As Foley says, *"What
you need is detachment, concentration, autonomy, and privacy, but what the
world insists upon is immersion, distraction, collaboration and company"*.[57]
This way of living becomes addictive and contemplation becomes analogous
to idleness.[58] The corollary of this is that our ability to perceive relationships
and connectedness becomes diminished, which, in turn, reduces our ability
to be creative.[59]

The nature, meaning and value of our creative endeavours are critically dependent on how we approach the creative process. Creative outputs can range from minor improvements of the existing condition, to superficial, ephemeral novelties, to outputs that are both meaningful and highly original. However, if we are to develop new, creative ways forward that achieve balance and moderation, and are far less destructive, we will need to cultivate more holistic outlooks – outlooks that valorize the rational and the intuitive. In this way, incremental change and continual improvement can be complemented by more radical, visionary ideas. And achieving the balance to allow creativity to flourish requires competent creative leadership.

Whether working alone or with others the creative process requires us to establish a certain distance from the details in order to be able to see the whole. This *standing back* enables the artist or designer to bring creativity and vision to the project at a meta level. In this way, the various, often disparate elements of a project can be seen, brought together and synthesized in a coherent manner that results in more than the sum of the parts. And this synthesis opens up the potential for an original and holistic contribution. The ability to *stand back* is related to our sense of individuality, which, in turn, is related to our desire for originality. And, of course, originality is a critical ingredient of creativity. While both rational/analytical and intuitive/imaginative thinking are related to this sense of separateness, the former is associated with isolation, power-seeking and competitiveness whereas the latter maintains a strong connection with others and the world. Individuality and originality should not be regarded *"as the prerogative of one hemisphere or the other: both exist for each other but in radically different ways, with radically different meanings"*.[60]

125

We can see from this discussion that when the rationalistic methods prevalent in group-based approaches are employed in creative endeavours not only do they tend to yield rather stereotypical or derivative outcomes but also, because they are more competitive, distinctiveness becomes a conscious and primary objective and creativity a means to that end. Hence, creativity is not being pursued for its own sake because there is a more deliberate focus on trying to be different, and this results in superficial novelty. Such activities load the dice, as it were, towards ways of thinking that can lead to incremental improvements but attempts at more creative outcomes are often trite and predictable, which is precisely the criticism made of this kind of work by experts such as Manzini. On the other hand, intuitive, right-hemisphere modes are effective in dealing with concrete realities, relationships, connections and integration. In this case, the creative process tends to be engaged in for its own sake and original ideas are inclined to emerge, rather than being actively sought. This more holistic way of thinking maintains a strong connection with the world so that, while being original and new, the creative work is more likely to resonate with enduring values, tradition, and more profound cultural ideas.

Creative Leadership: When subsumed into a collective, original ideas can become an inelegant lack-lustre compromise – which is the basis of the well-known saying: *A camel is a horse designed by a committee.* Other familiar sayings, which appear at first sight to be contradictory, are: *Too many cooks spoil the broth* and *Many hands make light work.* While both hold truth, they are expressing rather different things, and only the first relates to creativity. Many hands can make light work of the routine tasks that have to be done, but one chef has to be in charge of the kitchen. For collaborative group work to be effective, as Lanier has suggested, strong creative leadership is required.

126 The development of a new building calls on the expertise and creative input from many people, but all the different elements come together to form a coherent whole under the creative leadership of the architect. Similarly, filmmaking has input from many creative people – the costume designer, composer, set designer and so on – but the overall vision and creative leadership is provided by the director. In contrast, when creative vision and leadership is lacking, many individual contributions may yield little or no clear outcome. For example, in the early years of the twenty-first century, the *Occupy* movement arose as a rapidly generated social action to protest against bankers, corporations and an economic system associated with rising inequalities. However, it dissipated as quickly as it had arisen because it lacked any effective decision-making structure. There were many ideas but there was no clear leadership or synthesis, and so no viable alternative emerged.[61]

Effective creative leadership allows a collection of discrete parts to come together to form an integrated whole. When there are creative contributions by many different people, they only make sense as a whole if there is another *meta-level* creative contribution – this is the role of the curator, the architect, the designer or the film director. In all these cases, whether the creative contribution is related to a component within a large project, or whether it relates to the project as a whole, research and authoritative voices from the creative arts, from science and technology, and from psychology all indicate that this is best done by one person – one creator, one vision. And all such focussed creative endeavours require silence, solitude and freedom from distractions.

CONCLUSIONS

Group-based and solitary ways of working can both yield creative outputs but these will be quite different in character and significance. Collaborative work, because it emphasizes rationalistic, left-hemisphere thinking modes tends to produce results that are suited to incremental change and continual improvement. Not only does this foster a consequentialist morality, collaborative work tends to blur authorship and responsibility and obscure accountability. In addition, its attempts at more creative outcomes are often clichéd, derivative and banal. Solitary ways of working that draw on imaginative right-hemisphere thinking modes are better suited to holistic solutions and radical creativity. This type of creativity tends to be pursued for its own sake and is associated with a causative ethic that shifts the aim from improvement to aspiration. The outcomes may be more visionary but for that reason they will often be less immediately practical. Therefore, to implement the results of such creativity, to make a difference, we need to call on the participation and creative expertise of others. With strong creative leadership, our creative endeavours will then benefit from the virtues and strengths of both individual practices and communal contributions.

127

Today, we have important and urgent issues to deal with and if we are to come to grips with these agendas – including that of sustainability – many researchers are suggesting we need radical reform and fundamental systemic change. To achieve such change a form of creativity is required that reaches beyond incremental improvements. The arguments presented here suggest that such radical change and systemic innovation will require the kinds of visionary creativity that is the strength of solitary creative practices.

6

The Mesh freeing design from dominant dogmas

*All this ... would be of no more service to man than as an escape from
himself and his true aims, and a means of surrounding himself with
an ever closer mesh of distractions and useless activities.*

Hermann Hesse

INTRODUCTION

To create more responsible and constructive conceptions of material culture,
many of our current assumptions, conventions and dogmas have to be
overcome. As Ward has argued, *"Today we are in need of an 'unworlding' of
the world that has been made in the left hemisphere's image"*, which has
resulted in developments *"characterized by 'a loss of meaning in the
experienced world'"*.[1] These issues are explored here in relation to the
creation, interpretation and potential influence of material goods.

   The reality experienced by people is the world of relationships, empathy,
difference and moral responsibility. It is here that meaning is found, in human
connections and considered actions. Therefore, it is important to ensure that
the artefacts that make up our material world are conceived as fitting,
positive and potentially enduring contributions to human culture. Such
contributions can enrich our lives by enhancing human relationships and
quality of life through their making, use and maintenance; by being conceived

in ways that are attentive to the natural world that sustains us; and by contributing to thoughtful reflective ways of living through their presence and use. And we should strive to avoid design directions that promote socioeconomic disparities, inundate us with distractions, encourage consumption and foster social atomization.

Such considerations inevitably contest many prevailing directions in product design and production – especially those in the ever-burgeoning field of digital technologies and mobile devices that monitor and measure, and are usually founded on highly dubious, essentially utilitarian routes to human fulfilment and happiness.

A ONE-WAY LOGIC

The predominant worldview of late modernity remains firmly grounded in philosophical materialism and its close ally naturalism. This worldview is rooted in the idea that the person acts as a detached, objective observer and that 'the world out there' can be known through observation, data collection and standardized approaches to measurement.[2] But we are incapable of taking an entirely impartial, detached view of the world because we are intimately involved in it; we are part of, not independent observers of, reality.[3, 4] Hence, that which we regard as empirical evidence cannot be strictly objective because, to some degree, the observational data on which it is based is always mediated by our theories.[5] Evidence is always interpreted from a particular assemblage of facts – and the aims and intentions that prompt the formation of this assemblage will always include presumptions and prejudices.[6] As the philosopher Thomas Nagel has argued, *"Mind is not just an afterthought or an accident or an add-on, but a basic aspect of nature"*.[7] Our intuitive apprehensions of reality, which reach beyond the immediate, temporal, physical world of the senses, are inherent to the individual person. And yet the person – the subject – has no place in unified notions of science because the first-person viewpoint is eliminated from scientific explanations. But when it comes to people, there is a fundamental difference between explaining their behaviour as physical beings and understanding them as living persons within the world.[8]

The detached-observer view of reality that still dominates contemporary society and much techno-scientific development and production fails to recognize that our most profound understandings and beliefs about human existence – whether secular/humanist or religious/spiritual – affect our core sense of who we are, our view of the world and our conceptions of reality.

129

Moreover, the deep-seated bias of the detached view toward rational, analytical thinking makes the late-modern outlook both philosophically inadequate and extremely damaging. It takes insufficient account of the fact that a more holistic awareness is possible – one that includes belief, imaginative concepts, intuitive apprehensions and inspiration, all of which lie beyond the bounds of reason and empiricism but, nevertheless, are essential characteristics of being human and affect what and how we see. Consequently, appreciation and recognition of these aspects of human perception have declined, both in the public sphere and in academic discourse, in favour of evidence-based knowledge. Yet, it is these very same aspects of human perception that are so strongly connected to human values and notions of trust, loyalty, empathy and compassion[9, 10] – all of which require far greater prominence if we are to deal effectively with contemporary concerns about social injustice and environmental destruction. To be complete human beings, this imbalance will need to be addressed by restoring the importance and validity of the imagination, the emotional mind and intuition, which are critically tied to our ability to relate to others and the natural world.[11, 12]

The one-way logic of impersonal techno-scientific rationalism that dominates the late-modern era fails to recognize that as we change the world, the world changes us. Issues that arise in the subject, the first-person, affect and are affected by our actions.[13] Our hopes and anxieties, our ideas of what ultimately matters and gives life meaning, and our social values are all shaped by our interactions with others and the world. Lack of attention to these reciprocal relationships is intimately related to the rise of abstraction, delineation and classification that has distanced us from reality and created a quantified, categorized but ultimately impoverished world. It is a created notion of a world that is simpler and more comprehensible but also one that is starved of richness, texture and meaning. Primarily, it is a world that can be controlled, manipulated and made useful to our needs;[14] a world in which we become preoccupied with numerical evaluation, competitive ranking, and a crude neo-utilitarianism in which evidence-based policy-making is stripped of moral values and ideological principles.[15] This way of thinking is intimately wedded to a laissez-faire capitalist economic system that prioritizes technological innovation and market-based solutions and attempts to monetize virtually every aspect of society. But such a system is entirely inadequate when it comes to addressing matters of equity, justice and the common good. Economist and Nobel laureate Joseph Stiglitz says that in the US since the 1980s, all economic gains have gone to those in the top 10 per cent of the economy while the lower 90 per cent has stagnated; a similar if somewhat less severe picture has evolved elsewhere.[16] The former chief economist and senior vice president of the World Bank, François Bourguignon, says that since the latter half of the twentieth century, the developed economies in particular have experienced rising economic inequalities.[17] And Roy Jenkins, former British Chancellor of the Exchequer, has said:

> 'The market', in terms of protecting the environment or safeguarding
> schools, universities or Britain's scientific future, cannot run a whelk stall.
> And if asked which is under greater threat in Britain today, the supply of
> consumer goods or the nexus of civilised public services,
> I unhesitatingly answer the latter.[18]

In recent times we have witnessed enormous advances, growth and confidence in analysis and scientific explanations of the world – as it exists in discernible, material form. However, the prominence given to such thinking has been at the expense of ways of knowing that have been a critical part of the heritage of human wisdom for millennia, which have atrophied under the onslaught of modern thought.[19] This rupture in human understanding is linked to the notion of 'cognitive dualism', mentioned in Chapter 4, and the inadequacy and inappropriateness of scientific explanation to say anything significant about the emergent world of interrelationships, meanings and values that arise from the order of nature.[20]

131

TOWARDS A CO-EVOLVING PERSPECTIVE

In contrast to the intellectualized but deficient view of late modernity, we can also encounter the world in a direct way, as part of the lived experience of reality. In this view, we recognize that we are connected to the reality of existence in its complex, dynamic and ever-changing state. We learn to see ourselves as part of the greater whole and we relate to the world in its fullness – in its sights, sounds, smells, textures and tastes and through our face-to-face encounters with others. Meaning in life is not found in achieving some kind of predetermined objectives. Neither is it found in acquiring explicit forms of knowledge or some notion of 'truth'. As Eagleton has pointed out, it is found in the act of living and in living in a particular way; it is a form of practice.[21]

A telling example of deeper meanings associated with this intangible life-world, which contrasts markedly with the busy, efficient, productive world of techno-scientific rationalism, comes from Count Philippe Pozzo di Borgo, former head of France's Pommery champagne house, who was left a quadriplegic after a hang-gliding accident. He has said that for the first part of his life he was very healthy and productive but since his accident, which left him weak and dependent, he has acquired a very different perspective. He has recognized that being *"in the very weak world of survival, you discover you can live with great depth and relationship"*. He also talks of the tyranny of productivity, which yields a false picture of who we are as human beings.[22]

Instead of regarding ourselves as detached observers where our thoughts and actions are unidirectional, another view is possible. We begin to develop a quite different outlook when we recognize a more complementary, reciprocal relationship in which the externalization of ideas results in actions in the world that then inform and affect those ideas. Such a perspective points to a different awareness of reality; one that contests the modern empiricist-conditioned view that regards the person as a dispassionate spectator capable of translating scientific data about the natural world into things of meaning.[23] It sees human beings as part of the world – active participants in a co-evolutionary process of continuous change.[24] Analysis of details may be important, but we cannot gain a comprehensive and meaningful appreciation of the world and the wider significance and implications of our actions without taking a wider view, one that enables us to see how the different parts and details contribute to and affect the greater whole – both today and tomorrow. And such a view has to more fully acknowledge the critical importance of relationships, intuition, emotion, trust, benevolence, creativity and symbolism – because human values do not arise from data but from our imagination, beliefs, interrelationships and stories.[25]

132

DESIGN CONTRIBUTIONS AND IMPLICATIONS

While these co-evolutionary understandings may resonate with designers in terms of how works of design are created, they also raise important issues about how we view and interpret the role of designed goods and their potential to affect and influence people – positively or negatively – with respect to social and environmental concerns, as well as one's personal values and sense of well-being. Let us now consider these issues in terms of the design of material goods, the interpretation of materials goods and the potential influence of material goods.

The Design of Material Goods: Experienced designers will know that creative practice is itself a kind of co-evolutionary development – a two-way, mutually informing process of thinking and doing. It would be a mistake, therefore, to regard the artefacts of design – and of the creative arts in general – as mere manifestations or illustrations of preconceived ideas; such a view would fail to recognize the important contribution of the process itself in developing new insights (see Figure 6.1).

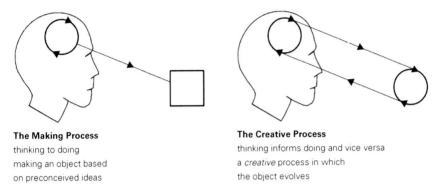

The Making Process
thinking to doing
making an object based
on preconceived ideas

The Creative Process
thinking informs doing and vice versa
a *creative* process in which
the object evolves

Figure 6.1 The Making Process and the Creative Process

Hence, creative practice is an example of a reciprocal, co-evolving way of knowing. Ideas are externalized through tangible means such as writings, sketches, drawings and study models, all of which serve to inform and develop the ideas. It is a process that brings together diverse elements and sometimes-contradictory concepts, and in which such conflicts and complexities become synthesized into a coherent whole. It calls upon and expresses the human imagination, leaps of insight, intuition, tacit knowledge, expertise, experience, aesthetic judgements, emotional responses and decisions that are, in part, subjective – but the inclusion of all these things is neither systematic nor orderly. Notably too, during the process of creating, these various facets and their interplay may or may not be consciously acknowledged by the designer. Furthermore, it is a process that seeks some kind of holistic integration and manifestation of ideas and insights. Indeed, the aesthetic experience itself is an encounter with the whole, where discrete parts and details are seen together and, hopefully, 'work' together in harmony. In striving to achieve this harmony, one has to trust in one's own intuitions and in the process itself, and also trust that creative, synthesized solutions will emerge. The poet Rainer Maria Rilke describes it this way:

Have patience with everything unresolved in your heart and to try to love the questions themselves as if they were locked rooms or books written in a very foreign language. Don't search for the answers, which could not be given to you now, because you would not be able to live them. And the point is, to live everything. Live the questions now. Perhaps then, someday far in the future, you will gradually, without even noticing it, live your way into the answer.[26]

In regard to these co-evolutionary practices, there are some important factors to bear in mind. To begin with, the intentionality of design, which by its very nature is an expression of human relationships and interpersonal attitudes, is not fixed. Our intentions can be altered, educated and can take new paths. They can be directed towards that which is virtuous, or that which is manipulative, unethical or irresponsible. If we aspire towards that which is meaningful, profound and enduring, then we must endeavour to *"address the horizon from which the other's gaze is seeking us ... to look the other person in the I".*[27] This is the nature of disciplined practice that strives towards virtue, goodness and deeper notions of meaning that can be expressed through, but can simultaneously transcend, the visible, explainable world of material things.

134   Additionally, in recent times, the boundaries of our view in design and, more generally, in the creative arts have not extended much beyond the artefact itself. Today, this is proving problematic, not just in terms of the environmental consequences but also existentially. Within such constrained boundaries, we may be capable of achieving some kind of aesthetic coherence, but the wider and deeper implications remain unconsidered. As Howes has argued, the modern period has seen an increasing transition towards a merely aesthetic validation of experience.[28] Kung makes the point that artefacts emerging from the creative arts in this period can, and to a large extent do, symbolize *meaninglessness*, but in a manner that is aesthetically completely meaningful; that is, internally harmonious.[29] Internal consistency and harmony might afford a certain aesthetic meaningfulness but this is hardly enough. Following on from the earlier discussion, we cannot gain a comprehensive and meaningful understanding of design and created works without taking a more holistic view, by which we attempt to see the broader- and longer-term implications of our activities. If we are to overcome the severely destructive tendencies of our contemporary condition, a far more profound sense of meaning is required. Traditionally, this is to be found through the lived experience – through a sense of purpose, fulfilment and flourishing, and by transcending routine tasks to take into account and reflect upon matters of ultimate concern. In other words, to recall Eagleton, meaning is to be found in living in a particular way – living as a form of practice that includes, as we shall see below, selflessness and self-discipline. And naturally this will involve and affect the way we do design, both what we design and how we design.

The Interpretation of Material Goods: The above understandings are relevant to the creative process and to our encounters with the results of that process, the works themselves and, more generally, to human-made and natural environments. Ward makes the point that aesthetic appreciation initiates alterations in consciousness,[30] and Stump and Cottingham emphasize the importance of philosophical reflection in revealing aspects of reality that lie beyond rationalistic arguments and technically expert knowledge;[31] their discussion concerns literary narrative but similar reflections can be directed towards works of design. It is through such reflections on the world that we find meaning in life. The arts, including the fine arts and applied arts like design, as well as music and poetry, speak to us by way of the creative, intuitive, aesthetic side of our nature rather than through logic. These forms of expression employ a different kind of language from the explanations and definitions of rational argument. They require sensitivity, awareness and affinity in both creator and recipient. They are allusive and evocative and they call upon the human imagination. They are not concerned with facts but with values and meanings, with what we choose to embrace and what we choose to reject, and with what transcends and transforms us. To become aware of these things, created works require our attention, our 'seeing' them fully and reflecting on their meaning. This entails concentration and appreciation of their presence and the aesthetic experience they afford, free from distractions and preconceptions. McGilchrist has explained that:

135

> attention is not just another 'function'. ... Its ontological status is something
> prior to functions and even to things. The kind of attention we bring to bear
> on the world changes the nature of the world we attend to, the very nature
> of the world in which those 'functions' would be carried out, and in which
> those 'things' would exist. Attention changes what kind of a thing comes
> into being for us: in that way it changes the world ... [but science] privileges
> detachment, a lack of commitment of the viewer to the object viewed.[32]

He also points out that attention is closely linked to values, which in turn affect the functions we perform and the purposes and ends to which we direct them.[33] Today, the countless diversions offered by digital media tend to hamper attention. Indeed, distractions and obstructions to attention have been a characteristic of modern society for decades. T. S. Eliot, in *The Dry Salvages,* indicted the media of his day for its constant barrage of distractions. He tells of a different reality, at the intersection of time with the timeless. It is a point realized through selflessness, self-surrender, observance and discipline, but one that can never be fully known or understood. It is here, in the present moment, that we find unity, reconciliation, right action and meaning, free of past and future. But for most of us it remains an aim, one never fully attained in this life.[34] Since this poem was published in 1941, the opportunities for distraction have mushroomed. Even so, it remains the case that through the creative arts we can express and appreciate ideas that serve as counterpoints and complements to the controlling logic of rational thought and the inexorable diversions offered by technological utility and progress.

The Potential Influence of Material Goods: In working towards more benevolent, equitable and compassionate futures, the arts, including design and our designed world, have a didactic role to play. Despite its diminishment in recent times, by being reduced in many quarters to an instrument of corporate capitalism, design has the potential to contribute in a far more significant way, especially at the local level where meaning is found through context and encounter. Design, along with other nonverbal arts – architecture, painting, sculpture and music – communicates aspects of being human that cannot be put into words but, nonetheless, can be perceived and felt. As Hart has said, they can provide *"fundamental clues as to what we are and what we are becoming"*.[35] Indeed, the didactic aspect of design has the potential to play a critical role in contributing to the development of more benign, less consumptive, less damaging ways of living. The power of design to influence, for good or ill, lies in the fact that we see and arrive at a dispositional attitude towards something before we consciously 'know'. It seems that the right cerebral hemisphere of the brain, associated with visual processing, holistic experiences, embodied knowledge, intuition and empathy,[36] is capable of processing information more quickly – by up to half a second – than the more articulate and assured left hemisphere. There is evidence to suggest that, instead of coming to conclusions about the world via systematic, rational consideration of observable information, we actually make up our minds more intuitively. We take in and almost instantaneously respond to the holistic view, and this occurs *prior to* interpretation and conscious reasoning. Only then do we look for reasons and arguments to make sense of and justify that understanding. These virtually instantaneous, instinctive impressions serve to inform our subsequent rationalizations. Moreover, these responses to visual stimuli, including design work, are not only pre-conscious and intuitive but they also touch us at a deeper level – imaginatively, affectively and existentially.[37, 38]

Scruton expresses this difference not with regard to left- and right-hemisphere brain functions but in terms of confrontations between the spiritual-religious traditions and modern science and the modern world, which he describes as a confrontation between the emotional and the intellectual sides of the human condition. He suggests that modern science's concern is with intellectual pursuits, which allow us to describe the nature of reality, whereas the traditional religious concern is with how we should live. With respect to the latter, and in accord with the arguments given above, he suggests that such beliefs *"are concerned with an emotional need that precedes rational argument"*, which shapes the conclusions in advance of any articulated reasons or explanation.[39]

137

In fact, the powerful effect of this 'prior to conscious knowledge' response has been recognized by designers for many years. Seymourpowell's *"classic design-dictum is that a successful new product has to have a certain quality, the 'I like it, I want it, what is it?' factor. In that one phrase alone they contradict the idea of consumption being the satisfaction of known, existing needs"*.[40] For this reason, while artists and designers may intuitively feel that a creative project is 'working' at this affective level, it may be difficult for them to explain it in rational terms or even describe it in words; indeed, they may feel there is little need to do so. This 'prior to interpretation, prior to words' response can go some way in helping us understand our attitudes and behaviours. Our belief about something does not simply rely on scientific approaches or on determining reasons for believing it. To a large extent, it seems our responses are contingent on a different mode of thinking – distinct from and occurring prior to, and at a deeper level than, declarative knowledge and logical articulation.

This way of understanding aligns with lived human experiences. Rather than being abstracted, detached and isolated, real-world encounters are holistic, synthetical and interrelated with context. A number of philosophical arguments support this view. Wittgenstein recognized that there are aspects of human knowing that cannot be expressed in words but which can be shown.[41] He also emphasized the importance of the context of use or practice in understanding the meaning of language[42, 43] and, of course, design itself is a form of language, a medium of communication. Similarly, Hick has argued that our actions in the world can only be determined to be meaningful if they are considered within the context in which they take place.[44] And Scruton maintains that human meaning is to be found in the living, contextualized world of persons as subjects – through the I–You encounter and our self-understanding – which cannot be replaced by scientific explanations of the human being. It is also to be found through taking responsibility for our actions, which involves values, moral principles and striving to live in a self-disciplined manner.[45]

The veracity of these deeper, meaning-related ways of knowing are dependent on and interconnected with one's own journey and with the transformations that can occur when due consideration is given to these 'inner' aspects of ourselves; that is, to ways of knowing that do not depend on external, empirical confirmation. By extending our outlook to include these personal, experiential facets of our lives, we develop in ourselves and gain a greater appreciation of the world around us.

138

In fact, there are many aspects of life that do not rely on physical evidence but require trust in our own intuitions as well as fidelity to the experiences of others or to tradition. For example, expressions of love between two people rely on truthfulness and mutual trust – there is no incontrovertible, observable evidence, data or proof. Similarly, when we attempt to learn a new skill, such as riding a bicycle or speaking a different language, despite our initial ineptitude, we have to trust that, with perseverance, we will be able to achieve a degree of proficiency. This is also a kind of evidence. It may not be objectively verifiable but it is evidence all the same – evidence that is accessible to the individual person and dependent for validation on personal experiences and responses. While such experiences are not fail-safe and require careful scrutiny, they are, nevertheless, a crucial aspect of one's individual development and can lead to new insights, personal transformation and radical change. We can see too that such evidence is not purely subjective – while it might be personally verifiable, we rely too on the fact that it is validated by others who have had similar experiences or reactions. As individuals, we could be deluded, but if others attest to similar experiences, this is less likely.[46]

To design, we have no choice but to draw on resources, experiences and modes of validation that fall outside the detached, evidence-based modes that characterize scientific research, but this does not mean our decisions are purely subjective. When we pay attention to context, tradition and human practices, we begin to understand the significance of artefacts in terms of their roles and meanings within a dynamic, continually adaptive human culture. We can reflect critically on these roles and meanings, and, especially today, there is a need to consider them in terms of their combined personal, social and environmental consequences. We cannot hope to fully appreciate these aspects of material culture and their implications for design if we aim to be detached and objective. Indeed, because design involves creativity, imagination and intuition, and because human meaning is to be found in the living world of experiences, design inescapably involves values. This means that, in doing design, we are asked to think about ethics, ideas of goodness and the good life, and even spiritual considerations because the design and production of artefacts inevitably involves questions about moral obligation, human dignity and the intrinsic worth of the individual.[47] We have seen earlier that intuitive, right-brain thinking is closely associated with caring and compassion. Related to this, the contemplative and spiritual traditions, which draw on intuitive apprehensions, are also closely associated with 'beyond self' priorities, beyond vested interests, and with an openness towards and concern for the plight of others.[48, 49] These modes of human thought and knowing, which in the West were once articulated through religion, lie beyond dogma and doctrine and beyond the rationalistic arguments of academic scholarship, and they are independent of formal education or training,[50] even though the contemplative tradition has long been associated with the life of learning.[51] Compassion is not developed through rational deliberation and conscious reasoning, but is bound up with our intuitive, unconscious capacity for empathy and emotional sensitivity towards other people. It is not based on principle but is intrinsic and irreducible, and critically, empathy is fundamental to morality.[52] Moreover, a life without contemplation and reflection is a life without stillness and inner growth; such a life tends to induce a sense of emptiness or ennui and a lack of rootedness.[53, 54]

It becomes apparent that the meanings of a designed artefact will be multi-layered. It may, at once, be utilitarian, aesthetic and symbolic. Consequently, its interpretation and appreciation can both include and transcend empirical analysis. Directly experiencing and reflecting upon the layered richness of created works can yield understandings that will differ from, but be complementary to, rational argument and explanation. Deeper insights will remain hidden if we restrict ourselves to analytical accounts and material descriptions and if we see creative works merely as physical manifestations of prefigured intentions. When we directly encounter them, and when we reflect upon their meanings and their broader significance, they can affect and heighten our awareness of the world and ourselves, and, in doing so, they can enrich our lives. Seymourpowell's remark recognizes the powerful impression that designed artefacts can have on people, but this was said in the context of design as a stimulus for acquisitiveness within a consumption-driven market system. However, this potency can be directed elsewhere – towards less consumptive, less damaging, more meaningful ends.

CREATING A MEANINGFUL MATERIAL CULTURE

This discussion suggests that any meaningful understanding of design has to recognize the importance of enduring values and those deeper understandings of reality that have shaped human societies for centuries. By including these more fundamental, intrinsic considerations, design can transcend the still-dominant perspective that regards detached objectivity and empirical data as the basis of reliable knowledge. Pragmatic concerns of utility and economy become contextualized within a broader frame of human purpose, morality and spiritual well-being – all of which lie beyond tangible evidence and proof. Such a direction recognizes that meaningful understandings of reality must include the lived experience, which on the one hand is relational and interdependent and on the other is individual – a personal journey amidst and a part of the greater whole.

When intellectual, rational understandings are complemented by emotional and intuitive awareness, we are able to appreciate reality as it is actually lived. These two kinds of cognition, in broad terms, are respectively associated with the left and right hemispheres of the brain.[55] Together, they yield a view of reality that not only seeks facts and reasons but also meanings, which historically was the realm of the world's great philosophical and spiritual traditions. In this regard, Cottingham points out a gross error in our contemporary interpretations of such traditions. Most modern debates about religion, he tells us, tend to be constructed in terms of the kinds of explanatory knowledge that science provides about the origins of the universe, but, "if the overwhelming evidence of scripture is any guide, it *must primarily be understood in the context of our urgent need to change our lives".*[56] And it is just such change, towards ways of living that offer more profound notions of personal fulfilment, that is needed to challenge the moral acceptability of continued consumerism and waste.

RECOVERY, RECEPTIVITY AND THE INADEQUACY OF CULTURE

To respond to these evolving understandings in a generous manner requires a receptive attitude – one open enough and humble enough to recognize the inadequacy of our contemporary worldview. And part of the project of developing a more comprehensive and inclusive worldview will be to cultivate a renewed attentiveness to traditional ways of knowing – ways that respond to intuitive apprehensions, subjective experiences, tacit knowledge and the human imagination. Historically, these ways of knowing have been expressed not merely through cultural endeavours but through spiritual and religious practices.

It is significant also that, unlike religion, culture and the artefacts of culture have never been able to amply unify the inner and the outer person, the spirit and the senses.[57] Therefore, if we are to pursue design in a manner that aims to unite theory and practice and the inner person with outer actions and the creation of objects, we must draw on something deeper than culture and its ever-changing patterns; and this more profound 'something', it seems, is to be found in the spiritual traditions of humanity. This, however, poses a major challenge today – not least because in contemporary society these traditions have become marginalized, fractured and diffuse. A distinctive characteristic of late-modern culture is the absence of a shared symbolic, spiritual tradition.[58] In academia these traditions also tend to be ignored: *"Almost every cultural theorist today passes over in silence some of the most vital beliefs and activities of billions of ordinary men and women, simply because they happen not to be to their personal taste".*[59] For many, such references are no longer welcome, appropriate or credible. Nevertheless, these aspects of human understanding, which surpass mundane phenomena, still have to be acknowledged and addressed if we are to 'get at' the deep sense of existential unease created by Western culture's relatively recent history. The sidelining of, and, in many cases, aggressive criticism of spirituality and religion is based, for the most part, on the false dichotomy of science *or* religion, whereby cosmological phenomena are either explained through science *or* through faith. But the intuitive spiritual sense, does not explain, nor is it concerned with physical phenomena and material facts, but with human meaning, values and ultimate purpose. The *phenomena of faith*, to use Scruton's term,[60] involve a life of inner reflection, contemplation and meditation; trust in active fidelity to the spiritual aspects of our personhood, which has many names, such as the Tao, Ultimate Reality or Ground of Being;[61] resistance to temptation and worldly things; and recognition of certain times, places, objects and words as sacrosanct – the experience of which is seen as mediating between the visible-physical and the invisible-metaphysical, apprehensions of which are sensed or known intuitively.[62] As McGilchrist says, *"We need metaphor or mythos in order to understand the world. Such myths or metaphors are not dispensable luxuries, or 'optional extras', still less the means of obfuscation: they are fundamental and essential to the process".*[63]

When reconceived to include these understandings, design can contribute to the recovery of more holistic ways forward. It can direct its efforts not just to the design of objects of practical utility but also to objects whose 'function' is concerned with inner values and a renewed validation of those things that may be intuitively apprehended but which defy empirical verification. Therefore, as an accompaniment and reflective complement to written explorations and arguments, some visual explorations of this direction have been included here. This dual approach recognizes that words and imagery represent two different ways of knowing, two different ways of appreciating the world. The first is linear, rational and explicit, the second holistic, intuitive and tacit. In spiritual traditions, words and imagery offer complementary experiences and complementary paths to understanding. Words require a level of literacy and are used in rituals such as liturgy, which are communal, social and institutional. In contrast, imagery is available to all and offers opportunities for individual, non-institutional acts of contemplation – in traditional places of religious practice, in the home, or in nature and places of solitude.[64]

The series of artefacts entitled *'Vestiges of Grace – forsaken paths to perception'* is shown in Figure 6.2 *Ithaca*, Figure 6.3 *Golgotha*, and Figure 6.4 *Xanadu*. Each piece refers to a faded Western tradition that pertains to humankind's ceaseless search for meaning – respectively mythology, Christianity, and Romanticism, the latter of which sought profundity and salvation not through traditional religious routes but through art.[65] Other examples could have been chosen, but these provide a useful basis for creative exploration and expression. Each artefact depicts an image evocative of its source – a past avenue to meaning and truth – but as a barely visible trace. Rendered only as faint impressions, this series speaks of the peripheral, virtually imperceptible role of these avenues in today's society. Thus, they allude to aspects of human knowing that have become marginalized in contemporary thought but are, nevertheless, critical to the development of more holistic and profound understandings. Contemplation of such avenues requires attentiveness, introspection and an amenable disposition. All these, however, tend to be hindered by the fast pace of modern life, the distractions of digital media, and the ubiquitous diversions of the market in the form of product promotion and advertising.

Hence, the *Vestiges of Grace* series offers a visual reminder of those things that have been devalued or even actively dismissed during the modern era. When accompanied by explanations and arguments, as included here, they offer a locus for reflecting on the effective absence of deeper notions of meaning and the consequences of this absence in contemporary affairs. And they provide a focal point for attentiveness, which, as we have seen, is an important ingredient in cultivating a more balanced, more holistic worldview – one that allows our endeavours to be at once just, caring and personally fulfilling.

CONCLUSIONS AND THE WAY FORWARD

143

In this chapter we have considered the limitations of the one-way logic of the detached observer. We have also considered philosophical arguments that suggest a more realistic understanding of the human condition is one in which we see ourselves as participants in a co-evolutionary process of continuous change. And we have seen that the creative design process is an example of just such a co-evolving process – as we externalize our thoughts through drawings, models and the like and respond to them, our ideas are informed and affected, leading to further externalizations. We have also seen that, in the modern era, the boundaries of our design activities have been too narrow and there is a need for a broader and deeper grounding than that offered by some form of internal aesthetic coherence. But we have also noted that culture alone is not up to the task of providing this grounding. Nevertheless, these deeper considerations are fundamental to the inner person, our values, the spiritual self and our perennial search for meaning. We have recognized too that meaning is to be found in our relationships with and empathy towards others, which is related to compassion and selflessness, as well as through inner reflection, contemplation and self-discipline. In addition, we have seen that the products of design are interpreted intuitively, holistically and virtually instantaneously, prior to rational thought and logical articulation. Consequently, it is important to acknowledge that the initial impact of an object can have a very powerful effect, which can be positive or negative, and used for good or ill.

Awareness of these critical issues about the nature of meaning and design allows us to bring new priorities to the discipline, which can potentially contribute to the development of more holistic perspectives. It becomes important to challenge dominant directions in design, whereby products are created to evoke emotional responses of curiosity and acquisitiveness – all aimed at boosting consumption. This path continues to flood an already saturated market with short-lived products and an increasing array of technological gadgets that offer endless possibilities for noise, distraction and entertainment. Such products, from TVs, game consoles and mobile phones to wearable technologies and implants, can be seen as severe obstacles to change and to the pursuit of more thoughtful, empathetic directions. They interrupt quietude, impede reflection and encourage individualism, consumption, self-centredness and atomization. Indeed, many of these directions, particularly evident in wearable devices, are simply contemporary developments of an early-modern, Bentham-style utilitarianism. Physiological monitoring and measurements are being interwoven with economic pursuits; physical motions and functions are being linked to health; and through shrewd marketing, the use of wearable monitoring devices is conflated with well-being and the pursuit of happiness.[66, 67] Such devices are being touted as 'wearable happiness';[68] one recent commentator on the business opportunity offered by these products suggested that *"the potential is strong for happier, healthier lives, and more successful organizations"*.[69]

In contrast to these directions, designers and others in the applied arts can explore ways of creating artefacts that encourage responses more fitting for today's context of social disparity and environmental destruction. Our creative contributions can be in far greater accord with more profound ideas of empathy, selflessness, care and inner reflection. As Eagleton, Scruton and others have discussed, the pursuit of meaning in life is a form of practice – a particular way of living in the world. This particular way of living falls into two, closely related modes. There is the outward focus, expressed through an empathetic, relational stance towards others and the world, which includes the communal and acknowledges the fact that we are social beings. And there is the inward focus, expressed through quieter, more contemplative

144

pursuits, which acknowledges that we are also individuals with a sense of self-identity and personhood. Both are present in traditional spiritual practices and contribute to what Ward refers to as a *"cultural ordering"* that is linked to ideas about living in a particular way – a certain way of behaving, a fittingness related to *"a series of associations, a web of ecological correspondences"*.[70]

For designers to constructively contribute to these directions, they will need to consider ways forward that take us down a quite different path from that which has dominated recent times. It must be a path that is in accord with and offers opportunities for stillness, silence and reflection. These are all associated with the nonverbal right hemisphere of the brain, which is also the part of us that sees the whole and is imaginative, intuitive and commensurate with empathy, meaning seeking and meaning making.

145

Vestiges of Grace

forsaken paths to perception

*If the doors of perception were cleansed everything
would appear to man as it is, infinite.*

*For man has closed himself up till he sees all things
thro' narrow chinks of his cavern.*

William Blake[71]

Ithaca

Always keep Ithaca in mind,
To arrive there is your destination.

C. P. Cavafy[72]

Figure 6.2

Ithaca

Golgotha

*He went out to the place of the Skull,
which in Aramaic is called Golgotha.*

John 19:17–18[73]

Figure 6.3
Golgotha

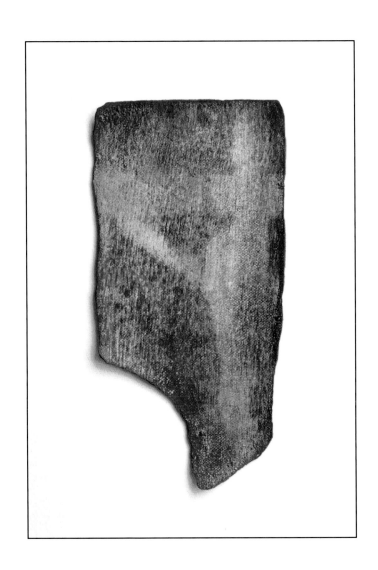

Xanadu

There is at this place a very fine marble
Palace, the rooms of which are all gilt.

The Travels of Marco Polo[74]

Figure 6.4

Xanadu

7
Rhythms movement, making and meaning

This is the way we sweep the floor
Sweep the floor, sweep the floor
This is the way we sweep the floor
So early in the morning

Traditional

Before becoming an academic, I spent many years in and around heavy industry. While still at school, and between later studies, I worked in the Bessemer converter shop, blast furnaces, rolling mills and galvanizing plants of the steelworks that was the lifeblood of my home town of Ebbw Vale in South Wales. One year I worked in the newly constructed industrial effluent plant where, as an improvement on emptying toxic sludge from the manufacturing process into the river, it was loaded into skips and dumped on the mountain. As an undergraduate, I worked with a blasting crew at Geevor, the last tin mine still operating in Cornwall. Set high above the shore, the headgear stood out starkly against sea and sky. Below the cliffs, the mining operation's rust-coloured tailings stained the waters and feathered the beaches. For several years I was a petroleum engineer with an oil major, working on drilling rigs around Groningen in the Netherlands and in the deserts of Oman. From the air, the once-pristine deserts were a criss-cross of truck tracks, seismic lines and pipelines. Each time rig operations were completed, the tailings ponds would be bulldozed over, burying hazardous chemicals along with thousands of gallons of drilling fluids.

All these environments were hard and coarse – places of iron and fire, roaring gantries, scarred hands on oily tools, rimed mugs and tobacco smoke. They were places of brute strength and rough language. To the newcomer, the noise, the moving machinery and the sense of danger could be overwhelming. It was invariably polluting and always blind to the consequences. These were man-made places, and in those days they were exclusively male. They were framed by materialism and driven by money, but the harshness and the long shifts forged a pride and a crude camaraderie. Men like warriors conquering the elements and using their ingenuity to wrestle steel from ore, tin from granite, oil from the depths. These were physical environments of action, urgency and progress, where mistakes were always bloody and sometimes fatal. In such surroundings, there was little opportunity, thought or quarter given to reflection, quietude and gentler things.

While the costs of heavy industry to the natural world may be severe, the work itself was often very fulfilling. You felt you were doing something substantial where tasks were being achieved by effort, ingenuity and sweat. They were industries that employed people across a whole range of abilities, from manual workers, skilled tradesmen and clerical staff to technicians, engineers and managers. Each had their place, played their role and earned a living. Everyone was part of something, which gave them a sense of belonging and identity. These industries created their own kinds of culture, wrought from the noise, dirt and machinery, the long hours and the day-to-day dynamics. And they offered their own kinds of reward – a sense of doing and achieving, and the dignity of work. You felt that your wages had been earned, a fair exchange.

In the years that followed, I came to see that there are other ways of thinking and other ways of acting, ways that cultivate more balanced understandings of what it is to be a human being living on a finite and fragile planet, ways that can be at once productive and contemplative, pragmatic and responsive, professional and perceptive. Ways that heed facts and values, action and reflection. These are the ways that must come to the fore if we are to counter the imperilling vandalism of vested interests, power and greed that with self-endorsed authority so carelessly and callously trample cultures, ecologies and humanity's deep-rooted wisdoms.

155

Industrialization has not only caused untold destruction of natural places, it has also trampled on critical aspects of our own being. And as the developed economies of the West have moved away from heavy industry and mass production, the directions taken do not suggest more balanced understandings or the prevalence of fairer, more just attitudes. In the transition from production to consumption and from products to services, many features of the workplace have changed. Some of the more positive aspects have been eroded – not least the availability of satisfying work across a wide range of abilities, and jobs that offer a sense of achievement and a decent wage. In this regard, Overell et al. conclude that the UK has a job-quality problem, an important aspect of which is a decline in autonomy due to rigid job specification and micro-management.[1] In many of today's jobs, employees have little discretion over how they work, and they feel more stressed and less trusted to make decisions. There is evidence, too, that employee skills are being poorly used. All these factors are detrimental to the idea of good work because they reduce one's sense of fulfilment. *"The evidence in favour of freeing employees from rigid rules, bureaucratic controls and superfluous procedures is overwhelming".*[2] Perhaps even more worrying is that studies from the UK and the US suggest that developments in digital technologies will lead to huge numbers of jobs being put at risk in coming decades.[3] Unless accompanied by radical, systemic reforms in our economy, such developments could lead to major unemployment and even greater economic disparities. Growth in unemployment and inequity would be accompanied by an erosion in the quality of life for many, social division and an increased burden on social and public sector provision.

156

NOVELTY AND TRADITION

In virtually all walks of life, modern society is inordinately preoccupied with technology, innovation, competition and choice, and with economic growth, which is how we have come to gauge progress. In this society, it seems we need a new, innovative product for every detail of our lives. The onus on business is to always be producing something new, no matter how trivial, as long as it will boost sales. These preoccupations are, of course, not only proving incredibly damaging but they are also the polar opposites of those values found in traditional societies where the obligation was to take as little as was needed from the natural environment and not let anything go to waste. Traditional ways of life were rooted to place, dependent on physical work, and respectful of conventions that had emerged over long periods of time. The slow pace of change allowed for new developments and practices, but these were fashioned by deep local knowledge to fit with needs and context. And these ways of life, within a particular landscape, shaped people's values, identity and sense of belonging and gave their lives meaning.[4] These are the factors that align many traditional ways of living with contemporary sustainability, not only culturally and environmentally but also economically, if we understand economy in its true sense, as the management of the material resources of a community. Traditional modes of living, because they do not encourage wants and consumption, require fewer external resources and expenditures, and they create far less waste. Therefore, in considering how we might design and produce in ways that are more enriching and less damaging, traditional practices have much to teach us. We can learn from their relationship to place; to identity and belonging; to the nature and pace of change; to values; and to notions of a meaningful life.

In the face of globalized, industrialized processes, many traditional practices have come to be seen as uncompetitive. While they may not be currently feasible in terms of a main, or indeed any, income generation, engagement in traditional practices can offer an important counterbalance to our busy, competitive, consumption-driven and increasingly digital lifestyles. In time, perhaps, such engagement can contribute to the development of new, more benign ways forward. Through focussed engagement, traditional practices offer ways of grounding our lives in context; they integrate us with place and, through physical activities, they help cultivate a sense of harmony and meaning. We saw in the previous chapter that it is through such engagement that we become changed – as we change the world the world changes us – and we start to develop different outlooks, different values and different priorities.

157

Here, I would like to consider ways of *making* and *doing* that are in keeping with more balanced, reflective and creative modes of being. Many of these are thousands of years old; they are in harmony with rather than at odds with nature and they can be beneficial to our own well-being. They also help foster the necessary conditions for creative insight and synthesis. In Chapter 3, in addition to *grassroots*, *contemplative* and *counterpoint design*, I mentioned *rhythmical objects*. At first glance, these appear to be more practical in nature, but, like the others, they also have an important symbolic role, as we shall see.

EQUITABLE AND RESPONSIBLE PRACTICES AND PRODUCTS

To deal effectively with environmental obligations while also creating good work, products need to be properly priced so that they reflect the true costs of their production. From a pragmatic perspective, when the full costs are taken into account, making practices and product use that are situated locally start to be more viable. Making and use not only can become integral ingredients of the community but also shipping, packaging, energy consumption and pollution can all be reduced. In addition, the quality of work – the making and maintenance processes – can be conceived as both meaningful and creative, building knowledge and skills and providing a sense of accomplishment. Such processes may be solitary activities, permitting silence, contemplation and thinking, or people may come together to work in groups, offering opportunities for social interaction, friendship, learning and confidence building. Either way, if they are local, they contribute to a material culture that both expresses and reflects personal, communal and local identity, and any detrimental effects can be recognized and rectified.

158 If goods are produced in this way as a commercial enterprise, rather than as a purely amateur or hobby activity, then, to be in accord with an ethos of sustainability, their production must be capable of supporting reasonable standards of living for individual makers and their families. This is generally not feasible in today's globalized economic system. Mass-produced products can be offered at far lower prices than locally produced, properly costed goods. This is only possible because the negative social and environmental impacts of mass production are not taken into account. The operations of global corporations are frequently linked to exploitative labour practices; gross disparities in income; the creation of immense quantities of disposable packaging and waste; and the international distribution of short-lived, disposable or irreparable products. The price differential between these two modes of production – local and global – reflects the hidden or 'externalized' costs of energy-intensive and often socially exploitative globalized practices. For a just, environmentally responsible future this differential will need to be addressed – through regulation, taxation or other means. If this were done, any revenues collected could be directed towards the remediation of harm and the encouragement of better, more intelligent ways forward. Such a direction requires strong, forward-looking governments capable of introducing policies and regulations that create a level playing field for local enterprises striving to act responsibly in their communities. This is exactly where visionary leadership could make a substantial difference to people's lives while simultaneously reducing the social divisions and inequities that have arisen in countries with developed economies since the 1980s. Such policies would also help reduce the enormous environmental impacts associated with consumerism and globalization.

Obviously, properly costed goods and services would mean higher retail prices for many things. People would be able to afford fewer things, which at first glance might seem an unattractive option in terms of individual choice and a thriving economy. However, this direction could not only be very positive, it also has to become part of the reimagining that is needed to deal with the growing social divisions and environmental crises facing us today. Properly priced goods and lower levels of consumption could have very productive outcomes for local economies. They could stimulate local businesses and markets, and local producers would receive fair remuneration; there would be good-quality local jobs with living wages, and an increased sense of local contribution, belonging and identity. This would help build social cohesion, community and, through the production and maintenance of local goods, a meaningful and distinctive material culture.

In such a scenario, the nature of goods would change. If we were paying substantially more for durable products, we would expect them to be well made, long lasting and repairable. Many of the products we now take for granted, including the many digital devices that have become so commonplace, would have to be redesigned to be serviceable and upgradable at the local level, even if their components continued to be mass produced at the international scale. Because of their enduring qualities as things, over time such products could become personally and culturally meaningful. They would carry with them the stories of their provenance and their history, and parts could be periodically replaced to keep up with technological developments. Enduring but evolving products would mean more services and employment at the local level, and fewer products being centrally produced and distributed. The concomitant reductions in new product acquisition would help counter the damaging effects of consumerism while simultaneously promoting local employment through making and service centres. If supported by policy and regulation that favour small, local enterprises, then good-quality jobs would be created that contribute to a highly variegated, distributed and hence collectively robust economy. This philosophy contrasts markedly with the state of affairs we have today where national economies are extremely vulnerable to changes in overseas markets

159

and where profits are drained from local communities to be directed towards bonuses and dividends for those with no interest in or commitment to the place where production and use of the products and services actually occur. People live in a particular locale and it is here, in a specific geographical location, that they work, bring up families, interact with neighbours, shop, go to school, and share experiences. Consequently, it is here where meaning is to be found, in the particularities of everyday encounters, work lives and leisure activities, in the joys and heartaches of lives lived. And it is here, at the local level, where it is possible to develop more meaningful renditions of material culture.

Digital processes and automated making and doing can undoubtedly accomplish many mundane tasks rapidly and effectively – and in certain fields may be necessary for achieving high-precision operations or for health or safety reasons. However, there is also a need for people to have satisfying work and for person-to-person contacts and connections. We must ask ourselves, therefore, what we believe work is for – is it just for creating profits or does it have value in its own right? With regard to the nature of material things, there is often a quality about the handmade and its relation to human creativity that is evident in the goods themselves.

160

They may lack machine-like accuracy and perfection yet they possess a character and an aesthetic that is preferred, as in this example by novelist Willa Cather: *"The thick clay walls had been finished on the inside by the deft palms of Indian women, and had that irregular and intimate quality of things made entirely by the human hand ... never quite evenly flat, never a dead white".*[5] Such artefacts can have a far stronger emotional effect on us because we recognize in them the human touch. There is a human connection that matters to us. The opportunities offered by automation, digital technologies and robotics are vast but there is a need to keep in mind that this human connection is important. These things may be reconciled if we strive to ensure a balanced approach at the local level where we can maintain face-to-face human contact and be directly aware of the implications of our activities.

Situated activities can both draw on and contribute to local knowledge, and with time, traditions become established that help sustain the values and beliefs of a culture. Traditions can be understood as representing context-related knowledge that has proved to be relevant, useful and important to people. This kind of knowledge, which becomes distilled and refined as it is passed down from one generation to another, is fundamentally grounded in human experiences and values. It finds expression in stories, music and song and also in local practices and material objects. Yet, *"less is known about the benefits of specific and readily available domestic arts and crafts"*;[6] in the social sciences, the artefact itself tends to be disregarded and, with it, qualities and characteristics integral to its making and use.[7] Domestic making practices are typically modest and unassuming and are often simply taken for granted, which may be one reason their positive contributions have not been extensively researched. Strikingly, however, many of these practices are conducive to periods of quietude and contemplation.

The rather frenzied preoccupations of modern life often mean there is little time for more reflective modes of being. However, we can point to various practices that have come down to us from pre- or non-modern cultures that support such modes; one example is the use of prayer and worry beads.[8] Their use often involves repetitive, 'disengaged' physical actions, which have the effect of inducing a calmer disposition. Significantly, these traditional ways of 'thinking-doing' can help us gain a broader, more comprehensive perspective. Neuroscientist Jaak Panksepp says that some aspects of folk-psychology may be able to teach us more about integrated ways of thinking than overly restrictive, systematic approaches that seek to analyze evidence-based, observable facts and behaviours. He points out that our dependency on language, words and logical rigour in modern scientific and cultural endeavours are obstacles to the attainment of more balanced understandings.[9] The primacy of left-hemisphere thinking modes not only hinders holistic understandings, it has also been associated with various medical conditions. Michel Odent, an obstetrician and childbirth specialist, argues that the technologizing of the birthing process can be linked to unforeseen negative effects later in life, including allergies and anorexia nervosa.[10] His research indicates that the increased use of technologies and drugs on delicate, vulnerable physiological systems may also have other serious consequences – potentially reducing the ability to socialize and the capacity for empathy and love, including a respect for the natural world.[11] Similarly, from the field of psychiatry, Iain McGilchrist links the predominance of left-hemisphere – discrete, analytical – thinking modes to an increased frequency of illnesses, again including anorexia nervosa.[12]

In contrast, there are direct, positive benefits to engaging in activities conducive to right-hemisphere, holistic thinking. Moreover, doing things for

161

ourselves at the local level can be inherently meaningful, contributing to the development of our values and our notions of the good. Sennett offers two interrelated arguments to support such practices. First, because the ecological crisis is a human-made problem linked to industrialization and technological expansion, to rely on technology to regain control may be an unreliable strategy. Second, expecting the general public to deal with the problems associated with manufactured products after the fact – once they have been produced and distributed – is highly problematic because the condition is then irreversible. Instead, he suggests that engagement in creating material things should start much earlier so that people gain a better, more comprehensive understanding of the processes involved. Making our material culture ourselves matters, he says, because of what we can learn about ourselves through the things we make. We learn to care about the right way to do things, the qualities of materials, the taste of well-cooked foods, and these things naturally lead us towards notions of the 'good' and spiritual and social values.[13] Essentially, craftsmanship is about doing a job well for its own sake, for its intrinsic rewards, not as a means to some other end. This stands in stark contrast to the ideologies of competition and market forces that have come to dominate most spheres of human activity today.[14] Research studies about creative occupations suggest that they are one of the essential ways in which a person can attain a sense of competence and achievement, express their true selves and achieve a sense of continuity in their lives.[15]

162

THE IMPORTANCE OF THE HUMAN TOUCH

For work to be creative and meaningful, for it to connect at a deeper level with people, it has to be of people – of the hand, the eye and the spontaneous, intuitive responses that are possible when working directly with materials. During the process of making, one has to 'see', 'listen', be responsive, and make decisions – not in a pre-planned, impositional way, but as the work unfolds. The maker has to allow the work to inform its emerging direction. Eisner puts it this way:

> *The work itself secures its own voice and helps set the direction. The maker is guided and, in fact, at times surrenders to the demands of the emerging forms. Opportunities in the process of working are encountered that were not envisioned when the work began but that speak so eloquently, about the process of emerging possibilities that new options are pursued. Put succinctly, surprise, a fundamental reward of all creative work, is bestowed by the work on its maker.[16]*

In this process, the tools we select are very important because they will fundamentally affect the nature of the outcome. If we use CNC routers, laser cutters and 3D printers, the designs will be pre-planned, predetermined and imposed on the material, irrespective of 'its own voice'. We become deaf to the materials themselves and, from the very start, we eliminate the element of surprise; the *"smart machine can separate human mental understanding from repetitive, instructive, hands-on learning. When this occurs, conceptual human powers suffer"*.[17] The result will be more precise but less intimate; a literal and figurative distance will be forged between the person and the work. The process will be efficient and repeatable but it will also be lifeless and sterile. This is because these kinds of tools are dependent solely on quantification – they are the tools of numbers, algorithms, measurement and automation. Ways of working that rely on the hand, the eye, the approximate and the responsive may be less efficient, repeatable and precise but it is these very features that imbue qualities that are warm, engaging and distinctive. The properties and particularities of handmade work are meaningful to us – they speak of our humanness and are reflective of context, place, receptivity and the knowledge and skills that constitute expertise. Swenarchuk refers to artisanal making processes as holistic technologies, in contrast to prescriptive technologies that are planned, organized, and controlled in ways detached from the making.[18]

163

Thus, making things by hand is an holistic endeavour and it is this notion that is critical to our understanding of what constitutes a meaningful human activity. Thinking and doing, rational and intuitive, responding and decision-making all become part of an indivisible, continuous process that flows and emerges. It is an integrated process that requires the maker to be fully engaged; we become one with the work itself, entirely absorbed in the activity, oblivious of time and self.[19] In this process, the object of our attention is, according to Borgmann, a 'focal thing' and the related activity that so absorbs us is a 'focal practice'. This kind of holistic practice can be understood as a meaning-making activity through which *"we are able to accomplish what remains unattainable when aimed at in a series of individual decisions and acts"*.[20] The latter may be rational and logical, but they lack the intuitive, tacit ways of knowing afforded through practice. Focal practices are meaningful because they help restore *"a depth and integrity to our lives that are in principle excluded with the paradigm of technology"*.[21] Creative, focal practices of engaged designing and making mediate between objective and subjective, analytical and synthetical ways of thinking, which can result in more balanced, holistic and meaningful outcomes.

TRADITIONAL PRACTICES, CONTINUITY AND CHANGE

When we work directly with materials, we automatically include in the process intuitive responses, decisions, feelings and aesthetic judgements. In this way, material artefacts become containers and expressions of human values. In traditional practices, values from past generations are carried, through present actions, into the future – like a runner in a relay race the maker briefly holds and then passes on the baton. Consciously or not, in the making there will be modification and transformation. While there is a sense of history and cultural identity tied to practice and place, there is no definitively 'original' design. Rather, there is slow, continual change, acceptance and enculturation. Knowledge, skills and values of former generations are brought into the present and carried forward. There is a sense of continuity, connectedness and community about such products, with less emphasis on novelty, innovation and 'originality'. Consequently, there is a downplaying of the 'me', the ego, which contrasts markedly with late modernity's prioritization of individualism. Inevitably, the maker's hand will leave its particular mark on the work, but this will be a consequence rather than a primary intention. Such approaches are typical of pre- or non-modern and, potentially, of after-modern outlooks, and they align well with sustainability and the common good.[22]

164

In today's meritocratic societies, immersed as they are in the neoliberal ideologies of free-market capitalism, there is a strong inclination to raise oneself above others, to demonstrate difference, advantage and position. Inseparable from this consumption-based system is the inclination to impose our will on the natural environment, to exploit it to suit our needs and desires. In contrast, traditional ways of living are more communal and tend to work with nature rather than against it. One example of this comes from New Mexico. The cultural norms among Pueblo Indian potters meant that traditionally they did not sign their work; designs belonged to the community as a whole. Similarly, making processes were collective endeavours that had been passed down through the generations. These were not individualistic meritocracies. Within this kind of culture, signing a piece would be claiming it for oneself, which was regarded as unseemly, lacking in discretion.[23] Things began to change with the construction of the railroad, which brought newcomers to the region in the nineteenth and twentieth centuries. As a consequence, the folk arts came to the attention of buyers from the eastern United States, so called 'Anglos'. Initially, however, these artefacts were not regarded as art objects worthy of signature, but either as crafts or simply as labour.[24] The signing of work only began in the twentieth century when it was realized that signed pieces would command higher prices when sold to tourists or collectors.[25]

In traditional cultures, an empathetic, communal spirit tends to permeate design and making, resulting in rather different outcomes from those typically encouraged in design schools. Rather than reward individual creative vision and originality, forms evolve over generations, resulting in refined, often very beautiful, functional designs that include everything from architecture, furniture and everyday goods to jewellery, textiles, clothing and religious objects. The truths manifested in such objects might not be verifiable through outward proofs but, nevertheless, they can be experienced, appreciated and known inwardly to be true. These local, anonymous designs, in contrast to products for mass production, are tailored to particular social and environmental conditions and are, therefore, uniquely suited to context. Significantly for this discussion, repetitive physical processes are often a characteristic feature of traditional making and use.

165

SILENCE, CONTEMPLATION AND REPETITIVE MAKING PRACTICES

Within the modern view we see ourselves as dispassionate observers of the world 'out there', a world that we are at liberty to plunder and spoil. Traditional practices resonate more strongly with the co-evolutionary understandings discussed in Chapter 6. This is because, through the focal practices so typical of traditional ways of making, we create favourable conditions for the occurrence of more synthetical modes of thinking. These practices require dedicated attention to both the process and the object being produced, and this affects the nature of the emerging object.[26] Hence, a reciprocal process arises – through our absorbed attentiveness we develop a deeper awareness of the world and the world becomes changed in a particular but important way, which then becomes included in the vista of our attention.

Many of these practices involve repetitions, through which the physical body and the intellectual side of our thinking become preoccupied with mundane tasks. This process frees the mind for other, more contemplative modes of thought. Betty Edwards, author of the classic text, *Drawing on the*

Right Side of the Brain, sets upside-down line drawing tasks for her students specifically to induce this kind of cognitive shift. She says, *"In order to gain access to the right hemisphere, it is necessary to present the left hemisphere with a task that it will turn down"*, it then tends to *"fade out"*. This, she says, leads to a mode of thinking and a state of being that is *"highly focussed, singularly attentive, deeply engaging, wordless, timeless, productive and mentally restorative"*.[27] Such mundane repetitive practices can help create conditions that are conducive to contemplation and the imagination. These thought processes are non-rationalistic, intuitive and first-person; that is, subjective. They are also restorative because they enable a more holistic view of reality, which allows us to put things in perspective and helps foster greater equilibrium and harmony in our actions and an improved sense of well-being. This wider view is especially important today because, as discussed earlier, the dangerously narrow modern outlook still dominates contemporary society.

Repetitive practices include domestic arts such as knitting and sewing, wood carving and whittling, and tasks such as raking and sweeping. We might, perhaps, also include the recent fashion of colouring books for adults, which are marketed as being relaxing, even therapeutic. These practices, as well as other common tasks like driving a car, require good hand–eye coordination, motor control, spatial awareness and decision-making, all of which take place in concert and are performed automatically; they do not rely on introspective reflection.[28] They require attention to the task at hand but also allow time for silence, solitude and thinking. Importantly, they facilitate an imperceptible transition into right-hemisphere thinking, which, being the creative mode, enables us to synthesize ideas and, perhaps, spontaneously see in our mind's eye resolution to some problem that has been bothering us; this is the 'Ah-ha' or Eureka moment of creative insight. As Edwards has said of her school days, *"art classes, cooking classes, sewing classes, ceramics, woodworking, metal working, and gardening provided welcome breaks in the academic day, with time for solitary thought. Silence is a rare commodity in modern classrooms, and drawing is an individual, silent, timeless activity"*.[29]

Repetitive physical movement and rhythms are critically important to these kinds of activities. *"This is repetition for its own sake ... the emotional payoff is one's experience of doing it again. There's nothing strange about this experience. We all know it; it is rhythm. Built into the contractions of the human heart, the skilled craftsman has extended rhythm to the hand and the*

166

eye".[30] Research among regular knitters indicates that these kinds of repetitive practices improve one's cognitive skills and abilities in areas such as mathematics, planning and organizing, as well as one's visual and spatial awareness and the ability to conceptualize three-dimensional spatial relationships.[31]

There is, however, something of a paradox here. While repetitive practices in making and use are conducive to contemplation, imagination and creative thinking, the practices and resulting objects are not necessarily intended to be innovative or especially original in their design. Indeed, the opposite may be the case – many traditional practices simply perpetuate well-established patterns, producing familiar artefacts for everyday use.

RHYTHMICAL OBJECTS AND MEANING

Objects whose making or use is achieved by engaging in focal practices that involve repetitions and rhythms are referred to here as *rhythmical objects*. These kinds of practices serve as a bridge between the rational and the intuitive, cultivating a more integrated outlook. The nineteenth-century American poet John Greenleaf Whittier refers to this state when he suggests that to give space for the inner, meaning-seeking side of us we must set aside sense-based knowledge and our preoccupations with material or worldly things.

167

> *Let sense be numb, let flesh retire;*
> *Speak through the earthquake, wind, and fire,*
> *O still, small voice of calm!*[32]

Ernest Hemingway alludes to this state when he writes of F. Scott Fitzgerald, *"He learned to think and could not fly any more because the love of flight was gone and he could only remember when it had been effortless".*[33] A. N. Wilson relates this uncreative, unimaginative state to modernity's pedantic preoccupation with materialism. He says, *"Materialism or Reductionism, or whatever you call it, the most boring, as well as the least accurate way of experiencing the world and recording experience, is the dominant mindset of the Western intelligentsia in our day"* and *"Human beings have an ineluctable tendency to think materially and literally, and … this is a sort of death".* He points out that a key to perception is the human imagination, which is the polar opposite of a scientific outlook anchored solely in empirical evidence.[34] Human meaning is to be found in this imaginative realm, which speaks of truths that cannot be found in data. These are the truths of empathy, love, attentiveness, compassion and caring. These are the truths of the novelist and the poet, the artist and the designer. They are the truths found in the stories of Dostoyevsky, Dickens and Gaskell, the verses of Blake and Rilke, and the paintings of Malevich and Rothko. The imaginative, attentive spirit is certainly apparent, too, in the work of groundbreaking designers like Rietveld, Rams and Sottsass, all of whom responded to the concerns of their time through form, materials and process. Today, however, there are quite different agendas to be addressed by design.

RHYTHMS, CONTEMPLATION AND MAKING

In musical composition, the term *ostinato* refers to the continuous repetition of a melodic fragment or rhythmical phrase. A number of contemporary composers – Glass, Reich, Adams, Bryars – use this kind of repetition in their work. It can have a powerful emotional effect on the listener and is often quite calming. Some years ago, while working on a recording at Leicester Polytechnic, Gavin Bryars recounts that he left a tape loop playing when he went for coffee. When he returned some time later, the students in the painting studio adjacent to the recording room were unusually quiet and subdued and moving more slowly; some were sitting quietly alone, some were even weeping.[35]

168

There are many historical and cultural examples of rhythm and repetition being used to quieten the intellectual mind, to induce calm or to facilitate contemplation. Nursery rhymes are recited to babies, often accompanied by a gentle rocking motion, to pacify and soothe them to sleep. These short songs, like the familiar *Rock-a-Bye-Baby*, employ rhyme and rhythm in repeated cycles. In the monastic traditions of Greece, *"one characteristic practice is to exclude noise, either in the outer world or in the mind, by repeating a single devotional phrase"*.[36] Many other contemplative traditions involve the repetition of prayers and mantras as well as repetitive physical movements, such as rocking back and forth[37] or the use of prayer beads where cycles of prayers are said while counting 'physically' by holding one bead after another. These techniques are concerned with embodied thought, as in this instruction by the fifth-century ascetic John the Solitary: *"Be careful not just to repeat them, but let your very self become these words. For there is no advantage in the reciting unless the word actually becomes embodied in you and becomes a deed"*.[38] Zarilli, discussing psychophysical practices in the performing arts of India, explains that, *"The formal years of training are understood gradually to reshape the actor's bodymind."* Techniques entail physical exercises, hand gestures and rhythmic patterns of movement.[39] We can also include physical, rhythmical practices like drumming as well as a host of practical activities that involve rhythmical body movements. MacCulloch tells us that early monasteries were *"hives of manufacturing"*; the community *"listened to a reader of Scripture, while systematically plaiting mats and ropes from reeds, an activity which one can see as the ancestor of the prayerful repetition of rosary beads, but which was also one of the staples of community income"*.[40]

RHYTHMICAL PRACTICES AND WELL-BEING

Malkina-Pykh demonstrates that a person's sense of well-being – their sense of happiness or satisfaction with life – can be significantly improved through therapies that involve rhythmic movements.[41] Her research into the relationship between body movement and psychotherapy is consistent with reported findings about well-being from people who regularly engage in practices like knitting. An example of this, from the field of health care, is offered by Odent, whom I mentioned previously in relation to the use of technology in modern childbirth. His research shows that for natural childbirth, intellectual ways of thinking should be suppressed; the birth process needs to be protected against forms of stimulation that encourage neocortical – that is, intellectual, rationalistic – brain activity. It seems that modern hospital practices often achieve the exact opposite. Not only are birthing rooms packed with specialized instruments, but hospital staff tend to ask questions of the birthing mother, give instructions and offer rational explanations. The birthing mother is observed by staff who directly face her and make eye contact. Environments are often relatively harsh, with bright lighting, commonly neon strips, hard surfaces and technological equipment. These, along with the presence of a male doctor, have the effect of stimulating neocortical activity and raising adrenaline levels. These are all hindrances to the calm, quiet conditions required for natural birth.[42] By contrast, he gives an example of a childbirth scenario from Paris in the 1950s that follows a pattern repeated in more traditional societies all around the world. Typically, there would be just one experienced midwife in the room with the birthing mother. The room would be warm, dimly lit and silent and the midwife would sit in a corner, knitting. Dismissed by modern science as mere folklore and old wives' tales, Odent demonstrates that these conditions provide an ideal environment for lowering neocortical activity and adrenaline in the mother. For these reasons, he argues, they are highly appropriate for natural childbirth; the labouring mother is safe and comfortable, and calmed

169

by the conditions. An important factor is the presence of only one other female, because with more people in the room the mother may feel observed. Somewhat surprisingly, the fact that the midwife is knitting is also important. Odent tells us that this repetitive activity is very effective in reducing hormone levels associated with stress. By knitting, the midwife ensures her own adrenaline levels are kept low and, because emotional states are contagious, this has a highly beneficial effect on the birthing mother – lowering her stress levels too.[43]

This example accords with Panksepp's view, referred to above, that folk psychology can teach us much about integrative ways of knowing. It accords too with research that shows knitting to be an effective stress reducer.[44] Riley explains that these benefits are also associated with quilting, sewing, weaving, spinning and other textile arts. However, it is also important to take into account the frequency of engagement. As one might expect, more regular practitioners – over three times a week – report increased gains in terms of a sense of calm, improved mental health, cognitive functioning and well-being. Significantly, engagement in such practices is particularly important to those whose day-to-day work involves use of computers and digital technologies; they report a need to switch off, disconnect and engage in hand skills and tactile practices.[45] Whereas the repetitive physical actions of traditional ways of working help quieten the mind and are positively associated with subjective well-being and happiness, there is a growing body of evidence to indicate that many contemporary activities involving the use of digital technologies negatively affect subjective well-being and are associated with higher levels of anxiety.[46]

These examples all demonstrate the need for a more balanced approach in our ways of encountering the world. It is noticeable that many of these disengaged actions, which are so conducive to holistic ways of thinking and being, have long been associated with the home and the domestic arts. In contrast, reductionism, instrumental views of the world and advanced technological approaches are associated with mass production, industry, and corporate environments. Consequently, if we are to develop more holistic, less damaging ways forward, there is much to learn from traditional cultures and the knowledge, skills and ways of being associated with their domestic arts, all of which have tended to be dismissed as old hat in modern times.

RHYTHMS, PHYSICAL ACTIONS AND OUTLOOK

Rhythms and repetitive physical activities seem to be important for many essential brain functions. For example, brain activity that controls arm movement is not based on spatial information but on rhythm.[47] These kinds of repetitive practices can generate a form of sensory overload of our everyday consciousness, from which emerges a new realization. We become oriented *"towards a deepening interiority"* in which the barriers between outer observation and inner imagination, the external and internal are lowered.[48] In other words, and in contrast to the modern predominantly Cartesian view, the subjective-objective division is bridged, allowing us to achieve a more unified outlook, one in which we see ourselves not as separate from the world but as an integral part of it. This leads to rather different priorities and values. Activities and objects that engage us physically and silently take the focus away from ourselves. They enable bigger-than-self thinking and invoke self-transcendence values associated with universalism and benevolence. This larger view is essential for empathy, for care and consideration of other people, other living things and the planet itself.[49] Repetitive practices and making things by hand may be time consuming, but therein lies their advantage. Preparing soup, for example, involves the peeling and repetitive chopping of vegetables. When we do this, we experience touch, smell, visual awareness, achievement, rhythm, control, understanding, and, in a busy world, the pleasure of time spent on the simple but fulfilling task of making something tangible. These are focal practices that offer direct experiences. Technology often erodes or even eradicates such experiences. The food processor may be convenient and time-saving, but we should ask ourselves, time saved for what? If approached with the right attitude, focussed, engaged activities that require our involvement and attentiveness not only accomplish productive tasks but also provide important opportunities for respite and contemplation.

171

In addition to personal benefits, these practices have social benefits. They employ methods of communicating to ourselves and to others via nonverbal means that are based on learned processes. They are representational activities that do not require speech. Intentionality is perceived and meaning is seen, both of which are critical elements of social interaction.[50] Knitting with others in a group can afford feelings of belonging and improved quality of life, and can dispel negative thoughts.[51]

Hence, the argument for supporting or engaging in these practices does not rest on efficiency of production or competitiveness in the marketplace but on the fact that, fundamentally, these are restorative practices. They conform to the three meaning-based elements of the *Quadruple Bottom Line of Design for Sustainability* discussed in Chapter 1: (1) *Personal Meaning* – well-being, holistic thinking, self-transcendence; (2) *Social Meaning* – empathy, social equity, community ethos; and (3) *Practical Meaning* – functional benefit, localization, pro-environmental values.[52] The fourth element, *Economic Means*, can here be understood as the enabling element. As I said earlier, rather than understanding economy in purely financial terms, it can be thought of in its fuller sense as the prudent management of resources of a community or a region, especially in terms of their sustained availability for local production, consumption or use. Local making practices can be creative, relatively inexpensive, small scale and can make use of locally produced, renewable materials.

ENGAGEMENT IN PRACTICE – RHYTHMICAL OBJECTS

To better understand the thinking processes, physical actions and experiences involved in repetitive, rhythmical making practices one has to actually engage in these practices for oneself. This was achieved here by creating a series of small functional objects from locally gathered wood. The tools employed in their making were simple and few – a pocketknife, sandpaper and wire wool. The objects were made by the repetitive process of whittling and their use also involves repetitive, rhythmical processes. They include knitting needles, crochet hooks, bodkins and sewing needles, drop spindles and a conductor's baton (see Figures 7.1–7.5).

On the face of it, these types of *rhythmical objects* are more explicitly pragmatic than the objects featured in earlier chapters; essentially, they are rudimentary tools. However, the approach to making is in keeping with an ethic that values locale, community and tradition and is, therefore, one that de-emphasizes individualism, innovation and context-less or uprooted originality. Quite clearly, there is nothing especially novel about their designs; there is merely a translation to the local. In some cases, their forms can be traced back thousands of years. In recent times we have seen many new ideas and much, perhaps too much, emphasis on progress and innovation. Frequently, these have been driven by financial objectives rather than being worthwhile in themselves. Consequently, many of those ideas and innovations lack depth and enduring meaning. By contrast, the examples of *rhythmical objects* included here adhere to traditional forms: They employ modest, non-damaging ways of making; they utilize small quantities of locally available materials; and they enable tasks to be achieved that range from the practical, such as the making of clothes, to the cultural in the form of music making. In their presence, their production and/or their use, these objects also help cultivate more contemplative ways of being. In turn, they allow for synthesis, meaning seeking and meaning making.

173

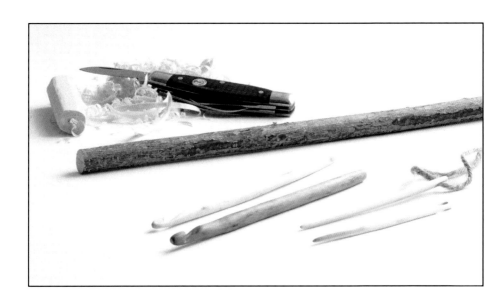

Figure 7.1

Crochet Hooks and Bodkins

whittled oak and birch

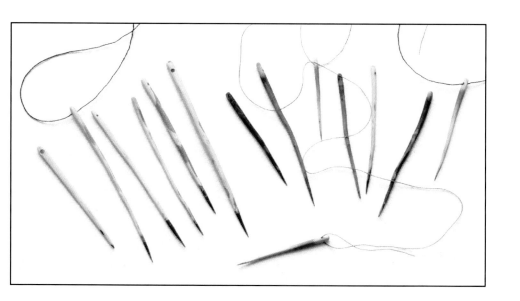

Figure 7.2

Sewing Needles

hawthorns and blackthorns

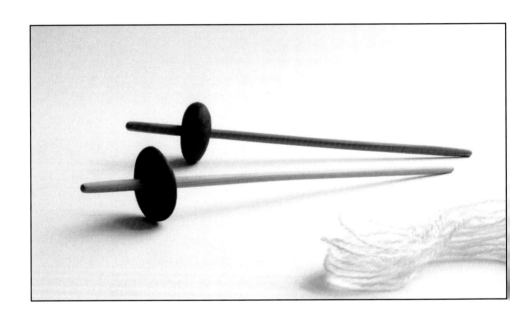

Figure 7.3

Drop Spindles

whittled cedar and pine, beach stones

Figure 7.4
Knitting Needles
whittled holly

Figure 7.5
Conductor's Baton
whittled oak and white birch

These practices and the objects they yield are not concerned with scientific or technological progress. And even though they are concerned with utility and offer some kind of functional agency, this is not their primary role. Likewise, they are not concerned with production efficiency, monetary profits and economic growth – they are not conceived as marketable goods. So, we might well ask, what kinds of objects are they, and what is their purpose and relevance today?

Primarily, they are objects of communication – they are signifiers of values and meanings related to environmental care, social responsibility and personal well-being. While all objects of design have some communicative function, these differ in that their visual statement and presence can be regarded as their *primary* function. They are concerned with revealing the inadequacies of the worldview of modernity, which includes many of today's late-modern perspectives. Objects, unlike words, enable a mode of communication that is instantaneous and aesthetic, which is to say it is a form of communication that addresses those very aspects of our nature that have been pushed aside by modernity's logic, rationalism and overly narrow notions of progress.

Ward has explained that signs are a way of producing mutual understandings. There is a qualitative relationship between that which is being signified and the sign, which here is an object. They can be regarded as markers that extract meanings from one situation or context and transfer those meanings and make them useful in others. Even though they might emerge from the particularities of place and time, their purpose is broader and, to an extent, generalizable. Hence, these kinds of objects can be understood as signs of, and contributors to, a world of shared meanings. As signs, they do not 'stand in' for that which is being referred to, but have abstract independence.[53] They refer to counter-perspectives, inner values and reflective modes of being, and, directly or by implication, are critiques of the currently dominant worldview that disregards or devalues these things.

179

GOING FORWARD

It is perhaps not entirely surprising that today there is renewed interest in traditional practices, not least because they are being seen as a positive complement to digital living. Their simplicity, affordability and portability, their connection to history and culture, and their manifest productivity all add to their appeal and contrast markedly with many contemporary technology-based activities. In recent years I have supervised or examined numerous PhD studies from all around the world that have focussed on traditional practices and their renewal, including projects in Indonesia, Iran, Malaysia, Thailand, Turkey and the UK. Activities like knitting are currently enjoying something of a renaissance, with a new social acceptability.[54] Our research has revealed that, in some places, such as New Mexico, traditional folk arts are thriving, producing distinctive products that include rugs and other woven goods, religious carvings and panel paintings, tinware, and ceramics. All these artefacts are relatively simple, they typically use local materials, and they can be practised either at home or in commercial settings.[55]

In the face of growing environmental concerns and economic uncertainties, this renewed interest in traditional practices is a sign of hope and restoration. In Canada, Anisef describes a wide variety of emerging practices and projects that explores craft in relation to cultural, environmental and economic sustainability.[56] A report from Denmark states, *"By using an approach rooted in tradition to give expression to new materials and technologies, craftspeople question our lifestyles and prototypes, and visualise how our sustainable futures might look"*.[57] If embedded in place and community and founded on enduring values, locally created goods and services offer ways of expressing and sustaining depth and meaning in the ordinary, everyday activities of our lives. And in finding meaning in our activities, we give meaning to our lives.

A more comprehensive, more balanced notion of design involves these other ways of seeing the world – these other ways of being that draw on human capacities largely ignored by the rational mind and which, at first, might seem irrelevant, tedious or uninteresting. But, as Sennett says, it is quite wrong to think of these practices as mindless.[58] Repetitive procedures and rhythms open up a different kind of consciousness and an awareness that is critically important for achieving a more integrated outlook. This is what is meant by the title of this book, *Design for Life* – it refers to a form of design and a kind of material culture that acknowledges, draws upon and helps cultivate our full humanity – the rational and the intuitive, the instrumental and the meaningful.

I mentioned in Chapter 1 that when dealing with notions of personal meaning, including more profound questions of ultimate concern or 'things that really matter', the words we use are not those of facts, information and empirical evidence but rather those of intimation, symbolism and metaphor. It is a form of language that points to that which may be intuitively apprehended and subjectively felt but lies beyond direct description, explanation or evidence. Yet, even though these deeper questions and apprehensions may elude precise characterization or empirical validation, they are critical features of being human. They give our lives meaning and are strongly connected to our values and beliefs. When we refer to these things, we typically use analogy and allegory through forms such as poetry, story, fable and parable. This is the language of the imagination and human creativity. Through such means, we are able to allude to deeper perceptions in ways that, though indirect, can be highly evocative. The literal meaning says one thing but points to another.

The language of design can play a similar role. Like story and poetry, design is also concerned with the imagination and creativity. The focus of design practice is on what could be, rather than what is. Consequently, while it draws on information and facts, it also invokes the language of intimation and conjecture. In doing so, individual objects can point towards deeper perceptions and be evocative of different, more constructive, less damaging lifestyles. In this regard, the small, hand-whittled objects featured in this chapter clearly do not represent a scalable alternative to the plethora of sophisticated products and production methods available to modern wealthy societies. We are not going to return to cottage-style industries where we rely on spinning our own thread and making our own clothes. Such a direction would not be practically feasible, economically viable or, for many, desirable, although it should be noted that this was, essentially, the direction advocated by Mahatma Gandhi for the liberation of the Indian people. He saw the spinning wheel (*charkha*) as a symbol of dignified human labour, decentralization, public service and a more just political and economic system, and handmade cloth (*khadi*) as a symbol of virtue and spiritual meaning.[59] While such directions may not be pragmatic or preferred, nevertheless, from this discussion a number of legitimate roles can be identified for the making and use of such objects in contemporary society. These can be summarized as practical, symbolic, complementary and resilient.

Practical: These objects, in their making and use, involve repetitive actions that have two distinct practical benefits. First, they lead to functional applications such as handspinning wool or creating hand-knitted garments. Such applications may not be economically viable at scale, but they do provide fulfilling and productive part-time or pastime occupations that lead to useful outcomes. Second, as we have seen, regular engagement in

181

rhythmical, repetitive occupations can improve subjective well-being as well as integrated thinking and creative insight.

Symbolic: These kinds of objects can play an important symbolic role in contemporary society. They can be understood as visible expressions of ways of thinking and being that are distinct from instrumental rationality and economic rationalism, which are not only closely interconnected but also dominate today's political, corporate and educational agendas. Instrumental rationality takes a direct approach to the solving of identified 'problems'. It is closely associated with achieving competitive edge within the neoliberal, free-market system fostered by the ideology of economic rationalism. In contrast, these objects are physical metaphors whose presence reminds us that to be fully human, it is important to acknowledge more than just rational, logical ways of thinking that emphasize analysis and evidential facts, and more, too, than economic considerations and the profit motive. These objects are physical symbols of other, complementary ways of thinking that are closely related to interiority, meaningfulness and values (see below).

Complementary: The making and use of these kinds of objects can be
182
constructively positioned as 'as well as' rather than 'an alternative to' contemporary, fast-paced, increasingly digital lifestyles; they offer 'time-out' periods. The physical, rhythmical, repetitive actions on which they depend can be calming, de-stressing and restorative, and this more relaxed state allows us to put things in perspective. In turn, this helps create conditions conducive to intuitive, meaning-seeking ways of thinking; synthesizing one's thoughts; creative insight; and pondering perennial questions about values and deeper notions of human meaning. And over time, such engagement will influence our outlook and our priorities.

Resilient: Within the local setting, the making and use of these kinds of artefacts represent a group of activities that could occupy people on a daily, weekly or seasonal basis. As full-time, dependable 'jobs for life' become increasingly rare and, perhaps, less rewarding, our notions of 'work life' may be able to transition towards more positive, varied collections of activities. Some of these may involve working for an employer, some may be a form of self-employment, and some may be highly productive but not necessarily part of a cash economy. Indeed, multi-skilled, versatile work-life endeavours that are sensitive to local conditions can be seen as a positive, more holistic, and more rewarding direction than that offered by the rigid, highly artificial 9-to-5 schedule that became the norm during the late-modern period. It is certainly less environmentally problematic than large-scale, heavy industries associated with resource extraction. In many respects, a more varied, multi-roled, production-oriented system is far closer to many traditional forms of living than the consumption-based, unsustainable lifestyles so prevalent today.

Hence, the repetitive, rhythmical tasks enabled by these objects encourage a slower, calmer demeanour, one that draws on intuitive and synthetical as well as rational and analytical ways of knowing. Achieving this more balanced view will be critical in realizing more mature, responsible and meaningful ways forward.

183

8
Seeds
designing for a new awareness

And other fell on good ground,
and did yield fruit that
sprang up and increased

Mark 4:8

In this concluding chapter I attempt to draw together the various threads I have discussed to show their interrelationships and to create an overall picture of the challenges facing design if it is to move in a direction that is more substantive and life enhancing. To do this, we must constantly shift our focus back and forth between the pragmatic and the philosophical, the particular and the general, the local and the global.

It will be clear by now that a very significant shift in priorities and practices is needed if we are to develop ways forward that are considerate of the effects our various endeavours have on natural places and systems, if we are to strive towards virtue and goodness in our dealings with other people, and if we are to create approaches that are personally fulfilling and meaningful. Such a shift involves not just new ways of doing but also new ways of thinking – a different outlook on life and on our duties towards ourselves, community, locale and the wider world. This kind of change is neither easy nor swift. It takes time for the emergence of new understandings to find broader acceptance and for new behavioural norms to take root. A large part of this will be learning to find a more equitable balance between, on the one hand, rationalism, intellectual pursuits and 'progress' and, on the other, intuition, experience and expertise. Also, we must pay greater attention to context, community and deeper questions about values, beliefs and purpose. And it is important to recognize that any such change will inevitably challenge established political, financial and corporate interests but, given the gross inequities and impacts that have arisen in recent decades, such contestation would appear justified.

LASTING CHANGE

Achieving better, lasting, and more meaningful ways of living is unlikely to result from grand schemes and masterplans that impose the will of ruling elites – be they political, corporate or religious – on ordinary people. Such narrow, inevitably biased ideologies usually create more problems than they solve. We have seen the tragic results of such impositions throughout history, but perhaps especially in the past century, as illustrated in Table 8.1. All these ideologies were, and in some cases still are, imposed on ordinary people and communities by top-down bureaucracies irrespective of local cultural norms, individual needs and preferences, and deep, situated knowledge, and all have proved to be socially, and in some cases environmentally, disastrous. This is not the way forward.

Human activities and a growing population are creating very serious damage to natural systems[1] and these, together with rising socioeconomic disparities, are fundamentally related to our economic system and the political agendas that support it. The so-called 'free market' is based on indiscriminate economic growth, is resource and energy intensive, and depends on, and therefore constantly encourages, excessive consumption habits.[2] Curtailing this will not be through the imposition of ideologies by ruling elites – not just because their own interests would be jeopardized but because such ideologies are invariably inadequate. Positive change will occur through education, dialogue, the development of new realizations, and by many people at the local level striving to do what they believe to be right and true, overcoming self-interest and greed, and working towards the common good. Unlike top-down diktats, small-scale, locally based initiatives can draw on local knowledge, be tuned to local conditions, and remain flexible, adaptive and dynamic. Through such means, we take responsibility for our own actions, overriding the all too easy excuses of realpolitik by which principles are set aside in favour of short-term expediencies. Through principled actions and striving to do the right thing, we exchange self-interest, greed and short-termism for integrity, ethics and the long view.

It is through such means, informed by context and situated knowledge, that behavioural norms and material expectations can change for the better, building a sense of community and creating the conditions for the development of a meaningful material culture. At the international, national and regional levels this will mean implementing policies that recognize the value of the local, enable the voice of community to be heard, support local enterprises, and prevent multinationals disregarding long-established customs and the welfare of those who live and work in a particular place. Policy changes are required that better serve the interests of small-scale endeavours, including

Table 8.1 **Grand Schemes and Their Consequences**

Grand Schemes	Consequences
Forcible Western Enculturation	• In countries such as Canada and Australia, children of indigenous people were taken from their homes and placed in residential schools by government or religious groups. • Forced to speak English, they were punished for speaking their own language. • This was a damaging imposition on cultures where history, customs and identity, as well as values, morality and beliefs, were passed down by word of mouth.
Communist Ideology and Western Reaction	• Communist ideology in the USSR resulted in totalitarian rule with major social restrictions and deprivations. • The West's paranoid fear of it led to McCarthyism in the US and an existential threat created by a Cold War that lasted decades.
China's One-Child Policy	• Implemented in 1979, this included mandatory birth control, termination of unauthorized pregnancies, and punitive measures for policy violation.[3] • It resulted in hundreds of millions of abortions and sterilizations and a huge gender imbalance, with some forty million more men than women by 2015 when the practice was halted.[4,5]
Corporate and Financial Globalization	• This exacerbates economic disparities in developed countries by disincentivizing wealth redistribution and social protection in the name of competitiveness.[6] • Due to this focus on growth, *Corporate Social Responsibility* is virtually irrelevant[7] – the term "*is either an oxymoron or hypocritical*".[8] • A focus on efficiency, which drives growth rather than reducing inequality and resource consumption, misleads the public, customers, and the companies themselves;[9] see Appendix 3.

the elimination of regulations that prevent local producers from competing with large corporations.[10]

THE GLOBAL AND THE LOCAL

From the international style of the 1920s and 1930s to the multinational corporations of today, modernity has increasingly taken us towards the global and the universal. In the process, modern society has tended to cut its ties with the local and has often ridden roughshod over the particularities that characterize contextualized customs, traditions and practices. It is becoming increasingly clear that this has been a great mistake, not to say a tragedy. As cultural historian and social critic Morris Berman has remarked, *"much was lost in the transition from the Middle Ages to modernity: craftsmanship, a deep appreciation of beauty, community, silence, and above all, a sense of spiritual purpose"*.[11]

Community, tradition, values worth passing on to the next generation, a sense of identity and deeper spiritual meanings are all found within specific contexts. They are tied to patterns of thought, practices and customs that are informed by the topography, climate, ecosystems and the human history and intercultural interactions of a specific place. When we focus on the local, the particular and the contextualized in an authentic manner and seek to do this to the best of our abilities, such work will be relevant at the local level and may also resonate with universal questions of ethics, virtue and notions of truth and, thus, will have universal appeal.[12] We saw examples of this in Chapter 4 with artist Grayson Perry and composer Arvo Pärt, whose creative works are tied to a particular place and culture but are, nevertheless, valued all over the world. While there may be no direct causal link, there will be correlation between a designer's creative work and their philosophy and beliefs, which are informed by and arise from their local culture.[13]

187

THINGS THAT MATTER

In choosing such a path, we must be aware too of the hurdles. If history is anything to go by, any attempt at change that gains momentum by espousing a markedly different way forward – no matter how ethical, virtuous and democratically elected – is likely be ridiculed, dismissed as naive, undermined and, if possible, suppressed by those in power and those with vested interests in maintaining the status quo. This, unfortunately, has been the case throughout history when people try to invoke positive change. In Haiti in 1804, for example, revolutionary leaders, brought to the region as slaves, strived to free themselves from French colonial rule. At the time, not only were unjust regimes the norm in this part of the world but the system was designed to ensure that governance and self-determination of any kind could not be claimed by certain groups.[14] Haiti was derided in highly pejorative terms in order to discredit it and to justify harsh counter measures; it was described in newspaper articles as *"a hopeless and absurd place … nothing more than a joke"*.[15] And it was made to pay dearly for its audacity – the French government demanded repayment for the loss of their property and, in a move that reverberates down the centuries, French banks offered loans to Haiti that essentially meant a future of continuous debt.[16]

Such approaches have continued in one form or another to the present day – notably through globalization and its attendant financialization, privatization and/or occupation of other peoples' territories; actions that are all embedded in colonialization and its history of exploitation of labour and land.[17] We see similar traits even in the recent history of Europe. For example, the left-wing Syriza party in Greece was elected in 2015 on a platform of anti-austerity, which challenged established ideologies of free-market capitalism. In reporting the election victory, the *Financial Times* of London underlined the potential threat posed to the established system by this leftist party: *"The most we can say is that if Greece's creditors blink, the significant demonstration effect to the rest of the eurozone will give rise to economic relief in the south and angst in the north, hardly furthering the cause of political unity"*.[18] The international financial and banking crisis of 2007–08, the common European currency and, internally, a history of financial mismanagement and corruption had resulted in Greece suffering severe financial and social deprivations.[19] This meant that Greece needed substantial help from Europe. But following the election, many commentators suggested that the loan conditions being imposed on Greece were both draconian and punitive.[20, 21, 22] Greece was forced to accept terms that many argued undermined its sovereignty, weakened its national democratic process, and would mean a never-ending debt situation; terms that the IMF subsequently declared to be unsustainable.[23, 24, 25]

While these issues are a long way from design, they do tell us something about the context in which design and production exist. And they tell us much about the difficulties of invoking significant change and working towards a system that is not only egalitarian and socially and environmentally responsible but also imaginatively reconceived to be more holistic in its outlook. Contemporary directions are often far too focussed on short-term financial gains – driven by consumerism, dependent on labour exploitation and resulting in debt, waste and burgeoning pollution. It is unethical and unsustainable, and sooner or later it will have to change. As Rebanks has said, "Modern life is rubbish for so many people. How few choices it gives them ... how much it asks of so many people for so little in return".[26] Our conceptions of things that matter and consequently our priorities will have to change if we are to address these issues at a deeper level. And if this change is to be substantive, it cannot but challenge established ideas and outlooks.

Today, when asked if something is true, we generally rely on modernity's long-enculturated but restricted ways of knowing that are evidence-based. The scientific method and the establishment of material evidence we believe allow us to know whether or not something is true. However, this question can be considered, and the answer formulated, in other ways. As Shortt puts it, "If you think that the only meaningful utterances are either mathematical or provable in a test tube, then you're rejecting ethics, aesthetics and much of culture, as well as spirituality".[27] Through one's upbringing, a lifetime of learning, direct awareness, first-person experiences, and personal feelings, there are things that one knows inwardly to be true. Often these are the things that matter most to us, yet there is no external evidence or scientific proof. These are the things we believe to be true, trust in, and live by – and there are many of them: the belief one has about the state of a relationship; the right way to act in a particular situation; one's religious or spiritual beliefs; and even if the composition of a particular painting 'works'. These beliefs depend for their validation not on external facts or proofs but one's own responses, experiences and internal transformation.[28] However, these beliefs are not entirely subjective because we call upon the responses and experiences of others to support the confidence we have in their validity.[29] Yet, it is these kinds of truths that today's reductive, rationalized 'accountabilities' too often ignore. In the process, they rip the heart out of human culture because fundamental aspects of being human are systemically excluded. As we often experience with modern bureaucracies and rationalized online systems, this omission results in a desiccated, functional husk that is preoccupied with details and mundanities but lacks empathy, deeper meaning or a greater sense of purpose and fulfilment.

These other ways of knowing need to be recognized, affirmed and incorporated into our decision-making so as to influence our priorities, our outlook and the nature of our activities. This will be best done at the

189

grassroots level where we have real, face-to-face encounters with others; are directly involved in context; and can take into account local knowledge and respond to local conditions. As it gains ground, such change will eventually mean reconstituting priorities and programmes at the policy level; hence, it is inescapably political. The discipline of design has a particularly constructive and potentially powerful role to play in furthering this kind of change, which is based in a more holistic idea of human understandings. This is because design is a discipline that attempts to bring together and synthesize the rational and the imaginative, the practical and the meaningful. And design has the ability to show the implications of alternative directions via tangible visualizations. In this regard, it has the ability to communicate in an instant, prior to conscious knowledge, and speak to us at the intuitive, emotional level. This powerful mode of communication will be important in helping to convey new realizations, open up new perspectives and cultivate different, more considerate and benign directions. In this endeavour, designers can develop more conceptual work as well as functional work, as the examples included in earlier chapters demonstrate.

'I WANT TO BE HAPPY'

There is something deeply self-contradictory about the idea of the individual pursuit of happiness within a competitive, consumption-based society. Competitiveness is about division. It is about being better than and distinguishing oneself from others. Consumption depends on advertising, which functions by sowing the seeds of discontent, keeping our minds firmly focused on the trivial details and differences between essentially identical products, creating petty jealousies and self-centred desires, promoting products as badges of social position, and selling the fallacy that happiness can be found through the acquisition of material things, experiences or services. These fictions and falsehoods, which have no upper limits, have been inveigled into our thinking for so long and from such an early age that they have become normalized – the way things simply are. The concerns here are not only environmental and social, they also lead to individual unhappiness. Unsurprisingly, they also fly in the face of age-old wisdom traditions from both the West and East that advocate a middle way between excess and poverty as the route to the greatest happiness.[30, 31] When it comes to happiness, Irving Caesar's lyrics, *"I want to be happy / but I won't be happy / Til I make you happy, too"*,[32] seem to be far truer than the messages of advertising. From classical Western philosophy we learn that happiness is found not only by avoiding the distractions and vices of wealth but also by seeking greater justice and by being concerned about the plight of others.[33] Concern for the welfare of others is also fundamental to Jewish and Christian teachings, for instance, in the injunction to *"love thy neighbour as thyself"*.[34, 35] Contemporary academic research also shows that individual happiness and one's sense of contentedness are very much dependent on the well-being of others – on reducing inequality and economic disparity across society.[36] The condition of others is important to us and to our own sense of happiness. This, however, seems to apply not just to those in our immediate circle – our family, friends and neighbours – but extends more broadly, encompassing complete strangers. In this regard, the work of American philosopher Samuel Scheffler supports points made in earlier chapters about the inadequacies of a consequentialist morality (see Chapters 4 and 5). Scheffler contends that features of human valuing include dimensions that are non-experientialist and non-consequentialist.[37] In other words we value things that we have no prospect of experiencing or benefitting from ourselves. Moreover, human valuing has a conservative dimension. There is, it seems, a *"conceptual connection between valuing something and wanting it to be sustained or preserved"*.[38] This relates directly to the notion of traditional practices because traditions are concerned with the handing down of beliefs, values and customs from one generation to another – that is, to preserving things we value beyond our own lifetime. Indeed, Scheffler's work suggests that our sense of happiness and well-being today is strongly related to events that will happen after our own lives have come to an end. It would appear that our happiness and the things we consider worthwhile are dependent on the idea that there will be a future not just for our loved ones and immediate community but for humanity itself. The prospect of this not being the case is likely to lead not only to a sense of grief and sadness but also to apathy and anomie.[39]

The plausibility of Scheffler's arguments raises important considerations about the nature of our present activities. There have been many scientific studies and there is much accumulated evidence to suggest that our collective actions, both in the recent past and continuing apace today, are jeopardizing the future prospects of humanity. It is clearly the case that these activities, which centre on the constant expansion and growth of consumption-based economies, are threatening ecosystems, reducing biodiversity and consuming natural resources at unprecedented rates.[40]

Knowing the dangers, our continued failure to act in any coordinated and substantial manner raises serious questions about the dominant values in our society, because it is these values that are allowing us to persist in such damaging activities. Scheffler's work suggests that, as the threat to the future becomes more acute and more apparent, our sense of existential angst, unhappiness and even despair will grow. It therefore becomes increasingly unreasonable not to act and not to change those things we know to be contributing to irrevocable harm.

The ideas and design explorations presented in this book are about doing things differently. They are about creating material goods in ways that are considerate of others and the environment by taking into account:

- the essential nature of material goods as things, which includes how they are made, used and eventually disposed of;
- the nature of the work created;
- the activities our goods enable, and the effects those activities have; and
- the contribution our goods make throughout their life cycle to community, the social good and the locale.

192 All these things involve empathy, love, compassion and caring. Of course, the production of useful goods also involves facts, function, effectiveness and economic viability. But to be in accord with deeper notions of human meaning and for our own personal happiness, these conventional priorities have to be addressed in ways that involve human values, the well-being and circumstances of other people, and the passing on of those values through tradition to ensure the well-being of those who will come after us.

THE COMPLEMENT OF PURPOSE

For a few years I was fortunate enough to teach on an annual two-week international programme on the island of Syros in the Aegean. A philosophy professor from Delft was teaching on the same course. In between our lectures, we would often drink coffee in the square below the grand belle époque town hall where we would wrestle over the finer points of design, technology and ethics. During one of these interludes in the teaching schedule, he mentioned that he particularly enjoyed coming to the island as part of his work because it created a good balance. I knew immediately what he meant. While we spent many hours each day in the classroom there was the opportunity also for conversation, learning from our Greek colleagues and, through the projects we were conducting, to visit different places and engage with and learn from local people about life on the island, the challenges they were facing and the opportunities they were creating. These encounters revealed ways of life, temperaments and outlooks that in many respects differed markedly from our own, and they enriched our own perspectives and understandings. Despite a busy schedule, we could also find time to think, read and reflect. And before classes or during the lunch break there was time to walk or swim.

I relate this here because our frenetic, production-focussed, consumer society expends enormous effort, time and money on promoting and providing purposeless leisure and often rather self-centred, entirely passive forms of entertainment. One compartment of our lives contains work, another contains leisure: two hours of TV after ten hours of work; two weeks in the sun after fifty in the office; a few years of retirement after a lifetime of labour. And in these designated leisure times we are offered endless choices, endless experiences, but without meaning or purpose. This is not to say that we cannot find a great deal of benefit in purposelessness – but the nature of that purposelessness matters. My reflections about working in Greece suggest a somewhat different notion of leisure from the prepackaged forms of tourism, recreation, entertainment and sport offered by the 'leisure industry'. It is one that is found within and amongst other things and, as such, it breaks down some of the compartmentalizations that characterize modern life. Indeed, these experiences in Greece, which integrated leisure with other activities and a sense of purpose, seem to be indicative of more general changes in our notions of leisure. In recent years, international tourism has been focussing far more on the culture of places, where context, history and tradition are seen as valuable assets.[41] And, since the 1980s, the annual number of people walking the traditional pilgrimage route known as the Camino de Santiago has risen from a few hundred to nearly a quarter of a million.[42]

Our ability to be constantly connected via digital devices is also breaking down conventional compartmentalizations about work and leisure. This can have some advantages, like staying in touch, allaying worries of family, or dealing with emergencies, but there are also significant disadvantages. If we are always connected, then wherever we are, we can never be wholly present. A message or a call inevitably takes us back to the routines, concerns and issues of *there*. This connectivity also means that work is able to fill more and more hours of our day. Consequently, work patterns and work intensities are changing. Doing and not doing, working and

193

resting, employment and leisure, action and reflection all become more fluid and intertwined, which is actually more akin to traditional patterns of living. In addition, while digital technologies may be breaking down separations, in their present incarnations they are accompanied by increased opportunities for distractedness. There are growing concerns about compulsive use patterns, especially in the use of smartphones by young people. Whether this kind of use is the result of anxiety and self-esteem issues or, as some researchers are suggesting, a medical condition known as *smartphone addiction*,[43] such dependencies and distractions run counter to the reflective modes of being that are associated with meaning and insight.

It is at times of pause, purposelessness and quietude that meaning is to be found – rather than in constant activity and purely instrumental endeavours. Indeed, as I have written elsewhere, deeper notions of meaning are found in that which is use-*less* rather than that which is use-*ful*.[44] Yet, somewhat paradoxically perhaps, it is also the case that this meaning only rings true when it is amongst other things and within a context of purpose – in the gaps, the in-between times. This is certainly the case in the creative process, where we can strive for hours trying to develop a creative direction by consciously focussing on research, sketching and idea development, but it is only when we look away, when we are not thinking about the task at hand, that creative insight occurs. In his poem *Via Negativa*, the Welsh clergyman and poet R. S. Thomas writes that, for him, God is found in these in-between places – in the spaces between the stars and the voids in our knowledge.[45] The sentiment is true even in a secular age, but we are perhaps more comfortable saying *meaning* is found in the interstices, in the in-between times and places, which actually may amount to the same thing. It is here, in periods of silence, when we are not doing or speaking, when we are at rest, that we often find ourselves, quite unintentionally, seeing things differently – from another, more holistic perspective. It is at just these times that we may gain deeper insights and find creative synthesis. Let us now consider this relationship between doing and not doing, silence and words, in the context of design.

194

DESIGN WORK

To this point I have explored three principal strands in terms of design and making: *Counterpoints, Vestiges of Grace* and *Rhythmical Objects*. The first two are attempts to use the power of creativity, image and object to 'make visible' important contemporary issues. Through their modes of expression and their content, they are arguments in form for the importance of the intuitive, subjective, experiential, aesthetic, emotional, imaginative and spiritual, all of which, as we have seen, have become devalued in modern times. Alongside and in balance with the rational and the objective, attention to these aspects of our humanity will be crucial for any substantive progress towards equity, environmental care and deeper meaning. In all these design examples, practical function is not the primary consideration. The aim is to create objects as visual, tangible statements that express concern and sorrow about the direction we have taken. They represent counterarguments and manifestations of fears, hopes and other priorities. These kinds of design objects are complements to systematic, text-based arguments, and alternatives to the *"letter"* that Blake said *"killeth"*.[46] They are also alternatives and complements to the materialism, rationalism and reductionism that, as we saw in Chapter 7, Wilson calls *"a sort of death"*. In these designs, the image and the object are both employed to 'get at' and express that which lies beyond words, description and explanation alone – the immediate, the experiential, and the silent connection between viewer and object. Such objects are indicative of another way of saying, another way of hearing, another way of knowing and, indeed, another way of being. Therefore, they are presented with complementary texts, both word and image are invoked, creating a balanced, holistic articulation of ideas.

195

As the name suggests, *Counterpoints* employ image and object as a way of creating arguments that contest and challenge current directions. *Vestiges of Grace* are gentler and more minimal – quieter expressions of that which has been lost, namely the rejected and, for many, largely forgotten spiritual heritage of the West that can bestow a sense of meaning, purpose and profundity in and through the material world. The third, *Rhythmical Objects*, is symbolic of, while being representational of, ways of working that are humble, meditative, practical and small scale. They are also implicitly representative of the importance of community and tradition.

All three design strands can help cultivate a sense of environmental care and social cohesion and cooperation while also providing a firm basis for belonging, identity and individual well-being. These various explorations address some of the major issues and perspective changes needed if designers are to contribute to the kinds of systemic shift that many are calling for. By showing what a more meaningful, lasting and less wasteful material culture might look like, designers can help invoke a shift in perspective. Indeed, given the severity of the environmental and social impacts of our current activities, one could argue that they have a moral responsibility to do so.

Perhaps one of the most important changes we can make as a society is to reduce our acquisitiveness, to consider how little we actually need, and learn to value other kinds of things. Here, I am referring to things like the purity of a mountain stream, birdsong in the spring, wildflowers in the hedgerows, and the buzz of insects as they gather nectar. In taking these for granted, we may be presuming too much; it is becoming increasingly clear that these aspects of life need to be valued anew. And here, too, designers can make a contribution. Familiar things can be presented in fresh ways so that they can be re-seen and re-appreciated. For example, in a society that is preoccupied by consumption and sees value primarily in that which can be packaged and bought, perhaps one way to draw attention to the things we overlook, their beauty and their preciousness, is to present them – obviously with irony – as priceless commodities. This is the basis of a fourth design strand that I have called *Seeds of Change* (Figures 8.1 to 8.3).

All these explorations and objects are about the making of meaning. They are concerned with questions of how we should live, the values we share, our relationships with community and place, the stories we tell, and our attitudes towards the natural world. Meaning is found not in the objects *per se* but in the life-world and the processes and activities that constitute that living – our work, relationships, leisure and reflection, and in living, dying, continuity and change. This is the world experienced by people, the world in which values, purpose and feelings matter. In all these areas we have choices, we can choose what meanings we make, what values we adhere to, what actions we take. We also have to bear in mind that this is a two-way process. Through our various activities and the ways we choose to live, we shape the world we have, and, in turn, this shapes who we are. Today, 'who we are' or 'who we have become' is having seriously destructive effects on the world – so there is a need to take a different course, to change who we are, the values we hold and the endeavours we pursue. There is a need to learn different ways of designing – to move away from design for seduction, acquisitiveness, status and disposal, and bring to the fore other values and create other meanings. The new norm has to become designing for moderation, permanence and universal notions of 'the good' – and this, in a nutshell, is *Design for Life*.

196

SILENCE AND WORDS

The objects I create in an attempt to advance and express ideas are part of a larger critical genre that challenges many aspects of contemporary design – its assumptions, its practices and its principal directions. Designers involved in this kind of work may focus on a variety of issues – society, environment, technology – but whatever their emphasis, this form of non-commercial design is an important and necessary component of disciplinary self-examination and progression. It is through such work that designers convey meanings, state positions or propose arguments – not in words but in the content, modes of expression, materials, making practices and aesthetics of the work itself. As with other forms of visual expression, to gain an understanding of the meaning of a piece of work, we have to look, see and silently reflect. Irrespective of the content and merits of any individual piece, the very existence of these critical and speculative forms of expression is a recognition of the limitations of language in articulating certain ways of knowing. Qualitative aspects of life and of material culture can be experienced and can be known but their fullness and their nuances cannot necessarily be adequately described. Even if description is attempted, it is not the same as the experience itself but is merely a translation of it into words. Linguistic description may offer insights, but is a complementary and necessarily sequential laying-out of issues rather than the immediate, holistic encounter one experiences when viewing a work of art or design. From McGilchrist's research[47] we can see that it is a category mistake to assume that we will always be able to put into words and fully describe and explain what we are able to do, see and know. As Eisner says, *"Some things can only be known through exemplification and through direct encounter"*.[48] Hence, for disciplinary advancement, for addressing contemporary issues and demonstrating alternative, positive directions forward, this kind of design work is essential.

197

Whether we are able to put these interpretive, qualitative forms of knowing into words is a separate issue entirely, one that is constrained by the limitations of language and also one that we are generally ill equipped to tackle because of modern society's bias towards explicit knowledge, facts and quantification. Yet, despite the difficulties, critical design discussion does have a vitally important role to play. It is a particular responsibility of design academics and design critics to move the design agenda, and perhaps especially the design research agenda, away from one that relies predominantly on rationalistic, evidence-based justifications and deterministic methodologies towards one that encourages and encompasses more nuanced, qualitative discussion. To be able to effectively discern design quality, and communicate design qualities, we must focus on the work itself – its critical agenda, form and aesthetic presence and its creative contribution to the field. In this way, we begin to change the design agenda from analysis, details and facts to one that focusses on holistic integration, appreciating the qualities of effective synthesis, and being comfortable speaking about the values and meanings manifested through a piece of work.

THE ROOTED AND THE ROOTLESS

In these explorations and arguments there is, of course, a certain irony, which needs to be acknowledged if design is to contribute effectively and appropriately to lasting change. This is the irony of an academic waxing on about the importance of localization, place, experience and tradition. First, today's universities are themselves products of the modern worldview. They are rather conservative institutions that, over the years, have divided up human knowledge into finer and finer specialisms. They favour the kinds of knowledge that can be verified through evidence and the scientific method and that have international impact rather than local relevance, all of which are inherent to their funding systems, publications recognition and reward systems. Second, the process of becoming 'educated' and working within this system frequently means becoming uprooted and, thereafter, being rootless. In my own career, I have worked for extended periods in Europe, the Middle East, North America and England. I have not lived back in my hometown in South Wales since the day I left to go to university. From parents and teachers alike, my upbringing was pervaded by the injunction to get an education, to get on and get out. After leaving, even if I had wanted to, there was no obvious way back. The steelworks and the mines had closed, and, like so many of Britain's industrial towns, a place that had once been thriving had entered a period of inexorable decline. And even if it had been possible, going back does not mean that one is still rooted in the same way to that place or that community. Once dislocated and educated elsewhere, something changes. One is now different and perceived to be so both by oneself and by those who remained. The fit is not what it was.

The paradox is that formalized, recognized education allows only one side of us to flourish. It develops our intellectual thinking and provides us with specialized knowledge in a particular sphere. The other side of us inevitably

198

becomes atrophied, separated, ungraspable and unlived. This is the place-based, contextualized side of us that is about identity and belonging, that has an intimate knowledge formed from a deep sense of familiarity with people and place, and that is filled with tacit ways of knowing and an abiding love of one's locale. This side of us is the product of ten thousand unspecified, unrecognized interminglings of sights, sounds, tastes, smells and textures. From time to time, during rare visits, they may arise as fleeting moments prompted by a long-forgotten taste or the scent of the earth after a heavy rain. But these once familiar, unremarkable sensations are now acknowledged only because they have become unaccustomed. One is forever unmoored – a citizen of anywhere and nowhere.

This way of being, experienced by so many people today, does however offer its own rewards and freedoms – and these are many. It would be churlish and misplaced to disparage the opportunities afforded by our formal education systems and, indeed, I would be the last to do so. Nevertheless, it is important to acknowledge that something is lost when people leave their roots, their locale and their community. This 'something' seems especially important in today's context, after decades of globalization, internationalization, mass migration and displacement. Place-based, community-based learning is sometimes the result of centuries of trial and error, and passing on of customs and traditions that embed knowledge, skills, values and meanings into specific ways of doing and particular, context-specific practices. Such knowledge may be the result of generations of contributions by people who have lived and worked in a certain place and learned through direct experience. This is not the result of formal, university courses or reading academic papers and books, but it is, nonetheless, important. It is important in its own right as deeply meaningful cultural knowledge, but it is also important because to effectively address today's critical environmental concerns we have to become much more oriented to the nuances and particularities of place and to recognize the significance of grassroots interventions based in local knowledge, skills and traditional ways of doing.[49, 50, 51]

Can these two worlds and these two kinds of knowledge – the rooted and the rootless – come together in a constructive and productive manner? Even if it may not be possible within one person, perhaps it may be possible among people – where there is mutual respect for the contribution of each and where there is a meeting of minds. These are the issues that have informed my own research and the various projects I have directed or been involved in, all of which have informed the ideas and design explorations included in this book. They suggest that, if design is to be relevant and at the forefront of current thinking about society, environment and the living of a meaningful life, then our ideas about what is of value, and consequently our education in design, has to change. To engage at the local level, learn from it and contribute to it demands commitment, deference to the knowledge, ways and will of others, and a sensitivity that emerges from time spent being silent, seeing, and seeking understanding. We must recognize that this is difficult to achieve, not to say justify, within our current system, and this deficiency does not go unnoticed. In conversation with a shopkeeper-musician in a town in central Turkey, I was struck not only by his deep knowledge of local customs and practices, but also by his view – from his own first-hand experience – of academic researchers. He told me that they often come to his town to do research, they ask questions of the local people, take photographs, and sometimes hold workshops. But these things, he felt, were not for the good of the local people; they made no lasting contribution. In his opinion, this was because the academics had no real commitment to the place – they were concerned with their own research and their own careers. Academics conduct their projects, write their papers, present them at conferences and get their doctoral degrees and their promotions. The local people who provide them with all this material see no benefit. It was a frank assessment which I knew was often only too true – not least because the incentives and reward systems of higher education serve to encourage this kind of outcome.

200

IMAGINATION, IMPULSE AND POSITIVE CHANGE

Constraints on the imagination are loosened in the arts – we are permitted, indeed we are required, to operate on impulse, and respond on impulse as a work develops.[52] This kind of process does not fit well within academia because it cannot be planned, the outcome cannot be predicted, and its basis cannot be justified through rational argument or by pointing to evidence. Nonetheless, it is fundamental and absolutely essential to the creative process. It is also essential to the development of a more just and caring society. To address the severe predicaments of our age we cannot simply rely on the findings of science. Scientifically established facts about the natural world are critical, but this is only one side of the story. The other side concerns ethics, imagination and creativity – these vital cultural ingredients inform our values, beliefs and knowledge and therefore they inform the activities that a society regards as worthwhile. As educational philosopher Maxine Greene has said, *"It may be the recovery of imagination that lessens the social paralysis we see around us and restores the sense that something can be done in the name of what is decent and humane"*.[53]

As I discussed in Chapter 6, aiming to achieve some kind of detached view that will yield objective, neutral results is an inherently misguided project because we are intimately involved in the world and part of the reality we are observing. Our observations are always subject to interpretation and affected by our theories. Attempting such an approach in practice-based design research and development is especially misplaced. Design is both an impulsive and a responsive process. To be truly creative, we should not hold some preconceived notion of the outcome then simply visualize it through drawings, models or prototypes. The creative process involves acting, observing and responding to what is observed. The work advances by the designer making creative decisions and engaging in actions, and making these decisions and actions in response to the emerging work. In this, the designer is not seeing the evolving work as a detached observer but is involved in it and is being affected by it. And to repeat Bouteneff's point, mentioned at the start of this book, *"some of the best research and insightful observations come from those who are deeply and personally involved in their subject, precisely by virtue of their engagement"*.[54]

201

For these reasons, design researchers within academia should be more confident in adopting practice-based approaches and should be prepared to defend these approaches based on first-person experiences, discussion of intentions and demonstrating – through the work itself – the relationships between aims and outcomes. Perhaps especially at the level of the design PhD, there is a need to develop practice-based approaches, together with supervisory and examiner experience, that support and are capable of constructively discussing such research. This will mean giving less priority to conventional design research approaches that focus on primary data acquisition through interviews and analytical methods, and paying far greater attention to creativity and design development, which form the very heart of a subject and are essential to the advancement of disciplinary knowledge. This, too, is part of the necessary shift towards new ways of engaging with the world, new ways of doing and the development of positive, equitable and environmentally conscious norms that also have the potential to be far more meaningful at a personal level.

A NEW DESIGN AGENDA

The important challenges we are confronting today, from rising inequities to environmental destruction, from questions of meaning to the emergence of more holistic perspectives, are challenges facing the whole of society. As such they need to inform design and take it in directions that are relevant, substantial and constructive. We do not need the vast numbers of ever new products that have become the norm and the expectation in the developed economies – least of all energy hungry, short-lived technological devices that distance us from each other and from the real world. We already have far too many of these damaging products, far too much vacuous choice, and far too much waste. But at the same time we have a dearth of meaning, no clear direction and no real sense of purpose, beyond the internal logic of a particular project or activity.

The issues facing us today – severe and worrying as many of them are – offer great opportunities for forging a different path, a creative path that calls upon and gives expression to the best of who we are and who we can be. A design agenda capable of addressing these issues will not mean more of the same, it will not be the agenda that has driven design in the past. The

202 design agenda of our present time has to be one that reintegrates and expresses our fullness as human beings – the rational and the imaginative, left and right, facts and values. It is a design agenda of complementarities, balance and multifarious, context-based initiatives that are considerate of people and planet. It is a design agenda that values tradition, moderation, continuity and relationships. And it is a design agenda that embraces the heritage of human wisdom and knowledge and is rooted in ways that down the centuries have proved resilient, enriching and environmentally respectful. It is these priorities and principles that are capable of weaving together the practical, the social and the spiritual in ways that are integrated, holistic, deeply meaningful and enduring.

AMONGST OTHER THINGS

Mass-production methods that employ mechanized and automated processes combined with low-cost labour in poorer countries allow us to purchase products that have an artificially low retail price. This does not mean that the cost of these products is low. The actual or true cost includes the environmental costs of energy intensive methods and the societal ills of labour exploitation. Most of these products are also short-lived, contributing to waste and the further impacts of product replacement. This is a formula for harm and decline and for creating a material culture that lacks intrinsic value and enduring meaning. These developments have resulted in a material culture that is constantly changing. Products are now endlessly replaceable – one ballpoint pen serves as well as another, the same is true for mobile phones, tablet computers, TVs, furniture, even automobiles. Consequently, individual products become stripped of any sense of evocation, memory or associative meaning – they are valued only for their utility or their brand identity, which itself is a mass-manufactured conceit.

In response to this state of affairs we must consider how we might design, produce and acquire material goods that are representative of more ethical practices and manifestations of meaningful, worthwhile human endeavours. By taking these concerns into account, our material goods can become expressions of processes that have a positive effect on human culture. In their making, use and after use, their environmental effects will be minimized and they will embody and inherently serve to sustain beliefs, knowledge and practices that a community or social group regard as important and worth sustaining.

Despite the many positive effects of ethically responsible local practices, however, it is rather obvious that such goods would be significantly more expensive than those coming from globalized mass-production systems that are exploitative of people and the natural environment. By ensuring appropriately sourced materials, fair wages, employment benefits and decent working conditions, the production costs of goods would, understandably and quite rightly, be substantially higher. Goods produced in a responsible, locally fitting manner would not be able to compete with globalized mass production if judged solely on price; assuming the continuation of the so called 'free-market' economy for the foreseeable future. While those who are relatively affluent may choose to pay higher prices for products they know to be environmentally and socially trustworthy, this will not be an option for the many who are less well off. There are a number of ways of addressing this concern.

In the longer term, with broader understanding of the issues and sufficient political will, economic policies and conditions could be adjusted to favour small, local producers rather than multinational corporations. They could support a culture of production and product care and maintenance, rather than one of consumption and waste. Such developments would help cultivate a different perspective – one in which we cease to regard materials goods as short-lived, easily replaceable, functional commodities. Things would be seen as lasting and as representative of local culture, history and identity, thereby fostering a greater appreciation of our material environment. Such goods might be more expensive initially but their longer lifespans and additional associations will contribute to a more meaningful way of living in which products are valued more fully.

In the shorter term, it could mean developing local approaches to production as part of a range of other activities. This approach is actually akin to many traditional ways of working. James Rebanks, whom I mentioned earlier, is a shepherd in the English Lake District employing traditional farming practices but, to make a living, he is also a UNESCO adviser, consultant and writer. He argues that many traditional practices are worth doing, even though they might not be viable when judged purely on economic grounds. They can be continued if people are prepared to do other or additional things to make a living. He points out that this has always been the case. If we do not do this, traditions die and the beliefs, values and customs they encompass die with them and people regret it.[55] Similarly, our research at Lancaster University demonstrates that traditional practices in less economically developed parts of the world are often sustained because they are one among various activities people do to support themselves and their families. Traditional weaving in Northern Thailand, for example, is generally carried out as a part-time activity, producing cloth for use by the weavers themselves and their family members or as a supplementary source of income.[56] An example from Sardinia indicates that other priorities – beyond the economic – are fundamental to the continuation of such practices. Chiara Vigo is one of the last people continuing an ancient craft – the harvesting and weaving of *byssus* or sea silk, made from the fibrous secretions of large clams. The craft goes back millennia. It is a difficult and time-consuming practice but it yields a fine woven cloth that shines like gold in sunlight. Even though it has been made for centuries, it seems that it has never been a commercial activity, and this continues to be the case today. She does not sell her woven products, saying *"It would be like commercialising the flight of an eagle. … It is sacred"*. Instead, she gives them away to people in need of her help. *Byssus* is believed to bring good fortune and fertility and thus it is woven too into the cultural fabric of the place, the folklore and religion. Chiara Vigo was taught the craft by her grandmother who had learned it from her mother, and she says that her daughter *"will have to continue this tradition so humankind can benefit from it"*.[57] Such approaches are not concerned with maximizing productivity, efficiency or profit, nor are they about automation, innovation or brand identity. Instead they are about doing things with care, to the best of one's ability and in ways that embody values. They are about doing things slowly, quietly and without fuss, in ways that are routine, normalized and part of a way of living in which making material culture – for one's own use, for one's family, for neighbours – is not necessarily part of a monetary economy but part of an economy of love, empathy and exchange. Only after these needs have been satisfied and if there is production to spare, might some goods be sold for monetary income. It is through such ways that – at the local level – we can create a material culture that is representative of deeper human values – a material culture created with commitment and love and replete with meaning. That is, a material culture that surpasses mere instrumental value and has intrinsic meaning because it is associated with the people who matter to us and the things we regard as worthwhile.

This is not to suggest that we cannot use innovative technologies and new methods – but their integration into traditional ways of making has to be carefully and sensitively considered if things that matter are to be preserved. Traditional practices are often the result of a fine balance that can be very fragile and where even a small change can upset a whole interrelated system. With care, however, the growing number of small, local design and making centres, such as MAKLab in Glasgow,[58] can offer opportunities for traditional skills to come together with new practices. For example, highly skilled handcarving techniques can be combined with 3D scanning and printing to create repeatable patterns for the ancient practice of lost-wax casting. This allows the patterns to be preserved in digital formats, which also enables them to be adjusted in size or detail and reproduced. Such methods can help preserve traditional practices and, potentially, even enhance them, allowing them to remain relevant in today's world.

The choice we face is not whether we need more or fewer products nor is it whether or not we should embrace new technologies and new methods. Clearly, we do require material goods and clearly, too, we should consider – but consider carefully – the use of new technologies and methods, as traditional practices have always done. Traditional practices may encompass generations of knowledge and know-how but they are also dynamic processes, always changing and adapting; they are not something to be preserved in aspic. The choice we face concerns the *kinds* of material goods we want, which includes the kinds of processes involved in their production. Do we want products that are cheap, unrepairable and disposable; that have

205

nothing to do with context; that are too often associated with social exploitation and environmental degradation; and that take the profits of production away from local communities? Or do we want products that have some relationship to the place where we live; that may be more expensive initially but are long-lasting and repairable; that create a range of local employment opportunities and build skills, relationships and self-respect; that result in decent wages that can support employees and their families; and are produced by enterprises that invest back into the community? The kind of material culture we create is a result of our will, the decisions we make, and the kinds of things we choose to value.

A LARGER VISTA

Common criticism of traditional practices suggests that, if one is not prepared to move forward – even though established ways of doing things may have proved themselves over generations to be effective, reliable and contextually fitting – then one is stuck in the past, destined to be 'left behind' as the world moves on. Such criticism suggests that there is something about change that is inherently good and unchallengeable. This is a highly partial view that has neither rational nor intuitive legitimacy. Nonetheless, it became the normative predisposition of modernity and largely remains the case today in late-modernity. Progress for its own sake has become sacrosanct – but unless we ask 'progress in what and why?', it remains an abstract, undefined notion. Needless to say, there are many circumstances where change is both necessary and beneficial. Progress in many areas can be extremely positive. However, the purpose and nature of change requires careful scrutiny when cultures, places and ways of life are affected; once displaced or dispersed, traditional ways of living and traditional practices, that are often inherently sustainable and deeply integrated with place, are lost forever. And this loss will include detailed knowledge about the local environment, wildlife and plants, as well as tried and true practices and patterns of living that have proved effective over time and that are often inseparable from beliefs and values.

206

It is important to view our continual striving for 'progress *per se*' within this larger vista, and to ask ourselves *why* change is needed, where it might be taking us, who benefits, and what we are trying to achieve. Unless we ask these kinds of questions, we can easily lose those things we value most. Moreover, in our rather myopic, consumption-based economy, what tends to happen is that certain aspects of a place or a culture become packaged and commodified – particular dishes in restaurants, certain houseware items, accessories or clothing, and local music – and are sold to visitors and tourists as 'authentic'. But a culture is more than discrete commodified elements that feed an already bloated consumer economy. These approaches only take. In contrast, many traditional ways of living and doing are about reciprocity. One often finds that methods that have developed over a long period of time have achieved a fit within the social and natural contexts such that there is both give and take – a symbiotic relationship that draws from and feeds back into the human culture, which itself has developed in an interdependent relationship with the physical environment. While these deeper aspects of tradition and culture are less visible and are non-commodifiable, they are essential to ways of living that are capable of sustaining, deepening and enriching things that matter – identity, beliefs, rituals, relationships, place and livelihoods.

207

Seeds of Change

designs for a new awareness

Broom

they took the blossoms of the oak,
and the blossoms of the broom,
and the blossoms of the meadowsweet,
and produced from them a maiden,
the fairest and most graceful that man ever saw.
And they baptized her, and gave her
the name of Blodeuwedd

The Mabinogion[59]

Figure 8.1
SEEDS OF CHANGE – Broom

Piñon Pine

Nine months after swallowing
the big piñon, she gave birth
to a baby boy, whom she named
Son of the Sun.
He was Montezuma.

A San Juan Pueblo Legend[60]

Figure 8.2
SEEDS OF CHANGE – Piñon Pine

Horse Chestnut

In the west country of England
the flowers are known as Candles.
It is said that the horse chestnut
keeps its candles burning to light
the fairies home after their dance.

Plant Lore[61]

Figure 8.3
SEEDS OF CHANGE – Horse Chestnut

Appendices

Appendix 1

confesión – *relic from a future past*

Imaginative ideas can suddenly appear unbidden, unplanned, and sometimes unwanted. Such was the case with the short piece of writing that was eventually incorporated into the object I have called *Confesión* (Figure 3.14). The idea came to me early one morning, in that half-awake state when one's mind is still suffused with dreams. I reached for my notebook, which is never far from my side, and wrote it down without deliberation. There it remained. I felt it was complete and in need of no further expansion or development. Retaining its raw, colloquial form seemed important because of its imagined provenance. The content was inescapably macabre but, even though I had written it, strangely, it seemed as if I had just set down something that was already there. The allusions may be chilling but the activities being described are not specific.

The inspiration to create a text-based object on a metal sheet came in part from the content of the piece and its reference to a lack of combustible matter, and in part from remembering an exhibition I had seen at the Wellcome Trust in London. *Infinitas Gracias* was a collection of Mexican votive paintings – a folk art through which people give thanks for prayers answered after illness or accident. These small paintings on metal panels feature imagery along with hand-written accounts of the incident depicted.

Consequently, the text of *Confesión* is in Mexican Spanish. This not only acknowledges the source that influenced the final form but also affects the viewer's experience of it as an object. Two rather different experiences can be envisaged. For those who understand the language and are of that culture, the text combined with the form offers a perceptual link to the source of inspiration and, potentially, some resonance with that traditional folk art. At the same time, the piece can be understood as presaging a dystopian future if we continue on our present course. On the other hand, for non-Spanish speakers, this way of presenting the text achieves a cognitive distancing – allowing the piece to be seen primarily as an object that, with its seal-like detail, appears to be some kind of legalistic document. Neither of these experiences – the potential resonance for those who are of that culture and the distancing for those who are not – would have been possible had the words been in English. However, for those who may be curious about the content, the English text is included below. Some time after this piece was completed, with the aid of an Arts Council England grant, it was transformed into a short film piece, performed by London-based actor Matt Prendergast, directed by Andrew Quick of Imitating the Dog theatre company, with technical production by Steve Wade. Links to this film are included in Appendix 4.

Confession: I'm not sure why we're even talking about this – it's not like it's new or weird anymore. Of course, we haven't always done it. There was a time, before my day though, when there were other things. Some of the old people still remember, when they were really young, when there were animal farms and fruit trees and stuff like that – and some people even say that they remember a time when the things that live in the water were caught and used as food. People used to eat that stuff. Can you imagine eating anything that came out of that filth? But all that was a long time ago. I've never seen any of that myself. Some people say that you can still find places, but I've never seen them and I've never met anybody who has. All I've known is what we do today. Of course, there are some things you don't do – there are rules. It's not like you can do anything you want. There are laws. It used to be that people found old stuff – on the beaches, in the pits – that they could burn, and they'd cook – but that's all used up now, you don't find that stuff anymore. So now it's just salted and kept dry – and after a while it's not bad. 'Course it's all got to be processed first – butchered, cut into strips – before it's salted. They do that down in the gorge, out of sight. People don't want to see that stuff going on. I couldn't do that job – down there – it's always in shadows and cold down there – that's why they do it, 'cos its cold – keeps the smell down. And the noise, all those women all day long. But you gotta live right? But man, I couldn't do that job, no way. Now I know it might sound strange coming from me, 'cos it's been this way ever since I can remember, but I still don't like it – I don't think it's what we

219

should be doing, you know. Tastes pretty good though, 'specially the drier stuff – the longer it's kept, the harder it gets – that stuff tastes pretty good. There's different names for the different types – there's a whole bunch of different types you can get – some of the really old stuff, the stuff that was smoked – that's supposed to be the best – but that's really expensive 'cos they can't make that anymore – nothing left to burn see.

04-04-84

220

Appendix 2

listening to the muse – *a personal reflection*

I lie half-awake on the emergence of dreams
in the half light of a new day

and in those unstructured thoughts
of non-chronological time
there is some kind of meshing,
unrecognized, unconscious,
some kind of synaptic flash of insight
that produces in the eye of the mind
a vision of an idea,
complete, perfect,
unwanting of refinement or explanation.
So it is yet without comprehension
– this will come.
Later.

Believe it.
Believe it to be true.
Have faith in it even though
it cannot yet be understood
it cannot yet be intellectualized, rationalized

or its meaning appreciated
– this will come.
Later.

But only if its truth is taken on trust.
One has to lean on this intuitive,
ungrasped insight,
stay with it, reflect on it,
persist.
And its meaning
will emerge.

222

Appendix 3 the inadequacies of corporate social responsibility

Former BP CEO, Lord Browne, argues that CSR and Public Relations (PR) departments are so ineffective, not to say irrelevant, because they are fundamentally disconnected from the company's main business operations and commercial purpose. Significant changes in a corporation's core activities are always based on the decisions of senior management, not 'out of touch' CSR departments. He says, *"The disconnect between CSR and commercial operations means that companies with superb CSR records can also be hugely damaging to society"*.[1] One recent example is the German car maker Volkswagen. On its CSR webpage the company states that, *"bearing its social responsibility has long been at the heart of our corporate culture. … This is how the Volkswagen Group supports a broad spectrum of projects which foster social development, culture and education whilst serving the needs of regional structural development, health promotion, sport and the conservation of nature"*.[2] Yet, in 2015, it was revealed that the company had been using an illegal 'defeat' device in millions of its diesel-fuelled cars that disengaged the emissions control system to give better driving performance. The device, designed to only activate during periodic state emissions tests, makes the car seem forty times cleaner.[3, 4, 5] The primary concern of the modern corporation is profit and this tends to override all other concerns, including environmental and social responsibilities.[6] In another recent case the former owner of the Peanut Corporation of America was jailed for 28 years for forging safety certificates and knowingly shipping contaminated products. These products had made hundreds of people ill and were linked to nine deaths. The judge in the case identified the desire for profits and simple greed as the major factors in the case.[7, 8]

224

Appendix 4 related websites

The Tell-Tale Notch, featured in the prologue of Chapter 2, is available as an audio-visual presentation at: www.youtube.com/watch?v=ZButVMMneKA

CONFESSION, a dramatization of the English text (Appendix 1) of *CONFESIÓN* (Figure 3.14) is available at: www.youtube.com/watch?v=GZ4CSiud76I

These video pieces were made with support of Arts Council England and Lancaster University. They are available at: www.stuartwalker.org.uk, along with news and additional work.

Notes

Prologue

1   Lawson-Tancred, H. C., trans. (2004) *Aristotle: The Art of Rhetoric*. Penguin Books, London, pp. 80–82.
2   Thompson, J. A. K., trans. (1976) *The Ethics of Aristotle: The Nicomachean Ethics*. Penguin Books, London.
3   Toye, R. (2013) *Rhetoric – A Very Short Introduction*. Oxford University Press, Oxford, pp. 34–42.
4   Hick, J. (1966) *Faith and Knowledge*, 2nd Edition. Fontana, Collins, Glasgow, pp. 244–245.

1 The Subject

1   Lanier, J. (2013) *Who Owns the Future?* Allen Lane, Penguin Books, London, p. 125.
2   Hartley, L. P. (1953) *The Go-Between*. Penguin Books, London, p. 5.
3   Bouteneff, P. C. (2015) *Arvo Pärt: Out of Silence*. St. Vladimir's Seminary Press, Yonkers, NY, p. 18.
4   Greene, M. (1995) *Releasing the Imagination: Essays on Education, the Arts and Social Change* [2000]. Jossey-Bass, Wiley, San Francisco, CA, pp. 4–5.
5   Walker, S. (2011) *The Spirit of Design: Objects, Environment and Meaning*. Routledge, Abingdon, Oxford.
6   Walker, S. (2014) *Designing Sustainability: Making Radical Changes in a Material World*. Routledge, Abingdon, Oxford.
7   Elkington, J. (1997) *Cannibals with Forks: The Triple Bottom Line of 21st Century Business*. Capstone Publishing Ltd., Oxford, pp. 70–94.
8   Siegel, L. (2009) 'Did Frank McCourt invent James Frey?' *The Daily Beast*, 20 July 2009, available at: http://www.thedailybeast.com/articles/2009/07/20/the-mother-of-all-memoirists.html, accessed 25 November 2015.

9 Grey, C. (2015) 'The future is not where the older generation seems to think it is'. *The Tablet* (London), 12 December 2015, p. 8.

10 Ibid.

11 Gamble, R. (2016) 'Traditionalist liturgies attract record numbers during Easter premium'. *The Tablet* (London), 14 April 2016, p. 30.

12 Atran, S. (2015) 'Youth, violent extremism and promoting peace'. Address to the UN Security Council, 23 April 2015, available at: http://blogs.plos.org/ neuroanthropology/2015/04/25/scott-atran-on-youth-violent-extremism-and-promoting- peace/, accessed 28 November 2015.

13 Ibid.

14 Taylor, C. (2007) *A Secular Age*. The Belknap Press of Harvard University Press, Cambridge, MA, p. 719.

2 A Narrowing

An earlier version of this chapter appeared in the *International Journal of Design for Sustainability*, Inderscience, Switzerland, Vol. 2, No. 4, pp. 283–296 (copyright 2014). With kind permission of Inderscience, Switzerland, who retain copyright of the original paper. Journal web page: http://www.inderscience.com/jhome.php?jcode=ijsdes#issue

1 Leopold, A. (1949) *A Sand County Almanac and Sketches Here and There*. Oxford University Press, London, pp. 67–68.

2 An audio-visual presentation of *The Tell-tale Notch*, with images and narration by the author, recorded at Robinwood Studios, Todmorden, and produced with the support of an Arts Council England grant, is available at: https://www.youtube.com/ watch?v=ZButVMMneKA.

3 Hague, W. (2007) *William Wilberforce: The Life of the Great Anti-Slave Trade Campaigner*. HarperCollins Publishers, London, p. 172.

4 Schama, S. (2009b) *A History of Britain, Volume 2: The British Wars 1603–1776*. The Bodley Head, London, p. 334.

5 Wakefield, J. (2016) 'Apple, Samsung and Sony face child labour claims'. *BBC News Online*, 19 January 2016, available at: http://www.bbc.co.uk/news/ technology-35311456, accessed 2 February 2016.

6 Gray, L. (2012) 'Rio +20: Nick Clegg defies Tories again by pledging environment key to growth'. *The Telegraph* (London), 15 June 2012, available at: http://www.telegraph. co.uk/earth/earthnews/9332404/Rio-20-Nick-Clegg-defies-Tories-again-by-pledging- environment-key-to-growth.html, accessed 31 January 2014.

7 Beckett, A. (2013) 'What is the "global race"?' *The Guardian* (London), 22 September 2013, available at: http://www.theguardian.com/politics/2013/sep/22/what-is-global- race-conservatives-ed-miliband, accessed 31 January 2014.

8 McGilchrist, I. (2009) *The Master and His Emissary: The Divided Brain and the Making of the Western World*. Yale University Press, New Haven, CT, pp. 259–269.

9 Ibid., p. 314.

10 Tarnas, R. (1991) *The Passion of the Western Mind*. Harmony Books, New York, NY, p. 226.

11 Armstrong, K. (2002) *Islam: A Short History*. Phoenix Press, London, p. 6.

12 Brotton, J. (2006) *The Renaissance*. Oxford University Press, Oxford, pp. 3–5.

13 McGilchrist, I. (2009) *The Master and His Emissary: The Divided Brain and the Making of the Western World*. Yale University Press, New Haven, CT, pp. 314–324.

14 Brotton, J. (2006) *The Renaissance*. Oxford University Press, Oxford, pp. 25–27.

15 Hampson, N. (1968) *The Enlightenment*. Penguin Books, London, pp. 25–28.

16 Brotton, J. (2006) *The Renaissance*. Oxford University Press, Oxford, p. 4.

17 Fernández-Armesto, F. and Wilson, D. (1996) *Reformation*. Bantam Press, London, pp. 103–108.

18 Schama, S. (2009a) *A History of Britain, Volume 1: At the Edge of the World? 3000 BC–AD 1603*. The Bodley Head, London, p. 267.

19 McGilchrist, I. (2009) *The Master and His Emissary: The Divided Brain and the Making of the Western World*. Yale University Press, New Haven, CT, p. 314.

20 The Quakers, or Society of Friends, with their emphasis on communal silence, are something of an exception among the Protestant movements arising from the Reformation.

21 Duffy, E. (1992) *The Stripping of the Altars: Traditional Religion in England 1400–1580*. Yale University Press, New Haven, CT, p. 381.

22 MacCulloch, D. (2013) *Silence: A Christian History*. Allen Lane, Penguin Group, London, pp. 129–136.

23 Hampson, N. (1968) *The Enlightenment*. Penguin Books, London, p. 130.

24 Schama, S. (2009c) *A History of Britain, Volume 3: The Fate of Empire 1776–2000*. The Bodley Head, London, p. 34.

25 Ibid., p. 267.

26 Rowson, J. and McGilchrist, I. (2013) 'Divided brain, divided world: why the best part of us struggles to be heard'. *Royal Society of Arts*, London, pp. 4–5, available at: http://www.thersa.org/__data/assets/pdf_file/0019/1016083/RSA-Divided-Brain-Divided-World.PDF, accessed 14 November 2013.

27 Yonge, C. D., trans. (1993) *The Works of Philo: Complete and Unabridged*. Hendrickson Publishers, Peabody, MA, p. 94.

28 Armstrong, K. (2008) *The Bible: The Biography*. Atlantic Books, London, pp. 50–51.

29 Gen. 4.

30 Taylor, C. (2007) *A Secular Age*. The Belknap Press of Harvard University Press, Cambridge, MA, pp. 300–301.

31 Hampson, N. (1968) *The Enlightenment*. Penguin Books, London, pp. 23–29.

32 McGilchrist, I. (2009) *The Master and His Emissary: The Divided Brain and the Making of the Western World*. Yale University Press, New Haven, CT, pp. 315–318.

33 Hampson, N. (1968) *The Enlightenment*. Penguin Books, London, p. 127.

34 Schwaabe, C. (2011) *Max Weber – The Disenchantment of the World*. Uhlaner, J. (trans.), Goethe-Institute. V., available at: http://www.goethe.de/ges/phi/prt/en8250983.htm, accessed 14 February 2014.

35 Edwards, P., ed. (1999) *James Cook: The Journals*. Penguin Books Ltd., London, pp. 542–547.

36 Hargett, J. M., trans. (1989) 'On the road in twelfth century China: the travel diaries of Fan Chengda (1126–1193)', pp. 46–47, Franz Steiner Verlag, Stuttgart; excerpt available at: http://bactra.org/Poetry/Su_Tung-po/Record_of_Stone_Bell_Mountain.html, accessed 2 February 2016.

37 Gay, P. (2007) *Modernism: The Lure of Heresy from Baudelaire to Beckett and Beyond*. Vintage Books, London, pp. 13, 434.

38 Corfield, P. J. (2008) 'All people are living histories – which is why history matters'. *Making History*, School of Advanced Studies, Royal Holloway, University of London, available at: http://www.history.ac.uk/makinghistory/resources/articles/why_history_matters.html, accessed 10 February 2014.

39 The novels of these years included Franz Kafka's *The Trial* (1925), which depicts a world of extreme instrumental rationality and burgeoning, impenetrable bureaucracy. Others, such as Hermann Hesse's *Der Steppenwolf* (1927), James Hilton's *Lost Horizon* (1933), Somerset Maugham's *The Razor's Edge* (1944), and Evelyn Waugh's *Brideshead Revisited* (1945), in their different ways, convey the idea of loss – a feeling that the spiritual sensibility had become somehow at variance with the contemporary

world. Aldous Huxley's *Brave New World* (1932) is a parody of techno-scientific utopia and Orwell's *1984* (1949) conveys the horrors of an oppressive totalitarian regime that takes an instrumental view of its citizenry.

40 Anon (1945) *Miracles of Invention and Discovery*. Odhams Press, London, p. 5.
41 Most scientific research is funded by the public purse and scientists can only pursue their activities with the approval of the taxpayer. Approval is usually based on an understanding that such research will eventually prove useful.
42 Bassler, B. (2014) *Exchanges at the Frontier*. BBC World Service, first broadcast 19:06, 8 February 2014.
43 Bakan, J. (2004) *The Corporation: The Pathological Pursuit of Profit and Power*. Constable and Robinson Limited, London, pp. 60–61.
44 Pratt, V., Brady, E., and Howarth, J. (2000) *Environment and Philosophy*. Routledge, London, pp. 81–84, extract available at: http://www.vernonpratt.com/thehumanbeing/individualism.htm, 12 February 2014.
45 Chaibong, H. (2000) 'The cultural challenge of individualism'. *Journal of Democracy*, Vol. 11, No. 1, pp. 127–134.
46 Brotton, J. (2006) *The Renaissance*. Oxford University Press, Oxford, pp. 3, 114.
47 Armstrong, K. (2002) *Islam: A Short History*. Phoenix Press, London, p. 6.
48 Chaibong, H. (2000) 'The cultural challenge of individualism'. *Journal of Democracy*, Vol. 11, No. 1, pp. 127–134.
49 Taylor, C. (2007) *A Secular Age*. The Belknap Press of Harvard University Press, Cambridge, MA, pp. 561, 717.
50 This European sense of positional superiority over other peoples, based on progress in science and technology and strongly connected to advancements in secularization and Western styles of democratic governance, is today being undermined by these very same developments. The scientific capability of the West has revealed that all living humans have a common maternal ancestor – this is based on research in genetics at Rice University in the United States (see note 51). This discovery from 'secular', objective scientific inquiry has been given the name "mitochondrial Eve" after the first woman in the book of Genesis in the Abrahamic religious traditions, which essentially makes the same point about human origins. As Longley has said, this "shoots down every claim to racial superiority. I find it a pleasing irony that this basic ethical insight about humanity from the book of Genesis has now been confirmed by Darwinian evolutionary biology" (see note 52).
51 Rice University (2010) '"Mitochondrial Eve": mother of all humans lived 200,000 years ago'. *ScienceDaily*, 17 August 2010, available at: www.sciencedaily.com/releases/2010/08/100817122405.htm, accessed 15 March 2014.
52 Longley, C. (2014) *Thought for the Day*. British Broadcasting Corporation, Radio 4, first broadcast 10 February 2014, transcript available at: http://www.bbc.co.uk/programmes/p01s272q, accessed 15 March 2014.
53 Said, E. W. (1978) *Orientalism* [2003]. Penguin Books, London, p. 7.
54 Young, R. J. C. (2003) *Postcolonialism*. Oxford University Press, Oxford, pp. 41, 60.
55 Taylor, C. (2007) *A Secular Age*. The Belknap Press of Harvard University Press, Cambridge, MA, pp. 300–301; Hampson, N. (1968) *The Enlightenment*. Penguin Books, London, p. 25.
56 Edwards, B. (2012) *Drawing of the Right Side of the Brain: A Course in Enhancing Creativity and Artistic Confidence*, 4th Edition. Souvenir Press, London, pp. 39–40.
57 See also Nagel, T. (2012) *Mind and Cosmos: Why the Materialist, Neo-Darwinian Conception of Nature Is Almost Certainly False*. Oxford University Press, Oxford, p. 4.
58 Heidegger, M. (1971) *Poetry, Language, Thought*. Hofstadter, A. (trans.), HarperCollins, New York, NY, p. 168.

59 McGilchrist, I. (2009) *The Master and His Emissary: The Divided Brain and the Making of the Western World.* Yale University Press, New Haven, CT, p. 321.

60 Lester, L. (2012) 'Risks and rewards of quantifying nature's "ecosystem services"'. *American Association for the Advancement of Science*, available at: http://www.eurekalert.org/pub_releases/2012-06/esoa-rar062112.php#, accessed 5 August 2013.

61 Rodwell, J. (2013) 'Aesthetic & spiritual responses to the environment: a two-day BESS workshop at York'. Biodiversity & Ecosystem Service Sustainability (BESS) Research Programme (2011–2017), Natural Environment Research Council (NERC), 3 July 2013, available at: http://www.nerc-bess.net/documents/BESS_NIA_Cultural_Ecosystem_Services_Workshop_Report.pdf, accessed 5 August 2013.

62 Fioramonti, L. (2014) *How Numbers Rule the World: The Use and Abuse of Statistics in Global Politics.* Zed Books, London, pp. 136–142.

63 Kayfetz, J. L. (2013) 'Poetry – and medicine'. 13 October 2013, available at: http://janetkayfetz.wordpress.com/2013/10/17/poetry-and-medicine/, accessed 27 January 2014.

64 Lutter, S. and Giljum, S. (2012) 'The issue'. *World Resources Forum*, Global Material Extraction and Resource Efficiency, available at: http://www.worldresourcesforum.org/issue, accessed 14 August 2013.

65 UNEP (2009) 'Facts and figures: global materials extraction (Fig. 2.1)'. Resource Panel, *United Nations Environment Programme*, available at: http://www.unep.org/resourcepanel/FactsFigures/tabid/106638/Default.aspx, accessed 14 August 2013; see also note 50.

66 Material intensity refers to the economic output per unit of materials extraction.

67 Lansley, S. (1994) *After the Gold Rush – The Trouble with Affluence.* Century Business Books, London, p. 134.

68 Schwartz, B. (2004) *The Paradox of Choice.* HarperCollins, New York, NY, pp. 109, 132–133.

69 In the early 1980s the CEOs of large US companies were paid approximately twenty times more than their lowest paid workers; today, this has risen to about 280 times. This state of affairs reflects a significant failing of the consumer capitalist system. Not only are such gross disparities unjust, they also undermine social cohesion and social capital and create a drain on the economy (see note 70). Wilkinson and Pickett suggest that in many cases the disparity between CEO income and average worker income exceeds a ratio of 500:1 (see note 71).

70 Longley, C. (2013) 'Being very wealthy can, as Jesus pointed out, be bad for the soul'. *The Tablet* (London), 10 August 2013, p. 5.

71 Wilkinson, R. and Pickett, K. (2009) *The Spirit Level: Why More Equal Societies Almost Always Do Better.* Allen Land, Penguin Books, London, pp. 232, 243.

72 Ibid.

73 Said, E. W. (2003) 'Preface' in *Orientalism* [2003]. Penguin Books, London, p. xiv.

74 Ibid.

75 Worldwatch Institute (2013) 'The state of consumption today'. *Worldwatch Institute*, Washington, DC, available at: http://www.worldwatch.org/node/810, accessed 14 August 2013.

76 Duffy, E. (2004) *Faith of our Fathers: Reflections on Catholic Tradition.* Continuum, London, pp. 1–3.

77 Paton, G. (2014) 'Religious education subjected to "rank discrimination"'. *The Telegraph* (London), 24 February 2014, available at: http://www.telegraph.co.uk/education/educationnews/10656555/Religious-education-subjected-to-rank-discrimination.html, accessed 3 March 2014.

78 Lloyd, S. (2013) 'RE: The truth unmasked – The supply of and support for religious education teachers: an inquiry by the All Party Parliamentary Group on Religious

230

Education'. *Religious Education Council of England and Wales*, London, March 2014, available at: http://religiouseducationcouncil.org.uk/images/stories/pdf/APPG_RE_The_Truth_Unmasked.pdf, accessed 3 March 2014.

79 Pagels, E. (2006) 'The Gospel of Thomas: new perspectives on Jesus' message' [Recorded lecture]. Sounds True Inc., Boulder, CO.

80 Dworkin, R. (2013) *Religion Without God*. Harvard University Press, Cambridge, MA, pp. 2–3.

81 Reid, K. (2013) 'From fragmentation to wholeness'. *Resurgence & Ecologist*, No. 279.

82 MacIntyre, A. (2007) *After Virtue*, 3rd Edition. Bristol Classical Press, Bloomsbury Academic, London, pp. 218–227.

83 Ibid.

84 Ibid., pp. 67–68.

85 Leopold, A (1949) *A Sand County Almanac and Sketches Here and There*. Oxford University Press, London, pp. 67–68.

86 Odent, M. (2013) *Childbirth and the Future of Homo Sapiens*. Pinter & Martin Ltd., London, p. 63.

87 Ibid.

88 Duffy, E. (2004) *Faith of our Fathers: Reflections on Catholic Tradition*. Continuum, London, p. 18.

89 MacIntyre, A. (2007) *After Virtue*, 3rd Edition. Bristol Classical Press, Bloomsbury Academic, London, p. 227.

90 Teather, S. (2014) 'Interview with Sarah Teather MP on the Sunday programme'. *BBC Radio 4*, Salford, 2 February 2014.

91 Walker, S. (2014) *Designing Sustainability: Making Radical Changes in a Material World*. Routledge, Abingdon, Oxford, p. 88.

92 Chomsky, N. (1997) 'The passion for free markets'. *Z Magazine*, May edition, available at: http://www.chomsky.info/articles/199705--.htm, accessed 11 March 2014.

93 Chaibong, H. (2000) 'The cultural challenge of individualism'. *Journal of Democracy*, Vol. 11, No. 1, pp. 127–134.

94 Fletcher, K. (2013) 'Sustainable fashion' in Walker, S. and Giard, J. (eds.) *The Handbook of Design for Sustainability*. Bloomsbury Academic, London, pp. 287–289.

95 Davison, A. (2013) 'Making sustainability up: design beyond possibility' in Walker, S. and Giard, J. (eds.) *The Handbook of Design for Sustainability*. Bloomsbury Academic, London, p. 43.

96 Nagel, T. (2012) *Mind and Cosmos: Why the Materialist, Neo-Darwinian Conception of Nature is Almost Certainly False*. Oxford University Press, Oxford, p. 12.

97 Ibid., p. 7.

231

3 Counterpoints

1 Lewis, C. S. (1947) *Miracles*. HarperCollins, London, p. 2.

2 E.g. CBC (2011) 'Canada pulls out of Kyoto protocol'. *CBCNews*, 12 December, available at: http://www.cbc.ca/news/politics/story/2011/12/12/pol-kent-kyoto-pullout.html, accessed 9 July 2013.

3 Cordeiro, W. P. (2003) 'The only solution to the decline in business ethics: ethical managers'. *Teaching Business Ethics*, Vol. 7, No. 3, pp. 265–277.

4 Odent, M. (2013) *Childbirth and the Future of Homo Sapiens*. Pinter & Martin Ltd., London, p. 26.

5 Hawken, P. (2009) 'Commencement: healing or stealing'. Commencement speech, University of Portland, available at: http://www.up.edu/commencement/default.aspx?cid=9456&pid=3144, accessed 9 July 2013.

6 Milton, J. (1674) *Paradise Lost*. Penguin Books, London, p. 20, line 686.

7 Hobsbawm, E. J. (1969) *Industry and Empire.* Penguin Books, London, pp. 15–16.
8 Smith, H. (2001) *Why Religions Matter: The Fate of the Human Spirit in an Age of Disbelief.* HarperCollins, New York, NY, pp. 191–199.
9 Rowson, J. and McGilchrist, I. (2013) 'Divided brain, divided world: why the best part of us struggles to be heard'. *Royal Society of Arts*, London, pp. 4–5, available at: http://www.thersa.org/__data/assets/pdf_file/0019/1016083/RSA-Divided-Brain-Divided-World.PDF, accessed 14 November 2013.
10 Heidegger, M. (1971) *Poetry, Language, Thought.* Hofstadter, A. (trans.), HarperCollins, New York, NY, p. 168.
11 Green, R. P. H., trans. (1997) *Saint Augustine: On Christian Teaching.* Oxford World Classics, Oxford University Press, Oxford, p. 67.
12 Ehrenfeld, J. and Hoffman, A. (2013) *Flourishing: A Frank Conversation about Sustainability.* Stanford University Press, Stanford, CA, pp. 104–105.
13 Comte-Sponville, A. (2007) *The Book of Atheist Spirituality: An Elegant Argument for Spirituality without God.* Huston, N. (trans.), Bantam Books, London, pp. 168–169.
14 Cottingham, J. (2005) *The Spiritual Dimension: Religion, Philosophy and Human Value.* Cambridge University Press, Cambridge, MA, pp. 8–13.
15 Merton, T. (1969) *Contemplative Prayer.* Doubleday, Random House, New York, NY, p. 57.
16 Eagleton, T. (2008) *The Meaning of Life.* Oxford University Press, Oxford, pp. 57–74.
17 Wilkinson, R. and Pickett, K. (2009) *The Spirit Level: Why More Equal Societies Almost Always Do Better.* Allen Land, Penguin Books, London, p. 22.
18 Wright, O. (2012) 'King blasts bankers over pay, service – and morality'. *The Independent* (London), 30 June 2012, available at: http://www.independent.co.uk/news/uk/politics/king-blasts-bankers-over-pay-service--and-morality-7900039.html#, accessed 7 May 2014.

232

19 Protess, B. and Silver-Greenberg, J. (2014) 'Credit Suisse pleads guilty in felony case'. *New York Times* (New York), 19 May 2014, available at: http://dealbook.nytimes.com/2014/05/19/credit-suisse-set-to-plead-guilty-in-tax-evasion-case/?_php=true&_type=blogs&hp&_r=0, accessed 19 May 2014.
20 Davies, C. (2011) 'David Chaytor jailed for 18 months over false expenses claim'. *The Guardian* (London), 7 January 2011, available at: http://www.theguardian.com/politics/2011/jan/07/mps-expenses-david-chaytor-jailed/print, accessed 7 May 2014.
21 Cumming-Bruce, N. (2014) 'Vatican tells of 848 priests ousted in decade'. *New York Times* (New York), 6 May 2014, available at: http://www.nytimes.com/2014/05/07/world/europe/vatican-tells-of-848-priests-ousted-in-last-decade.html?_r=0, accessed 7 May 2014.
22 Halliday, J. (2013) 'Police could have stopped Jimmy Savile in the 1960s, says official report'. *The Guardian* (London), 12 March 2013, available at: http://www.theguardian.com/media/2013/mar/12/jimmy-savile-metropolitan-police, accessed 7 May 2014.
23 O'Carroll, L. (2013) 'Senior Met officer sentenced to 15 months for phone-hacking leak'. *The Guardian* (London), 1 February 2013, available at: http://www.theguardian.com/media/2013/feb/01/april-casburn-sentenced-15-months-phone-hacking, accessed 7 May 2014.
24 Farhi, P. (2014) '*Washington Post* wins Pulitzer Prize for NSA spying revelations; *Guardian* also honored'. *Washington Post* (Washington, DC), 14 April 2014, available at: http://www.washingtonpost.com/politics/washington-post-wins-pulitzer-prize-for-public-service-shared-with-guardian/2014/04/14/bc7c4cc6-c3fb-11e3-bcec-b71ee10e9bc3_story.html, accessed 7 May 2014.
25 Taylor, C. (2007) *A Secular Age.* The Belknap Press of Harvard University Press, Cambridge, MA, pp. 95, 599.

26 Berners-Lee, M. and Clark, D. (2013) *The Burning Question*. Profile Books, London, p. 12.

27 Porritt, J. (2007) *Capitalism as if the World Matters*. Routledge, London, p. 105.

28 Jackson, T. (2009) *Prosperity Without Growth: Economics for a Finite Planet*. Routledge, London, p. 5.

29 Piketty, T. (2014) *Capital in the Twenty-First Century*. Harvard University Press, Cambridge, MA, pp. 255–258.

30 Young, R. J. C. (2003) *Postcolonialism*. Oxford University Press, Oxford, p. 3.

31 Williams, R. (1983) *Keywords: A Vocabulary of Culture and Society* [2014]. HarperCollins, London, pp. 100–102.

32 Graham, M., Hogan, B., Straumann, R. K., and Medhat, A. (2014) 'Uneven geographies of user-generated information: patterns of increasing informational poverty'. *Annals of the Association of American Geographers*, Vol. 104, No. 4, pp. 1, 5, available at: http://www.oii.ox.ac.uk/people/?id=165, accessed 19 May 2014.

33 Graham, M. (2014) *Four Thought*. BBC Radio 4, British Broadcasting Corporation, 18 May 2014, available at: http://www.bbc.co.uk/programmes/b0435j93, accessed 19 May 2014.

34 Baker-Smith, D., trans. (2012) 'Introduction' to *Utopia* by Thomas More [1516]. Penguin Books, London, p. xi.

35 MacCulloch, D. (2013) *Silence: A Christian History*. Allen Lane, Penguin Group, London, p. 90.

36 Green, R. P. H., trans. (1997) *Saint Augustine: On Christian Teaching*. Oxford World Classics, Oxford University Press, Oxford, p. 72.

37 Mortley, R. (1986) *From Word to Silence*. Bond University, Australia, available at: http://epublications.bond.edu.au/word_to_silence_I/, p159 accessed 13 June 2013.

38 Lewis, C. S. (1947) *Miracles*. HarperCollins, London, p. 2.

39 James, W. (1902) *The Varieties of Religious Experience*. The Modern Library, Random House, New York, NY, p. 7.

40 MacCulloch, D. (2013) *Silence: A Christian History*. Allen Lane, Penguin Group, London, pp. 66–67.

41 Mortley, R. (1986) *From Word to Silence*. Bond University, Australia, available at: http://epublications.bond.edu.au/word_to_silence_I/, p159 accessed 13 June 2013.

42 Scruton, R. (2014) *The Soul of the World*. Princeton University Press, Princeton, NJ, pp. 33–36, 77.

43 Said, E. W. (2003) 'Preface' in *Orientalism* [2003]. Penguin Books, London, p. xix.

44 McGilchrist, I. (2009) *The Master and His Emissary: The Divided Brain and the Making of the Western World*. Yale University Press, New Haven, CT, pp. 237, 300.

45 Wolin, R. (2013) 'Emmanuel Lévinas'. *Encyclopædia Britannica*, available at: http://www.britannica.com/EBchecked/topic/337960/Emmanuel-Levinas, accessed 10 April 2014.

46 Said, E. W. (1978) *Orientalism* [2003]. Penguin Books, London, p. 14.

47 Sim, S. (2007) *Manifesto for Silence: Confronting the Politics and Culture of Noise*. Edinburgh University Press, p. 56.

48 Merton, T. (1969) *Contemplative Prayer*. Doubleday, Random House, New York, NY, p. 16.

49 Latour, B. (2004) 'Why has critique run out of steam?' in *The Norton Anthology of Theory and Criticism*, 2nd Edition. W. W. Norton & Co., New York, pp. 2272–2302.

50 Scruton, R. (1994) *Modern Philosophy: An Introduction and Survey*. Reed International Ltd., London, pp. 29–31.

51 Walker, S. (2014) *Designing Sustainability*. Routledge, London, pp. 7–23.

52 Armstrong, K. (2005) *A Short History of Myth*. Canongate, Edinburgh, UK, pp. 2–23.

53 Armstrong, K. (2005) *A Short History of Myth*. Canongate, Edinburgh, UK.

233

54 McGilchrist, I. (2009) *The Master and His Emissary: The Divided Brain and the Making of the Western World*. Yale University Press, New Haven, CT, p. 86.

55 Eagleton, T. (2014) *Culture and the Death of God*. Yale University Press, New Haven, CT, p. 50.

56 MacCulloch, D. (2013) *Silence: A Christian History*. Allen Lane, Penguin Group, London, p. 213.

57 Armstrong, K. (2005) *A Short History of Myth*. Canongate, Edinburgh, UK, pp. 2–4.

58 Ibid., pp. 10, 32–33.

59 Ehrenfeld, J. and Hoffman, A. (2013) *Flourishing: A Frank Conversation about Sustainability*. Stanford University Press, Stanford, CA, p. 104.

60 Breton Connelly, J. (2014) *The Parthenon Enigma*. Head of Zeus Ltd., London, pp. xxii, 328–329.

61 Odent, M. (2013) *Childbirth and the Future of Homo Sapiens*. Pinter & Martin Ltd., London, p. 14.

62 McGilchrist, I. (2009) *The Master and His Emissary: The Divided Brain and the Making of the Western World*. Yale University Press, New Haven, CT, pp. 428–429.

63 Durbin, R. J., Waxman, H. A., Harkin, T., Rockefeller IV, J. D., Blumenthal, R., Markey, E. J., Brown, S., Reed, J., Boxer, B., Heitkamp, H., Merkley, J., and Pallone, F. (2013) 'Gateway to addiction: a survey of popular electronic cigarette manufacturers and target marketing to youth'. Available at: http://media.cleveland.com/health_impact/other/Report%20-%20E-Cigarettes%204%2014%2014.pdf, accessed 10 July 2014.

64 Doward, J. (2014) 'Tobacco giant "tried blackmail" to block Ugandan anti-smoking law'. *The Guardian* (London), 12 July 2014, available at: http://www.theguardian.com/business/2014/jul/12/bat-blackmail-uganda-smoking-law-tobacco, accessed 13 July 2014.

65 Fulcher, J. (2004) *Capitalism*. Oxford University Press, New York, NY, p. 10.

66 Jones, R. (2014) 'Wonga's fake legal letters passed to police'. *The Guardian* (London), 26 June 2014, available at: http://www.theguardian.com/business/2014/jun/26/wonga-fake-legal-letters-passed-police, accessed 10 July 2014.

67 Shiva, V. (2013) 'The seeds of suicide: how Monsanto destroys farming'. *Asian Age and Global Research*, 5 April 2013, available at: http://www.globalresearch.ca/the-seeds-of-suicide-how-monsanto-destroys-farming/5329947, accessed 30 May 2014.

68 Todhunter, C. (2013) 'Genetically engineered "terminator seeds": death and destruction of agriculture'. *Global Research*, Montreal, Canada, available at: http://www.globalresearch.ca/genetically-engineered-terminator-seeds-death-and-destruction-of-agriculture/5319797; accessed 6 August 2013.

69 Ahmed, I. (2012) 'KILLER SEEDS: the devastating impacts of Monsanto's genetically modified seeds in India.' *Global Research*, Montreal, Canada, available at: http://www.globalresearch.ca/killer-seeds-the-devastating-impacts-of-monsanto-s-genetically-modified-seeds-in-india/28629, accessed 6 August 2013.

70 Odent, M. (2013) *Childbirth and the Future of Homo Sapiens*. Pinter & Martin Ltd., London, pp. 106–107.

71 Howse, C. (2014) 'A peek at the catechism would be useful for any commentator on religion'. *The Tablet* (London), 5 July 2014, p. 10.

72 Clark, M. J. (2014) *The Vision of Catholic Social Thought: The Virtue of Solidarity and the Praxis of Human Rights*. Fortress Press, Minneapolis, MN, pp. 110–114.

73 Fulcher, J. (2004) *Capitalism*. Oxford University Press, New York, NY, p. 14.

74 Paton, G. (2014) 'Religious education subjected to "rank discrimination"', *The Telegraph* (London), 24 February 2014, available at: http://www.telegraph.co.uk/education/educationnews/10656555/Religious-education-subjected-to-rank-discrimination.html, accessed 3 March 2014.

75 Lloyd, S. (2013) 'RE: the truth unmasked – The supply of and support for Religious Education teachers: an inquiry by the All Party Parliamentary Group on Religious

Education'. *Religious Education Council of England and Wales*, London, March 2013, p. 4, available at: http://religiouseducationcouncil.org.uk/images/stories/pdf/APPG_RE_The_Truth_Unmasked.pdf, accessed 3 March 2014.

76 MacCulloch, D. (2013) *Silence: A Christian History*. Allen Lane, Penguin Group, London, p. 7.

77 Sim, S. (2007) *Manifesto for Silence: Confronting the Politics and Culture of Noise*. Edinburgh University Press, pp. 38, 59, 76.

78 Levitan, L., Cox, D. G., and Clarvoe, M. B. (2014) 'Avoiding pollution and saving farmers money by recycling agricultural plastic films'. CALS Impact Statement, Cornell University, Ithaca, NY, available at: http://vivo.cornell.edu/display/individual16665, accessed 31 May 2014.

79 Powell, A. (2012) 'Trouble afloat: ocean plastics Even in the most remote locations, the buildup of timeless debris grows'. *Harvard Gazette*, available at: http://news.harvard.edu/gazette/story/2012/02/trouble-afloat-ocean-plastics/, accessed 31 May 2014.

80 Rollo, K. (1997) 'Agricultural plastics – Boon or bane?' *Cornell Waste Management Institute*, Cornell University, Ithaca, NY, available at: http://cwmi.css.cornell.edu/agwaste.html, accessed 31 May 2014.

81 Herro, A. (2013) 'New bans on plastic bags may help protect marine life'. *Worldwatch Institute*, Washington, DC, available at: http://www.worldwatch.org/node/5565, accessed 31 May 2014.

82 USGS (2014) 'Environmental health, toxic substances – Biomagnification'. United States Geological Survey, *US Department of the Interior*, Washington, DC, available at: http://toxics.usgs.gov/definitions/biomagnification.html, accessed 10 June 2014.

83 Thompson, R. C. (2013) 'Written evidence submitted by Professor Prof. Richard C. Thompson (WQ17) [Water Quality 17]'. *Science and Technology Committee – Written Evidence*, House of Commons, UK Parliament, London, 28 February 2013, available at: http://www.publications.parliament.uk/pa/cm201213/cmselect/cmsctech/writev/932/contents.htm, accessed 13 July 2014.

84 EPA (2012) 'The Great Lakes today: concern – four toxic contaminants'. *US Environmental Protection Agency*, Washington, DC, available at: http://www.epa.gov/greatlakes/atlas/glat-ch4.html, accessed 10 June 2014.

85 Sim, S. (2007) *Manifesto for Silence: Confronting the Politics and Culture of Noise*. Edinburgh University Press, pp. 38, 50, 76.

86 Hansell, A. L., Blangiardo, M., Fortunato, L., Floud, S., et al. (2013) 'Aircraft noise and cardiovascular disease near Heathrow airport in London: small area study'. *British Medical Journal (BMJ)*, 347:f5432, available at: http://www.bmj.com/content/347/bmj.f5432, accessed 9 October 2013.

87 Duffy, E. (2004) *Faith of Our Fathers: Reflections on Catholic Tradition*. Continuum, London, p. 1.

88 Ward, B., trans. (1973) *The Prayers and Meditations of St. Anselm with the Proslogion*. Penguin Books, London, p. 244.

89 Walker, S. (2014) *Designing Sustainability*. Routledge, Abingdon, Oxford, pp. 54–71.

90 McGilchrist, I. (2009) *The Master and His Emissary: The Divided Brain and the Making of the Western World*. Yale University Press, New Haven, CT, p. 207.

91 Piketty, T. (2014) *Capital in the Twenty-First Century*. Harvard University Press, Cambridge, MA, p. 571.

92 Treanor, J. (2012) 'UBS corrupt payments exposed as bank pays £940m to settle Libor claims'. *The Guardian* (London), available at: http://www.theguardian.com/business/2012/dec/19/ubs-pays-libor-fixing-claims, accessed 27 April 2014.

93 Business Times (2014) 'Tech giants settle suit over no-poaching deal'. *The Business Times* (Singapore), available at: http://www.businesstimes.com.sg/print/1073763, accessed 27 April 2014.

94   Griffith, T., trans. (2000) *Plato: The Republic*. Ferrari, G. R. F. (ed.), Cambridge
     University Press, Cambridge, pp. 50–56.
95   Said, E. W. (1978) *Orientalism* [2003]. Penguin Books, London, p. 14.
96   Skidelsky, R, and Skidelsky, E. (2012) *How Much is Enough: Money and the Good
     Life*. Other Press, New York, NY, p. 210.
97   Davison, A. (2001) *Technology and the Contested Meanings of Sustainability*. State
     University of New York Press, Albany, NY, p. 29.
98   Thackara, J. (2005) *In the Bubble: Designing in a Complex World*. MIT Press,
     Cambridge, MA, p. 18.
99   E.g. Cox, S. (2014) 'Sebastian Cox: Designer and Craftsman', available at: http://
     sebastiancox.co.uk, accessed 10 June 2014.
100 E.g. Meroni, A., ed. (2007) *Creative Communities: People Inventing Sustainable Ways
     of Living*. Edizioni Poli.design, Milan.
101 Hawken, P. (2007) *Blessed Unrest*. Penguin Group, New York, NY.
102 Walker, S. (2014) *Designing Sustainability*, Routledge, London, pp. 24–86.
103 Buchanan, R. (1989) 'Declaration by design: rhetoric, argument, and demonstration in
     design practice' in Margolin, V. (ed.) *Design Discourse: History, Theory, Criticism*.
     The University of Chicago Press, Chicago, pp. 93–94.
104 Ibid., p. 94.
105 Walker, S. (2011) *The Spirit of Design*. Routledge, London.
106 Walker, S. (2014) *Designing Sustainability*. Routledge, London.
107 Walker, S. (2011) *The Spirit of Design*. Routledge, London, p. 151.
108 Walker, S. (2014) *Designing Sustainability*. Routledge, London, pp. 52–53.
109 Gaver, W. (2012) 'What should we expect from research through design?'
     Proceedings of the SIGCHI Conference on Human Factors in Computing Systems,
     5–10 May 2010, Austin, TX.
110 Shortt, R. (2016) *God Is No Thing: Coherent Christianity*. Hurst & Company, London,
     p. 63.
111 Ibid.
112 MacCulloch, D. (2013) *Silence: A Christian History*. Allen Lane, Penguin Group,
     London, pp. 129–136; Schama, S. (2009a) *A History of Britain, Volume 1*. The Bodley
     Head, London, p. 267.
113 Duffy, E. (2004) *Faith of Our Fathers*. Continuum, London, p. 2.
114 Turkle, S. (2011) *Alone Together: Why We Expect More from Technology and Less
     from Each Other*. Basic Books, New York, NY, pp. 15, 227–228; Carr, N. (2010) *The
     Shallows*. Atlantic Books, London, p. 116; Torrecilals, F. L. (2007) 'Four in ten young
     adults are mobile-phone addicts'. *The Medical News*, 27 February 2007, available at:
     www.news-medical.net/news/2007/02/27/22245.aspx, accessed 20 October 2010.
115 Ward, G. (2014) *Unbelievable*. I. B. Taurus, London, p. 82.
116 Renton, A. (2015) 'What would you pay to be happy?' *The Observer* (London), 10 May
     2015.

236

4 The Shift

An earlier version of this chapter was presented as a keynote address at the *Unmaking
Waste* conference in Adelaide, South Australia, 22–24 May 2015 and published in
proceedings. With kind permission of *Unmaking Waste 2015*, available at: http://
unmakingwaste2015.org/?page_id=2865, accessed 22 September 2015.

1   Gay, P. (2009) *Modernism: The Lure of Heresy for Baudelaire to Beckett and Beyond*.
    Vintage Books, London, p. 298.

2 Korten, D. C. (2006) *The Great Turning: From Empire to Earth Community*. Berrett-Koehler Publishers Inc., CA, pp. 68–70.

3 Holden, M. (2015) 'Cameron's conservatives vow tough new strike laws'. *Reuters* (London), 10 January 2015, available at: http://uk.reuters.com/article/2015/01/10/uk-britain-conservatives-unions-idUKKBN0KJ0EJ20150110, accessed 10 January 2015.

4 China Labor Watch (2014) 'iExploitation: Apple's supplier Jabil Circuit exploits workers to meet iPhone 6 demands'. China Labor Watch Report, *China Labor Watch*, 24 September 2014, available at: http://www.chinalaborwatch.org/upfile/2014_09_25/2014.09.25%20iExploitation%20at%20Jabil%20Wuxi%20EN.pdf, accessed 5 January 2014.

5 Kara, S. (2014) 'Tainted Carpets: slavery and child labor in India's hand-made carpet sector'. *FXB Center for Health and Human Rights*, Harvard School of Public Health, Harvard University, Boston, MA.

6 Wadsworth, M. (2007) 'IKEA exposed over "child labour" and green issues'. *The-Latest*, available at: http://www.the-latest.com/ikea-exposed-over-child-labour-and-green-issues, accessed 5 January 2014.

7 Oliver, J. G. J., Janssens-Maenhout, G., Muntean, M., and Peters, J. A. H. W. (2014) *2014 Report*. PBL Netherlands Environmental Assessment Agency, The Hague, p. 4.

8 Armenteras, D. and Finlayson, D. M., eds. (2012) 'Biodiversity'. *GEO5 – Global Environmental Outlook: Environment for the Future We Want*, p. 135, available at: http://www.unep.org/geo/pdfs/geo5/GEO5_report_full_en.pdf, accessed 26 January 2015.

9 Hickey, W. (2013) 'Apple avoids paying $17 million in taxes every day through a ballsy but genius tax avoidance scheme'. *Business Insider*, 21 May 2013, available at: http://www.businessinsider.com/how-apple-reduces-what-it-pays-in-taxes-2013-5?IR=T, accessed 5 January 2014.

10 Needhidasan, S., Samuel, M., and Chidambaram, R. (2014) 'Electronic waste – An emerging threat to the environment of urban India'. *Journal of Environmental Health Science and Engineering*, Vol. 12, No. 36, published online 20 January 2014, available at: http://www.ncbi.nlm.nih.gov/pmc/articles/PMC3908467/, accessed 29 January 2015.

11 Leonard, A. (2010) *The Story of Stuff*. Constable and Robinson Ltd., London, pp. 184–189.

12 Piketty, T. (2014) *Capital in the Twenty-First Century*. Harvard University Press, Cambridge, MA, pp. 298–300.

13 Lillford, P. (2015) 'The Secret Life of Packaging'. *The Food Chain*, BBC World Service, broadcast 23 January 2015.

14 Kristeva, J. (1995) *New Maladies of the Soul*. Guberman, R. (trans.), Columbia University Press, New York, NY, p. 27.

15 Klein, N. (2014) *This Changes Everything: Capitalism vs. the Climate*. Allen Lane, London, pp. 87–91.

16 Skidelsky, R. and Skidelsky, E. (2012) *How Much Is Enough: Money and the Good Life*. Other Press, New York, NY, pp. 210–211.

17 Klein, N. (2014) *This Changes Everything: Capitalism vs. the Climate*. Allen Lane, London, pp. 56–63, 87.

18 Fischer-Kowalski, M., Swilling, M., von Weizsäcker, E.U., Ren, Y., Moriguchi, Y., Crane, W., Krausmann, F., Eisenmenger, N., Giljum, S., Hennicke, P., Romero Lankao, P., Sirihan Manalanq, A., and Sewerin, S. (2011) 'Decoupling natural resource use and environmental impacts from economic growth – A report of the working group on decoupling to the International Resource Panel'. *United National Environmental Programme*, pp. xiii, 7, 30, available at: http://www.unep.org/resourcepanel/decoupling/files/pdf/decoupling_report_english.pdf, accessed 27 November 2014.

19 Neumark, D., Zhang, J., and Ciccarella, S. (2008) 'The effects of Wal-Mart on local labor markets'. *Journal of Urban Economics*, No. 63, pp. 422, 428.

20 Irwin, E. G. and Clark, J. (2007) 'The local costs and benefits of Wal-Mart'. *Downtown Economics*, Center for Community & Economic Development, University of Wisconsin Extension, Madison, WI, available at: http://fyi.uwex.edu/downtowneconomics/files/2012/07/local-cost-and-benefits-of-walmart.pdf, accessed 25 November 2014.

21 Tweed, K. (2013) 'Global e-waste will jump 33 percent in the next five years'. *IEEE Spectrum*, 17 December 2013, available at: http://spectrum.ieee.org/energywise/energy/environment/global-ewaste-will-jump-33-in-next-five-years, accessed 29 November 2014.

22 Gorz, A. (2010) *Ecologica*. Seagull Books, London, p. 145.

23 Fischer, D. (2013) '"Dark money" funds climate change denial effort'. *Scientific American*, 23 December 2013, available at: http://www.scientificamerican.com/article/dark-money-funds-climate-change-denial-effort/, accessed 13 February 2015.

24 RFF (2016) 'RFF's decision to divest'. *The Rockefeller Family Fund*, available at: http://www.rffund.org/divestment, accessed 23 March 2016.

25 Williams, R. (2014) 'Divine understanding: An exploration of the fundamental connection between faith and human perception spans neuroscience, philosophy and theology': a book review of *Unbelievable: Why We Believe and Why We Don't* by Graham Ward, *The Tablet* (London), 20/27 December 2014, p. 38.

26 Miller, H. (1957) *Big Sur and the Oranges of Hieronymus Bosch*. New Directions Publishing Corporation, New York, NY, p. 25.

27 Nicoll, M. (1950) *The New Man* [1972]. Penguin Books, Baltimore, MD, p. 164.

28 Science strives to provide a natural explanation of worldly phenomena and, even if such an explanation is not presently available, it presupposes that, sooner or later such an explanation will be forthcoming if further research is conducted. This presupposition is what drives scientific knowledge forward. However, the presupposition itself is not scientific, is not founded on human reasoning powers or evidence-based research and is not provable; rather, it is a belief – a form of faith or trust in the veracity of the scientific endeavour.

29 Duffin, J. (2009) *Medical Miracles. Doctors, Saints, and Healing in the Modern World*. Oxford University Press, Oxford, pp. 183–190, available at: http://inters.org/religion-medicine-and-miracles, accessed 28 November 2014.

30 Greene, G. (1938) *Brighton Rock*. Vintage, London, p. 151.

31 Scruton, R. (2014) *The Soul of the World*. Princeton University Press, Princeton, NJ, pp. 32–40.

32 Cottingham, J. (2014) *Philosophy of Religion: Towards a More Humane Approach*. Cambridge University Press, New York, NY, pp. 6–7.

33 Ward, G. (2014) *Unbelievable: Why We Believe and Why We Don't*. I. B. Taurus, London, p. 7.

34 Scruton, R. (2014) *The Soul of the World*. Princeton University Press, Princeton, NJ, p. 48.

35 Chesterton, G. (1908) *Orthodoxy*. Image Book, Doubleday, New York, NY, pp. 10, 44.

36 Zipes, J., trans. & ed. (2014) 'Introduction: rediscovering the original tales of the Brothers Grimm' in Zipes, J. (trans. and ed.) *The First Complete Edition: The Original Folk & Fairy Tales of the Brothers Grimm*, Princeton University Press, Oxford, pp. xxxv–xxxvi.

37 Ibid., p. xxv.

38 Moore, R. K. (2014) 'The localization movement. Creating a viable local economy. Challenging the new world order'. *Centre for Research on Globalization*, 27 February 2014, available at: http://www.globalresearch.ca/the-localization-movement-creating-a-

viable-local-economy-challenging-the-new-world-order/5371155, accessed 13 February 2014.

39 Daly, H. (2007) *Ecological Economics and Sustainable Development: Selected Essays of Herman Daly.* Edward Elgar, Cheltenham, UK, pp. 12–24.

40 Yunus, M. (2007) *Creating a World Without Poverty.* Public Affairs, New York, NY, pp. 49–56.

41 Strauss, C. F. and Fuad-Luke, A. (2008) 'The slow design principles: a new interrogative and reflexive tool for design research and practice' in Cipolla, C. and Peruccio, P. P. (eds.) *Changing the Change Proceedings.* Politecnico di Milano, Italy, pp. 1440–1453, available at: http://www.allemandi.com/university/ctc.pdf, accessed 25 November 2014.

42 Evans, M., Walker, S., Cassidy, T., and Twigger Holroyd, A. (2014) 'Design routes: envisioning the future of culturally significant designs, products and practices'. AHRC Funded Research Project, available at: http://imagination.lancs.ac.uk/activities/Design_Routes, accessed 25 November 2014.

43 Nugraha, A. (2012) 'Transforming tradition: a method for maintaining tradition in a craft and design context'. PhD dissertation, Aalto University, School of the Arts, Design and Architecture, Helsinki, Finland.

44 Perry, G. (2014) 'Making meaning in the arts: Grayson Perry in conversation with Prof. Charlie Gere'. Lancaster Institute for the Contemporary Arts, Lancaster University, 28 November 2014.

45 Bouteneff, P. C. (2015) *Arvo Pärt: Out of Silence.* St. Vladimir's Seminary Press, Yonkers, New York, NY, p. 14.

46 Klein, N. (2014) *This Changes Everything: Capitalism vs. The Climate.* Allen Lane, London, p. 59.

47 Ward, G. (2014) *Unbelievable: Why We Believe and Why We Don't.* I. B. Taurus, London, p. 77.

48 Nicoll, M. (1950) *The New Man* [1972]. Penguin Books, Baltimore, MD, pp. 88–89.

49 Edwards, B. (2012) *Drawing of the Right Side of the Brain: A Course in Enhancing Creativity and Artistic Confidence*, 4th Edition. Souvenir Press, London, p. 247.

50 McGilchrist, I. (2009) *The Master and His Emissary: The Divided Brain and the Making of the Western World.* Yale University Press, New Haven, CT, p. 65.

51 Scruton, R. (2014) *The Soul of the World.* Princeton University Press, Princeton, NJ, p. 76.

52 Merton, T. (1969) *Contemplative Prayer.* Doubleday, Random House, New York, NY, pp. 57–58.

53 Van Nes, N. (2010) 'Understanding replacement behaviour and exploring design solutions' in Cooper, T. (ed.) *Longer Lasting Products: Alternatives to the Throwaway Society.* Gower Publishing Limited, Farnham, UK, p. 109.

54 Ruskin, J. (1838) *The Poetry of Architecture.* Part I 'The Cottage', pp. 8, 19–20, available at: http://www.gutenberg.org/cache/epub/17774/pg17774.txt, accessed 30 November 2014.

55 Perry, G. (2014) 'Making meaning in the arts: Grayson Perry in conversation with Prof. Charlie Gere'. *Lancaster Institute for the Contemporary Arts*, Lancaster University, 28 November 2014.

239

5 Creativity

1 Miller, H. (1957) *Big Sur and the Oranges of Hieronymus Bosch.* New Directions Publishing Corporation, New York, NY, p. 13.

2 Cain, S. (2012) *Quiet.* Penguin Books, London, pp. 73–74.

3 Figgis, M. (2013) 'Why British film is all kitsch 'n' sink'. *The Observer* (London), 22 June 2013, available at: http://www.guardian.co.uk/film/2013/jun/22/mike-figgis-defeatist-british-film-industry, accessed 23 June 2013.

4 Feist, G. J. (1999) 'Autonomy and independence' in Runco, M. A. and Protzker, S. R. (eds.) *Encyclopedia of Creativity*, Vol. 1, 2nd Edition, pp. 157–162.

5 Hughes, R. (1980) 'Episode 8. The future that was'. *The Shock of the New*, BBC TV Series, London, 56:34–57:13, available at: https://www.youtube.com/watch?v=AFc1BeS0vKI, accessed 20 December 2015.

6 Lanier, J. (2006) 'Digital Maoism'. *Edge*, May 2006, available at: http://edge.org/conversation/digital-maoism-the-hazards-of-the-new-online-collectivism, accessed 5 October 2014.

7 Ibid.

8 Lanier, J. (2010) *You Are Not a Gadget: A Manifesto*. Allen Lane, Penguin Group, London, p. 56.

9 Lanier, J. (2006) 'Digital Maoism'. *Edge*, May 2006, available at: http://edge.org/conversation/digital-maoism-the-hazards-of-the-new-online-collectivism, accessed 5 October 2014.

10 Lanier, J. (2010) *You Are Not a Gadget: A Manifesto*. Allen Lane, Penguin Group, London, pp. 126–132.

11 Norman, D. A. and Verganti, R. (2014) 'Incremental and radical innovation: design research vs. technology and meaning change'. *Design Issues*, Vol. 30, No. 1, p. 79.

12 Ibid.

13 Coutts, L. M. and Gruman, J. A. (2012). 'Applying social psychology to organizations' in Schneider, F. W., Gruman, J. A., and Coutts, L. M. (eds.) *Applied Social Psychology: Understanding and Addressing Social and Practical Problems*, p. 238. Sage, Los Angeles, CA.

14 Lanier, J. (2006) 'Digital Maoism'. *Edge*, May 2006, available at: http://edge.org/conversation/digital-maoism-the-hazards-of-the-new-online-collectivism, accessed 5 October 2014.

15 Coutts, L. M. and Gruman, J. A. (2012). 'Applying social psychology to organizations' in Schneider, F. W., Gruman, J. A., and Coutts, L. M. (eds.) *Applied Social Psychology: Understanding and Addressing Social and Practical Problems*, p. 238. Sage, Los Angeles, CA.

16 Oxford English Dictionary, Oxford University Press, 2016 Online Edition, accessed via Lancaster University Library.

17 Zeckhauser, R. (2013) 'The wisdom of crowds and the stupidity of herds'. Presentation to School of Information, Harvard Kennedy School, University of Michigan, 21 March 2013, available at: http://stiet.cms.si.umich.edu/sites/stiet.cms.si.umich.edu/files/The%20Wisdom%20of%20Crowds%20and%20the%20Stupidity%20of%20Herds%20Presentation%20Results.pdf, accessed 29 September 2014.

18 Cain, S. (2012) *Quiet*. Penguin Books, London, pp. 88–89.

19 Bisadi, M., Mozaffar, F., and Hosseini, S. B. (2012) 'Future research centers: the place of creativity and innovation'. *Asia Pacific International Conference on Environment-Behaviour Studies* (AicE-Bs2012 Cairo), Giza, Egypt, 31 October–2 November 2012. Published in *Procedia – Social and Behavioural Sciences*, Vol. 68, pp. 240–241.

20 Baldry, C. and Barnes, A. (2012) 'The open-plan academy: space, control and the undermining of professional identity'. *Work Employment Society*, Vol. 26, No. 2, pp. 229, 240.

21 Cottingham, J. (2014) *Philosophy of Religion: Towards a More Humane Approach*. Cambridge University Press, New York, NY, p. 6.

22 McGilchrist, I. (2009) *The Master and His Emissary: The Divided Brain and the Making of the Western World*. Yale University Press, New Haven, CT, pp. 65, 259–260.

23 Manzini, E. (2013) 'Against Post-It design: to make things happen'. Personal correspondence, available for DESIS Lab Coordinators and Operations Managers at: http://www.desis-network.org/sites/default/files/newsletters/10/DESISnewsletter10. html.

24 Coutts, L. M. and Gruman, J. A. (2012). 'Applying social psychology to organizations' in Schneider, F. W., Gruman, J. A., and Coutts, L. M. (eds.) *Applied Social Psychology: Understanding and Addressing Social and Practical Problems*, p. 238. Sage, Los Angeles, CA.

25 Zeckhauser, R. (2013) 'The wisdom of crowds and the stupidity of herds'. Presentation to School of Information, Harvard Kennedy School, University of Michigan, 21 March 2013, available at: http://stiet.cms.si.umich.edu/sites/stiet.cms.si.umich.edu/files/ The%20Wisdom%20of%20Crowds%20and%20the%20Stupidity%20of%20 Herds%20Presentation%20Results.pdf, accessed 29 September 2014.

26 Coutts, L. M. and Gruman, J. A. (2012). 'Applying social psychology to organizations' in Schneider, F. W., Gruman, J. A., and Coutts, L. M. (eds.) *Applied Social Psychology: Understanding and Addressing Social and Practical Problems*, p. 238. Sage, Los Angeles, CA.

27 Cornwell, J. (2014) *The Dark Box*. Profile Books, Books, p. 53.

28 C. W. and A. J. K. D. (2013) 'Was tulipmania irrational?' *The Economist* (London), 4 October 2013, available at: http://www.economist.com/blogs/freeexchange/2013/10/ economic-history, accessed 11 November 2014.

29 Taylor, C. (2007) *A Secular Age*. The Belknap Press of Harvard University Press, Cambridge, MA, p. 89.

30 Arrington, M. (2010) 'Digg's biggest problem is its users and their constant opinions on things'. Available at: http://techcrunch.com/2010/05/12/diggs-biggest-problem-are-its-users-and-their-constant-opinions-on-things/, accessed 19 October 2014.

31 Variety Staff (1966) 'Review: "Casino Royale"'. *Variety*, 31 December 1966, available at: http://variety.com/1966/film/reviews/casino-royale-1200421405/, accessed 3 November 2014.

32 TV Guide (n. d.) '"Casino Royale" 1967 review'. *TV Guide*, available at: http://movies. tvguide.com/casino-royale/review/110477, accessed 3 November 2014.

33 Ebert, R. (1967) 'Casino Royale'. *RogerEbert.com*, available at: http://www.rogerebert. com/reviews/casino-royale-1967, accessed 11 November 2014.

34 Sheldrake, R. (2012) *The Science Delusion*. Coronet, Hodder & Stoughton, London, pp. 37–38.

35 Lanier, J. (2010) *You Are Not a Gadget: A Manifesto*. Allen Lane, Penguin Group, London, p. 50.

36 Edwards, B. (2012) *Drawing of the Right Side of the Brain: A Course in Enhancing Creativity and Artistic Confidence*, 4th Edition. Souvenir Press, London, p. 40.

37 Cottingham, J. (2014) *Philosophy of Religion: Towards a More Humane Approach*. Cambridge University Press, New York, NY, p. 6.

38 McGilchrist, I. (2009) *The Master and His Emissary: The Divided Brain and the Making of the Western World*. Yale University Press, New Haven, CT, p. 65.

39 Sim, S. (2007) *Manifesto for Silence: Confronting the Politics and Culture of Noise*. Edinburgh University Press, p. 50.

40 MacCulloch, D. (2013) *Silence: A Christian History*. Allen Lane, Penguin Group, London, p. 220.

41 Franck, F. (1973) *The Zen of Seeing Seeing/Drawing as Meditation*. Vintage Books, New York, NY, p. xii.

42 Cain, S. (2012) *Quiet*. Penguin Books, London, p. 84.

241

43 Baldry, C. and Barnes, A. (2012) 'The open-plan academy: space, control and the undermining of professional identity'. *Work Employment Society*, Vol. 26, No. 2, pp. 229, 240.

44 Scollard, J. R. (1987) *The Self-Employed Woman*. Pocket Books, Simon and Schuster, New York, NY, p. 87.

45 MacCulloch, D. (2013) *Silence: A Christian History*. Allen Lane, Penguin Group, London, p. 17.

46 Edwards, B. (2012) *Drawing of the Right Side of the Brain: A Course in Enhancing Creativity and Artistic Confidence*, 4th edition. Souvenir Press, London, p. 4.

47 See Scruton, R. (2014) *The Soul of the World*. Princeton University Press, Princeton, NJ, p. 47.

48 Ares (2014) 'Ecodesign – Your future: how ecodesign can help products smarter'. *The Ecodesign Directive*, Report No. 1206343, 16 April 2014, The Directorate-General for Enterprise & Industry and The Directorate-General for Energy, European Commission, p. 3, available at: http://ec.europa.eu/geninfo/query/index. do?queryText=How+ecodesign+can+help&query_source=GROWTH&summary= summary&more_options_source=restricted&more_options_date=*&more_options_ date_from=&more_options_date_to=&more_options_language=en&more_options_f_ formats=*&swlang=en, accessed 23 March 2016.

49 Donne, J. (1990) 'Meditation XVII: Nunc lento sonitu dicunt, morieris' in Carey, J. (ed.) *The Major Works including Songs and Sonnets*. Oxford University Press, Oxford, p. 344.

50 Duchamp, M. (1957) 'The creative act'. Session on the Creative Act, Convention of the American Federation of Arts, April 1957, Houston, TX, available at: http://www. wisdomportal.com/Cinema-Machine/Duchamp-CreativeAct.html, accessed 25 November 2014.

51 Ibid.

52 Thackara, J. (2005) *In the Bubble: Designing in a Complex World*. MIT Press, Cambridge, MA.

53 Buchanan, R. (1989) 'Declaration by design: rhetoric, argument, and demonstration in design practice' in Margolin, V. (ed.) *Design Discourse: History, Theory, Criticism*. The University of Chicago Press, Chicago, IL, pp. 93–94.

54 SFMOMA (2011) 'Less and more: the design ethos of dieter rams'. San Francisco Museum of Modern Art, 29 June 2011, available at: http://www.sfmoma.org/about/ press/press_exhibitions/releases/880, accessed 3 November 2014.

55 McGilchrist, I. (2009) *The Master and His Emissary: The Divided Brain and the Making of the Western World*. Yale University Press, New Haven, CT, p. 314.

56 Ibid., p. 237.

57 Foley, M. (2010) *The Age of Absurdity: Why Modern Life Makes It Hard to Be Happy*. Simon & Schuster Ltd., London, p. 94.

58 Sim, S. (2007) *Manifesto for Silence: Confronting the Politics and Culture of Noise*. Edinburgh University Press, p. 64.

59 Edwards, B. (2012) *Drawing of the Right Side of the Brain: A course in enhancing creativity and artistic confidence*, 4th Edition. Souvenir Press, London, p. xvii.

60 McGilchrist, I. (2009) *The Master and His Emissary: The Divided Brain and the Making of the Western World*. Yale University Press, New Haven, CT, p. 309.

61 Gitlin, T. (2014) 'Where are the Occupy protesters now?' *The Guardian* (London), available at: http://www.theguardian.com/cities/2014/jun/17/where-occupy-protesters-now-social-media, accessed 11 November 2014.

6 The Mesh

A shorter version of this chapter appeared as Design for the Living World: advancing beyond modern dogmas to create meaningful 'goods' in the Journal for Mesoamerican Studies *Ketzalcalli*, 2014, No. 2, pp. 9–20, Kommission Verlag für Ethnologie, Hannover, Germany.

1 Ward, G. (2014) *Unbelievable: Why We Believe and Why We Don't*. I. B. Tauris, London, p. 81.
2 Davies, W. (2015) *The Happiness Industry: How the Government and Big Business Sold Us Well-Being*. Verso, London, p. 23.
3 Mortley, R. (1986) *From Word to Silence*. Bond University, Australia, available at: http://epublications.bond.edu.au/word_to_silence_I/, p160, accessed 13 June 2013.
4 Cottingham, J. (2014) *Philosophy of Religion: Towards a More Humane Approach*. Cambridge University Press, New York, NY, pp. 2–3.
5 Ibid., pp. 19–20.
6 Ward, G. (2014) *Unbelievable: Why We Believe and Why We Don't*. I. B. Tauris, London, p. 17.
7 Nagel, T. (2013) *Mind and Cosmos: Why the Materialist Neo-Darwinian Conception of Nature is Almost Certainly False*. Oxford University Press, Oxford, p. 16.
8 Scruton, R. (2014) *The Soul of the World*. Princeton University Press, Princeton, NJ, pp. 31–32.
9 McGilchrist, I. (2009) *The Master and His Emissary: The Divided Brain and the Making of the Western World*. Yale University Press, New Haven, CT, p. 170.
10 Ward, G. (2014) *Unbelievable: Why We Believe and Why We Don't*. I. B. Tauris, London, p. 77.
11 Ibid., p. 75.
12 Odent, M. (2013) *Childbirth and the Future of Homo Sapiens*. Pinter & Martin Ltd., London, pp. 124–125.
13 Ibid., p. 33.
14 Cottingham, J. (2014) *Philosophy of Religion: Towards a More Humane Approach*. Cambridge University Press, New York, NY, pp. 2–7.
15 Davies, W. (2015) *The Happiness Industry: How the Government and Big Business Sold Us Well-Being*. Verso, London, p. 17.
16 Macalister, T. (2015) 'Joseph Stiglitz: unsurprising Jeremy Corbyn is a Labour leadership contender'. *The Guardian* (London), 26 July 2015, available at: http://www.theguardian.com/politics/2015/jul/26/joseph-stiglitz-jeremy-corbyn-labour-leadership-contender-anti-austerity, accessed 27 July 2015.
17 Bourguignon, F. (2015) *The Globalization of Inequality*. Princeton University Press, Princeton and Oxford, pp. 117–118.
18 Campbell, J. (2014) *Roy Jenkins: A Well-Rounded Life*. Jonathan Cape, London, p. 666 referring to an article in the *Times* (London) of 8 April 1988.
19 Armstrong, K. (2007) *The Bible: The Biography*. Atlantic Books, London, pp. 168–175.
20 Scruton, R. (2014) *The Soul of the World*. Princeton University Press, Princeton, NJ, pp. 31–30.
21 Eagleton, T. (2007) *The Meaning of Life*. Oxford University Press, Oxford, pp. 50, 93.
22 Pozzo di Borgo, P. (2014) Interview in 'To Die with Dignity?' *Heart and Soul*, BBC World Service, London, broadcast 30 September 2014.
23 Mortley, R. (1986) *From Word to Silence*. Bond University, Australia, available at: http://epublications.bond.edu.au/word_to_silence_I/, p. 160, accessed 13 June 2013.
24 Ward, G. (2014) *Unbelievable: Why We Believe and Why We Don't*. I. B. Tauris, London, p. 72.

25 Palmer, M. and Wagner, K. (2013) 'ValuesQuest: the search for values that will make a world of difference'. Discussion paper, *Club of Rome*, p. 11, available at: http://www.clubofrome.org/cms/wp-content/uploads/2013/02/VALUESQUEST-The-search-for-values-that-will-make-a-world-of-difference.pdf, accessed 8 September 2013.

26 Rilke, R. M. (1903) *Letters to a Young Poet*. Soulard, R., Jr. (ed.), Scriptor Press, Malden, MA, p. 14, available at: https://kbachuntitled.files.wordpress.com/2013/04/rainer-maria-rilke-letters-to-a-young-poet.pdf, accessed 12 April 2015.

27 Scruton, R. (2014) *The Soul of the World*. Princeton University Press, Princeton, NJ, pp. 31–75.

28 Howes, G. (2007) *The Art of the Sacred: An Introduction to the Aesthetics of Art and Belief*. I. B. Taurus, London, p. 131.

29 Ibid., p. 27.

30 Ward, G. (2014) *Unbelievable: Why We Believe and Why We Don't*. I. B. Tauris, London, p. 62.

31 Cottingham, J. (2014) *Philosophy of Religion: Towards a More Humane Approach*. Cambridge University Press, New York, NY, pp. 2–7. Cottingham here reinforces his argument by referring to Stump, E. (2010) *Wandering in Darkness*, Oxford University Press, Oxford, pp. 26–27.

32 McGilchrist, I. (2009) *The Master and His Emissary: The Divided Brain and the Making of the Western World*. Yale University Press, New Haven, CT, p. 28.

33 Ibid., pp. 28–29.

34 Eliot, T. S. (1963) *Collected Poems 1909–1962*. Faber and Faber, London, pp. 213–214.

35 Hart, R. (1979) *Unfinished Man and the Imagination*, Herder and Herder, New York, NY, p. 19, quoted in Howes, G. (2007) *The Art of the Sacred: An Introduction to the Aesthetics of Art and Belief*. I. B. Taurus, London, pp. 160–161.

36 McGilchrist, I. (2009) *The Master and His Emissary: The Divided Brain and the Making of the Western World*. Yale University Press, New Haven, CT, pp. 55–59, 309.

37 Ward, G. (2014) *Unbelievable: Why We Believe and Why We Don't*. I. B. Tauris, London, pp. 10–12, 77.

38 Rowson, J. and McGilchrist, I. (2013) 'Divided brain, divided world: why the best part of us struggles to be heard'. *Royal Society of Arts*, London, pp. 4–5, available at: http://www.thersa.org/__data/assets/pdf_file/0019/1016083/RSA-Divided-Brain-Divided-World.PDF, accessed 14 November 2013.

39 Scruton, R. (2014) *The Soul of the World*. Princeton University Press, Princeton, NJ, p. 1.

40 Gardener, C. and Sheppard, J. (1989) *Consuming Passion: The Rise of Retail Culture*. Routledge, Abingdon, p. 53.

41 Wittgenstein, L. (1922) *Tractatus Logico-Philosophicus*. Kegan Paul, Trench, Trubner & Co., Ltd., London, p. 90, available at: https://www.gutenberg.org/files/5740/5740-pdf.pdf, accessed 8 June 2015.

42 Wittgenstein, L. (1953) *Philosophical Investigations*, 3rd Edition. Basil Blackwell, Oxford, p. 10.

43 Cottingham, J. (2014) *Philosophy of Religion: Towards a More Humane Approach*. Cambridge University Press, New York, NY, p. 10.

44 Hick, J. (1989) *An Interpretation of Religion: Human Responses to the Transcendent*. Yale Unity Press, New Haven, CT, pp. 130–131.

45 Scruton, R. (2014) *The Soul of the World*. Princeton University Press, Princeton, NJ, pp. 76–77.

46 Cottingham, J. (2014) *Philosophy of Religion: Towards a More Humane Approach*. Cambridge University Press, New York, NY, pp. 21–22.

47 Ibid., p. 29.

48 Pagels, E. (2003) *Beyond Belief*. Vintage Books, New York, NY, p. 9.

49 Merton, T. (1969) *Contemplative Prayer*. Doubleday, Random House, New York, NY, p. 16.

50 MacCulloch, D. (2013) *Silence: A Christian History*. Allen Lane, Penguin Group, London, p. 120.

51 Merton quoted in Furlong, M. (1980) *Merton: A Biography*. Harper and Row, San Francisco, CA, p. 22.

52 McGilchrist, I. (2009) *The Master and His Emissary: The Divided Brain and the Making of the Western World*. Yale University Press, New Haven, CT, p. 86.

53 Furlong, M. (1971) *Contemplating Now*. Hodder & Stoughton, London, p. 13 (quoted in Sim, 2007, p. 64).

54 McGilchrist, I. (2009) *The Master and His Emissary: The Divided Brain and the Making of the Western World*. Yale University Press, New Haven, CT, p. 314.

55 Odent, M. (2013) *Childbirth and the Future of Homo Sapiens*. Pinter & Martin Ltd., London, pp. 114, 124–125.

56 Cottingham, J. (2014) *Philosophy of Religion: Towards a More Humane Approach*. Cambridge University Press, New York, NY, p. 16.

57 Eagleton, T. (2014) *Culture and the Death of God*. Yale University Press, New Haven, CT, p. ix.

58 Howes, G. (2007) *The Art of the Sacred: An Introduction to the Aesthetics of Art and Belief*. I. B. Taurus, London, p. 150.

59 Eagleton, T. (2014) *Culture and the Death of God*. Yale University Press, New Haven, CT, p. ix.

60 Scruton, R. (2014) *The Soul of the World*. Princeton University Press, Princeton, NJ, p. 11.

61 Chidester, D. (2000) *Christianity: A Global History*. HarperCollins, New York, NY.

62 Ibid.

63 McGilchrist, I. (2009) *The Master and His Emissary: The Divided Brain and the Making of the Western World*. Yale University Press, New Haven, CT, p. 441.

64 MacCulloch, D. (2013) *Silence: A Christian History*. Allen Lane, Penguin Group, London, pp. 110–112.

65 Scruton, R. (2016) *Confessions of a Heretic*. Notting Hill Editions, London, pp. 2–3.

66 Davies, W. (2015) *The Happiness Industry: How the Government and Big Business Sold Us Well-Being*. Verso, London, pp. 24–26.

67 EAston (2015) 'Hitachi developed a wearable device that can measure happiness'. *WT VOX*, 2 September 2015, available at: https://wtvox.com/2015/02/hitachi-developed-a-wearable-device-that-can-measure-happiness/, accessed 20 June 2015.

68 Elfenbein, E. (2014) 'Wear are we going? The future of wearable happiness'. *The Coca-Cola Company*, 15 May 2014, available at: http://www.coca-colacompany.com/innovation/wear-are-we-going-the-future-of-wearable-happiness, accessed 23 June 2015.

69 Galer, S. (2015) 'Health, wealth and happiness: are we just a wearable away from having it all?' *Forbes*, 2 April 2015, available at: http://www.forbes.com/sites/sap/2015/04/02/health-wealth-and-happiness-are-we-just-a-wearable-away-from-having-it-all/, accessed 21 June 2015.

70 Ward, G. (2014) *Unbelievable: Why We Believe and Why We Don't*. I. B. Tauris, London, pp. 42–43.

71 Blake, W. (1790) 'The marriage of heaven and hell – A memorable fancy'. *The Selected Poems of William Blake* [1994], Wordsworth Editions Ltd. Ware, Hertfordshire, UK, p. 201.

72 Cavafy, C. P. (2013) *Selected Poems*. Connolly, D. (trans.), Aiora Press, Athens, p. 25.

73 Gospel of John, New Testament, *The Holy Bible – New International Version*, Hodder and Stoughton, London, 1978, p. 144.

245

74 Marco Polo and Rustichello of Pisa (ca. 130) *The Travels of Marco Polo*, Volume 1
    [2004]. Chapter LXI, 'Of the City of Chandu [Xanadu], and the Kaan's Palace There'.
    [p. 632 of PDF file] available at: http://hudsoncress.net/hudsoncress.org/html/library/
    history-travel/marco-polo-vol1.pdf, accessed 25 October 2015.

7 Rhythms

1   Overell, S., Mills, T., Roberts, S., Lekhi, R., and Blaug, R. (2010) 'The employment
    relationship and the quality of work'. Provocation paper 7, The Good Work Commission,
    The Work Foundation, London, pp. 72–73, available at: http://www.goodworkcommission.
    co.uk/Assets/Docs/ReportsWithCovers/07.EmploymentRelationshipQualityOfWork.pdf,
    accessed 14 September 2015.
2   Ibid.
3   Deloitte (2014) 'London Futures – Agiletown: the relentless march of technology and
    London's response'. *Deloitte LLP*, London, p. 5.
4   Rebanks, J. (2015) *The Shepherd's Life: A Tale of the Lake District*. Allen Lane, Penguin
    Random House, London, pp. 18–41.
5   Cather, W. (1927) *Death Comes for the Archbishop* [1990]. Vintage Classics, Random
    House, New York, NY, pp. 33–34.
6   Riley, J., Corkhill, B., and Morris, C. (2013) 'The benefits of knitting for personal and
    social wellbeing in adulthood: findings from an international survey'. *British Journal of
    Occupational Therapy*, Vol. 76, No. 2, p. 50.
7   Sennett, R. (2008) *The Craftsman*. Penguin, London, p. 7.
8   Walker, S. (2006) *Sustainable by Design – Explorations in Theory and Practice*.
    Routledge, Abingdon, Oxford, pp. 44–50.
9   Panksepp, J. (1998) Appendix B: 'The brain, language, and affective neuroscience' in
    Affective Neuroscience: The Foundations of Human and Animal Emotions. Oxford
    University Press, Oxford, p. 335.
10 Odent, M. (2013) *Childbirth and the Future of Homo Sapiens*. Pinter & Martin Ltd.,
    London, pp. 38–39.
11 Ibid., pp. 22, 26, 58.
12 McGilchrist, I. (2009) *The Master and His Emissary: The Divided Brain and the Making
    of the Western World*. Yale University Press, New Haven, CT, p. 405.
13 Sennett, R. (2008) *The Craftsman*. Penguin, London, pp. 2–8.
14 Ibid., pp. 27, 31–32.
15 Riley, J., Corkhill, B., and Morris, C. (2013) 'The benefits of knitting for personal and
    social wellbeing in adulthood: findings from an international survey'. *British Journal of
    Occupational Therapy*, Vol. 76, No. 2, p. 51.
16 Eisner, E. W. (2002) *The Arts and the Creation of Mind*. Yale University Press, New
    Haven, CT, p. 7.
17 Sennett, R. (2008) *The Craftsman*. Penguin, London, p. 39.
18 Franklin, U. M. (2006) *The Ursula Franklin Reader: Pacifism as a Map*. Between the
    Lines, Toronto, ON, p. 17.
19 Sennett, R. (2008) *The Craftsman*. Penguin, London, p. 174.
20 Borgmann, A. (1984) *Technology and the Character of Contemporary Life* [1987].
    The University of Chicago Press, Chicago, IL, p. 207.
21 Ibid., p. 208.
22 Sennett, R. (2008) *The Craftsman*. Penguin, London, p. 288.
23 Fischer, A. (2015) Personal communication, 24 September 2015. Andrea Fischer,
    Director, *Andrea Fisher Fine Pottery*, Santa Fe, NM.
24 Nunn, T. M. (2001) *Sin Nombre: Hispana and Hispano Artists of the New Deal Era*.
    University of New Mexico Press, Albuquerque, NM, p. xi.

25 Fischer, A. (2015) Personal communication, 24 September 2015. Andrea Fischer, Director, *Andrea Fisher Fine Pottery*, Santa Fe, NM.

26 McGilchrist, I. (2009) *The Master and His Emissary: The Divided Brain and the Making of the Western World*. Yale University Press, New Haven, CT, p. 28.

27 Edwards, B. (2013) *Drawing of the Right Side of the Brain: A Course in Enhancing Creativity and Artistic Confidence*, 4th Edition. Souvenir Press, London, p. xxvii.

28 Ward, G. (2014) *Unbelievable: Why We Believe and Why We Don't*. I. B. Tauris, London, p. 46.

29 Edwards, B. (2013) *Drawing of the Right Side of the Brain: A Course in Enhancing Creativity and Artistic Confidence*, 4th Edition. Souvenir Press, London, p. xxiv.

30 Sennett, R. (2008) *The Craftsman*. Penguin, London, p. 175.

31 Riley, J., Corkhill, B., and Morris, C. (2013) 'The benefits of knitting for personal and social wellbeing in adulthood: findings from an international survey'. *British Journal of Occupational Therapy*, Vol. 76, No. 2, p. 55.

32 Whittier, J. G. (1892) 'The Brewing of Soma'. *The Poetical Works in Four Volumes*, available at: http://www.bartleby.com/372/197.html, accessed 29 July 2015. I am grateful to A. N. Wilson's passing reference to the last line of this quotation (see note 34, p. 74), which prompted me to seek out the source and led me to this poem.

33 Hemingway, E. (1964) *A Moveable Feast* [2000]. Vintage Books, London, p. 129. This quotation is from an edition edited by Hemingway's wife from an early manuscript. The so-called 'restored edition' by Arrow Books, London, (2011) offers a different rendering of this passage, which alters the meaning.

34 Wilson, A. N. (2015) *The Book of the People*. Atlantic Books, London, pp. 118–122.

35 Bryars, G. (1993) 'Jesus' Blood Never Failed Me Yet'. Audio CD Liner Notes. Point Music, Universal Music Group, Santa Monica, CA.

36 MacCulloch, D. (2013) *Silence: A Christian History*. Allen Lane, Penguin Group, London, pp. 111–112.

37 Brown, S. M. (1981) *Higher and Higher: Making Jewish Prayer Part of Us*. United Synagogue of America, Department of Youth Activities, New York, NY, p. 58–59.

38 Brock, S. (1979) 'JOHN THE SOLITARY, "ON PRAYER"'. *The Journal of Theological Studies*, Vol. 30, No. 1, pp. 84–101.

39 Zarrilli, P. B. (2011) 'Psychophysical approaches and practices in India: embodying processes and states of "being–doing"'. *New Theatre Quarterly*, Vol. 27, No. 3, p. 256.

40 MacCulloch, D. (2013) *Silence: A Christian History*. Allen Lane, Penguin Group, London, p. 76.

41 Malkina-Pykh, I. G. (2015) 'Effectiveness of rhythmic movement therapy: case study of subjective well-being'. *Body, Movement and Dance in Psychotherapy*, Vol. 10, No. 2, pp. 106–120.

42 Odent, M. (2013) *Childbirth and the Future of Homo Sapiens*. Pinter & Martin Ltd., London, pp. 76–78.

43 Ibid., pp. 80–82.

44 Utsch, H. (2007) 'Knitting and stress reduction'. PhD study, Department of Clinical Psychology, Antioch University New England, Keene, NH.

45 Riley, J., Corkhill, B., and Morris, C. (2013) 'The benefits of knitting for personal and social wellbeing in adulthood: findings from an international survey'. *British Journal of Occupational Therapy*, Vol. 76, No. 2, pp. 50–52.

46 Lepp, A., Barkley, J. E., and Karpinski, A. C. (2014) 'The relationship between cell phone use, academic performance, anxiety, and satisfaction with life in college students'. *Computers in Human Behavior*, Vol. 31, pp. 344, 348.

47 Myers, A. (2012) 'A different drummer: Stanford engineers discover neural rhythms drive physical movement'. *Stanford*, available at: http://engineering.stanford.edu/print/node/36844, accessed 16 July 2014.

247

48 Ward, G. (2014) *Unbelievable: Why We Believe and Why We Don't*. I. B. Tauris, London, p. 67.

49 Common Cause (2011) *The Common Cause Handbook – A Guide to Values and Frames for Campaigners, Community Organisers, Civil Servants, Fundraisers, Educators, Social Entrepreneurs, Activists, Funders, Politicians, and Everyone in Between*. Public Interest Research Centre, Machynlleth, Wales, p. 16.

50 Ward, G. (2014) *Unbelievable: Why We Believe and Why We Don't*. I. B. Tauris, London, pp. 50–51.

51 Riley, J., Corkhill, B., and Morris, C. (2013) 'The benefits of knitting for personal and social wellbeing in adulthood: findings from an international survey'. *British Journal of Occupational Therapy*, Vol. 76, No. 2, pp. 51–56.

52 Walker, S. (2014) *Designing Sustainability: Making Radical Changes in a Material World*. Routledge, Abingdon, Oxford, pp. 42–43.

53 Ward, G. (2014) *Unbelievable: Why We Believe and Why We Don't*. I. B. Tauris, London, pp. 55–56.

54 Riley, J., Corkhill, B., and Morris, C. (2013) 'The benefits of knitting for personal and social wellbeing in adulthood: findings from an international survey'. *British Journal of Occupational Therapy*, Vol. 76, No. 2, p. 51.

55 Field research conducted in September 2015 as part of an Arts and Humanities Research Council (UK) funded project entitled *Design Routes: Culturally Significant Designs, Products and Practices*, conducted by Prof. M. Evans, Manchester Metropolitan University, Prof. T. Cassidy, Leeds University and Prof. S. Walker, Lancaster University.

56 Anisef, J. (2011) *Tracing Emerging Modes of Practice: Craft Sector Review*. Ontario Arts Council, Toronto, ON, pp. 15–36.

57 Pagh, J. (2011) 'Sustainability by design: crafts'. Ministry of Foreign Affairs of Denmark, Copenhagen, Denmark, p. 1, available at: http://www.denmark.dk/en/menu/About-Denmark/Danish-Design-Architecture/Design/Sustainability-By-Design/, accessed 6 November 2015.

58 Sennett, R. (2008) *The Craftsman*. Penguin, London, p. 175.

59 Mukherjee, R., ed. (1993) *The Penguin Gandhi Reader*. Penguin Books India (P) Ltd., New Delhi, India, pp. 84, 182.

8 Seeds

1 IPCC (2014) *Climate Change 2014 Synthesis Report Summary for Policymakers*, p. 2. Available at: https://www.ipcc.ch/pdf/assessment-report/ar5/syr/AR5_SYR_FINAL_SPM.pdf, accessed 25 August 2015.

2 Klein, N. (2014) *This Changes Everything: Capitalism vs. The Climate*. Allen Lane, London, pp. 85–90.

3 China Labor Watch (2014) 'iExploitation: Apple's supplier Jabil Circuit exploits workers to meet iPhone 6 demands'. China Labor Watch Report, *China Labor Watch*, 24 September 2014, available at: http://www.chinalaborwatch.org/upfile/2014_09_25/2014.09.25%20iExploitation%20at%20Jabil%20Wuxi%20EN.pdf, accessed 5 January 2014.

4 Alton, D. (2015) 'China's one-child catastrophe'. *Catholic Herald* (London), 5 November 2015, available at: http://www.catholicherald.co.uk/issues/november-6th-2015/chinas-one-child-catastrophe/, accessed 5 November 2015.

5 Phillips, T. (2015) 'China ends one-child policy after 35 years'. *The Guardian* (London), 29 October 2015, available at: http://www.theguardian.com/world/2015/oct/29/china-abandons-one-child-policy, accessed 20 October 2015.

6 Bourguignon, F. (2015) *The Globalization of Inequality*. Princeton University Press, Princeton and Oxford, pp. 186–187.

7   Browne, J. (2015) *Connect: How Companies Succeed by Engaging Radically with Society*. W. H. Allen, London, pp. 135–141.

8   Ehrenfeld, J. R. and Hoffman, A. (2013) *Flourishing: A Frank Conversation about Sustainability*. Stanford University Press, Stanford, CA, pp. 50–51.

9   Ibid.

10 Scruton, R. (2012) *Green Philosophy: How to Think Seriously about the Planet*. Atlantic Books, London, p. 396.

11 Berman, M. (2014) 'The American Sage'. *Dark Ages America*, 16 November 2014, available at: http://morrisberman.blogspot.co.uk/2014/11/the-american-sage.html, accessed 27 October 2015.

12 Bouteneff, P. C. (2015) *Arvo Pärt: Out of Silence*. St. Vladimir's Seminary Press, New York, NY, p. 14.

13 Ibid., p. 16.

14 Salt, K. N. (2015a) Quoted from 'Haiti aid: throwing good money after bad?' *Newshour Extra*, BBC World Service, London, broadcast 7 August 2015.

15 Dubois, L. (2011) *Haiti: The Aftershocks of History*. Metropolitan Books, New York, NY, pp. 1–2.

16 Salt, K. N. (2015a) Quoted from 'Haiti aid: throwing good money after bad?' *Newshour Extra*, BBC World Service, London, broadcast 7 August 2015.

17 Salt, K. N. (2015b) 'Ecological chains of unfreedom: contours of black sovereignty in the Atlantic world'. *Journal of American Studies*, Vol. 49, No. 02, pp. 267–286.

18 Ruxton, D. (2015) 'Media reaction to Syriza's victory in Greek general election'. *The Irish Times* (Dublin), 28 January 2015, available at: http://www.irishtimes.com/news/world/europe/media-reaction-to-syriza-s-victory-in-greek-general-election-1.2079844, accessed 9 August 2015.

19 Fisk, R. (2015) 'Greece debt crisis: EU "family" needs to forgive rather than punish an impoverished state'. *The Independent* (London), 6 July 2015, available at: http://www.independent.co.uk/news/world/europe/greece-debt-crisis-live-referendum-eu-family-needs-to-forgive-rather-than-punish-an-impoverished-state-10370181.html, accessed 9 August 2015.

20 E.g. ibid.

21 Jones, O. (2015) 'We must stop Angela Merkel's bullying – or let the forces of austerity win'. *The Guardian* (London), 28 January 2015, available at: http://www.theguardian.com/commentisfree/2015/jan/28/syriza-merkel-economic-greece-europe, accessed 9 August 2015.

22 Peston, R. (2015) 'Why has the ECB punished Greece?' *BBC Business News Online*, 5 February 2015, available at: http://www.bbc.co.uk/news/business-31148199, accessed 9 August 2015.

23 Evans-Pritchard, A. (2015) 'Greece is being treated like a hostile occupied state'. *The Telegraph* (London), available at: http://www.telegraph.co.uk/finance/economics/11735609/Greece-news-live-Crucified-Tsipras-capitulates-to-draconian-measures-after-17-hours-of-late-night-talks.html, accessed 10 August 2015

24 Nardelli, A. (2015) 'IMF: austerity measures would still leave Greece with unsustainable debt'. *The Guardian* (London), 30 June 2015, available at: http://www.theguardian.com/business/2015/jun/30/greek-debt-troika-analysis-says-significant-concessions-still-needed, accessed 9 August 2015.

25 Farell, H. (2015) 'The euro zone was supposed to strengthen European democracy. Instead, it's undermining it'. *Washington Post* (Washington, DC), 13 July 2015, available at: https://www.washingtonpost.com/blogs/monkey-cage/wp/2015/07/13/the-euro-zone-was-supposed-to-strengthen-european-democracy-instead-its-undermining-it/, accessed 3 July 2016.

26 Rebanks, J. (2015) *The Shepherd's Life: A Tale of the Lake District*. Allen Lane, Penguin Random House, London, p. 97.

27 Shortt, R. (2016) *God Is No Thing: Coherent Christianity*. Hurst & Company, London, p. 16.

28 Cottingham, J. (2014) *Philosophy of Religion: Towards a More Humane Approach*. Cambridge University Press, New York, NY, p. 21.

29 Ibid., p. 22.

30 Griffith, T., trans. (2000) *Plato: The Republic*. Ferrari, G. R. F. (ed.), Cambridge University Press, Cambridge, p. 342.

31 Armstrong, K. (2001) *Buddha*. Viking, Penguin Group, New York, NY, pp. 66–71.

32 Caesar, I. and Youmans, V. (1924) *JazzStandards.com*, available at: http://www. jazzstandards.com/compositions-2/iwanttobehappy.htm, accessed 11 August 2015. Song lyrics available at ST Lyrics: http://www.stlyrics.com/lyrics/teafortwo/iwanttobehappy.htm, accessed 11 August 2015.

33 Griffith, T., trans. (2000) *Plato: The Republic*. Ferrari, G. R. F. (ed.), Cambridge University Press, Cambridge, p. 342.

34 Lev 19:18 KJV.

35 Matt 19:19 KJV.

36 Wilkinson, R. and Pickett, K. (2009) *The Spirit Level: Why More Equal Societies Almost Always Do Better*. Allen Lane, Penguin Books, London, pp. 29, 222.

37 Scheffler, S. (2013) *Death and the Afterlife*. Oxford University Press, Oxford, p. 32.

38 Ibid., p. 22.

39 Ibid., p. 40.

40 E.g. IPCC (2014) *Climate Change 2014 Synthesis Report Summary for Policymakers*. Available at: https://www.ipcc.ch/pdf/assessment-report/ar5/syr/AR5_SYR_FINAL_SPM.pdf, accessed 25 August 2015.

41 Rebanks, J. (2015) *The Shepherd's Life: A Tale of the Lake District*. Allen Lane, Penguin Random House, London, p. 229.

42 Caminoteca (2015) 'Number of pilgrims arrived to Santiago from 1985'. *Pilgrim's Office in Santiago*, available at: http://caminoteca.com/en/about-the-camino/statistics, accessed 6 September 2015.

43 Jeong, S., Kim, H., Yum, J., and Hwang, Y. (2015) 'What type of content are smartphone users addicted to?: SNS vs. games'. *Computers in Human Behavior*, Vol. 54, pp. 10–17. Online edition 18 July 2015, available at: http://www.sciencedirect.com/science/article/pii/S0747563215300467, accessed 7 September 2015.

44 Walker, S. (2006) *Sustainable by Design: Explorations in Theory and Practice*. Routledge, London, p. 202.

45 Thomas, R. S. (1993) 'Via negativa' in *Collected Poems 1945–1999*. Phoenix, London, p. 220.

46 Blake, W. (1825) *Illustrations of the Book of Job*, Plate 2: 'Job and His Family'. Blake Archive, p. 55, available at: http://www.blakearchive.org/exist/blake/archive/object.xq?objectid=bb421.1.spb.03&java=no, accessed 26 July 2015.

47 McGilchrist, I. (2009) *The Master and His Emissary: The Divided Brain and the Making of the Western World*. Yale University Press, New Haven, CT.

48 Eisner, E. W. (2002) *The Arts and the Creation of Mind*. Yale University Press, New Haven, CT, p. 165.

49 Van der Ryn, S. and Cowan, S. (1996) *Ecological Design*. Island Press, Washington, DC, pp. 65, 68, 79.

50 Scruton, R. (2012) *Green Philosophy: How to Think Seriously about the Planet*. Atlantic Books, London, pp. 309, 318, 396.

51 Klein, N. (2014) *This Changes Everything: Capitalism vs the Climate*. Allen Lane, London, p. 86.

52 Eisner, E. W. (2002) *The Arts and the Creation of Mind*. Yale University Press, New Haven, CT, p. 4.

53 Greene, M. (1995) *Releasing the Imagination: Essays on Education, the Arts and Social Change* [2000]. Jossey-Bass, Wiley, San Francisco, CA, p. 35.

54 Bouteneff, P. C. (2015) *Arvo Pärt: Out of Silence*. St. Vladimir's Seminary Press, New York, NY, p. 18.

55 Rebanks, J. (2015) *The Shepherd's Life: A Tale of the Lake District*. Allen Lane, Penguin Random House, London, pp. 210–211.

56 Chudasri, D. (2015) 'An investigation into the potential of design for sustainability in the handicrafts of Northern Thailand.' Poster for the Design PhD Conference 2015 Lancaster, Lancaster Institute for the Contemporary Arts, Lancaster University, 30 April 2015.

57 Paradiso, M. (2015) 'Chiara Vigo: The last woman who makes sea silk'. *BBC News Magazine Online*, 2 September 2015, available at: http://www.bbc.co.uk/news/ magazine-33691781, accessed 2 September 2015.

58 MAKLab (2015) 'Design. Prototyping. Making'. *MAKLab Limited*, available at: http://maklab.co.uk/, accessed 3 September 2015.

59 Broom: The birth of Blodeuwedd is recounted in the story of 'Math the Son of Mathonwy' in the collection of Welsh legends known as *The Mabinogion*, (Lady Charlotte Guest, trans.), 1849, Blackmask Online [2002], p. 109, available at: http://aoda.org/pdf/mbng.pdf, accessed 29 October 2015.

60 Piñon Pine: *A San Pueblo Legend* is recounted in Lanner, R. M. (1981) *The Piñon Pine: A Natural and Cultural History*. University of Nevada Press, Reno, NV, pp. 86–87.

61 Horse Chestnut: The story of the 'candles' of the horse chestnut tree is recounted in Watts, D. C. (2007) *Dictionary of Plant Lore*. Academic Press: Elsevier, Waltham, MA.

251

Appendix 3: The Inadequacies of Corporate Social Responsibility (CSR)

1 Browne, J. (2015) *Connect: How Companies Succeed by Engaging Radically with Society*. W. H. Allen, London, pp. 135–141.

2 Volkswagen (2015) 'CSR projects'. *Volkswagen Group*, available at: http://www. volkswagenag.com/content/vwcorp/content/en/sustainability_and_responsibility/ CSR_worldwide.html, accessed 20 September 2015.

3 Davenport, C. and Ewing, J. (2015) 'VW is said to cheat on diesel emissions; US to order big recall'. *New York Times* (New York), 18 September 2015, available at: http://www.nytimes.com/2015/09/19/business/volkswagen-is-ordered-to-recall-nearly-500000-vehicles-over-emissions-software.html, accessed 20 September 2015.

4 Brooks-Pollock, T. (2015) 'Volkswagen ordered to recall 500,000 cars after software masks emissions'. *The Independent* (London), 19 September 2015, available at: http://www.independent.co.uk/life-style/motoring/motoring-news/volkswagen-ordered-to-recall-500000-cars-after-software-masks-emissions-10508892.html, accessed 20 September 2015.

5 Ruddick, G. (2015) 'VW scandal: carmaker admits 11m vehicles are involved'. *The Guardian* (London), 22 September 2015, available at: http://www.theguardian.com/ business/2015/sep/22/vw-scandal-escalates-volkswagen-11m-vehicles-involved, accessed 22 September 2015.

6 Bakan, J. (2004) *The Corporation: The Pathological Pursuit of Profit and Power*. Constable and Robinson Ltd., London, pp. 60–61.

7 Blinder, A. (2015) 'Georgia: 28-year sentence in tainted peanut case'. *New York Times* (New York), 21 September 2015, available at: http://www.nytimes.com/2015/09/22/us/

georgia-28-year-sentence-in-tainted-peanut-deaths.html?_r=0, accessed 21 September 2015

8   BBC News (2015) 'US salmonella outbreak: peanut boss jailed for 28 years'. *BBC News Online* (London), 21 September 2015, available at: http://www.bbc.com/news/world-us-canada-34321181, accessed 22 September 2015.

Sources of quotations at the beginning of each chapter

Ch. 1   Longfellow, H. W. (1882) *Hyperion*, Project Gutenberg, Salt Lake City, UT, available at: http://www.classicly.com/download-hyperion-pdf, accessed 2 January 2016, p. 121.

Ch. 2   Defoe, D. (1719) *Robinson Crusoe* [2008], Vintage, London, p. 107.

Ch. 3   Austen, J. (1817) *Persuasion* [2009], Penguin Books, Penguin Group (Australia), Melbourne, Victoria, p. 176.

Ch. 4   Shakespeare, W. (ca. 1597) *Henry IV, Part 2.*

Ch. 5   Author

Ch. 6   Hesse, H. (1927) *Steppenwolf*, Penguin Essential edition, Penguin Books, London, p. 123. With permission from Suhrkamp Verlag, Frankfurt am Main (copyright Hermann Hesse, all rights reserved).

Ch. 7   *The Mulberry Bush*, English nursery rhyme, traditional.

Ch. 8   *Gospel of Mark 4:8*, Holy Bible, King James Version.

Bibliography

Ahmed, I. (2012) 'KILLER SEEDS: the devastating impacts of Monsanto's genetically modified seeds in India'. *Global Research*, Montreal, Canada, available at: www.globalresearch.ca/killer-seeds-the-devastating-impacts-of-monsanto-s-genetically-modified-seeds-in-india/28629, accessed 6 August 2013.

Alton, D. (2015) 'China's one-child catastrophe'. *Catholic Herald* (London), 5 November 2015, available at: www.catholicherald.co.uk/issues/november-6th-2015/chinas-one-child-catastrophe/, accessed 5 November 2015.

Anisef, J. (2011) *Tracing Emerging Modes of Practice: Craft Sector Review*. Ontario Arts Council, Toronto, ON.

Anon (1945) *Miracles of Invention and Discovery*. Odhams Press, London, p. 5.

Ares (2014) 'Ecodesign – Your future: how ecodesign can help products smarter'. *The Ecodesign Directive*, Report No. 1206343, 16 April 2014, The Directorate-General for Enterprise & Industry and The Directorate-General for Energy, European Commission, p. 3, available at: ec.europa.eu/geninfo/query/index.do?queryText=How+ecodesign+can+help&query_source=GROWTH&summary=summary&more_options_source=restricted&more_options_date=*&more_options_date_from=&more_options_date_to=&more_options_language=en&more_options_f_formats=*&swlang=en, accessed 23 March 2016.

Armenteras, D. and Finlayson, D. M., eds. (2012) 'Biodiversity'. *GEO5 – Global Environmental Outlook: Environment for the Future We Want*, p. 135, available at: www.unep.org/geo/pdfs/geo5/GEO5_report_full_en.pdf, accessed 26 January 2015.

Armstrong, K. (2001) *Buddha*. Viking, Penguin Group, New York, NY.

Armstrong, K. (2002) *Islam: A Short History*. Phoenix Press, London.

Armstrong, K. (2005) *A Short History of Myth*. Canongate, Edinburgh, UK.

Armstrong, K. (2008) *The Bible: The Biography*. Atlantic Books, London.

Arrington, M. (2010) 'Digg's biggest problem is its users and their constant opinions on things'. *TechCrunch Inc.*, Palo Alto, CA, 12 May 2010, available at: techcrunch.com/

2010/05/12/diggs-biggest-problem-are-its-users-and-their-constant-opinions-on-things/, accessed 19 October 2014.

Atran, S. (2015) 'Youth, violent extremism and promoting peace'. Address to the UN Security Council, 23 April 2015, available at: blogs.plos.org/ neuroanthropology/2015/04/25/scott-atran-on-youth-violent-extremism-and-promoting-peace/, accessed 28 November 2015.

Baker-Smith, D., trans. (2012) *Utopia* by Thomas More [1516]. Penguin Books, London.

Baldry, C. and Barnes, A. (2012) 'The open-plan academy: space, control and the undermining of professional identity'. *Work Employment Society*, Vol. 26, No. 2, pp. 229, 240.

Bassler, B. (2014) *Exchanges at the Frontier*. BBC World Service, first broadcast 8 February 2014.

BBC News (2015) 'US salmonella outbreak: peanut boss jailed for 28 years'. *BBC News Online* (London), 21 September 2015, available at: www.bbc.com/news/world-us-canada-34321181, accessed 22 September 2015.

Beckett, A. (2013) 'What is the "global race"?' *The Guardian* (London), 22 September 2013, available at: www.theguardian.com/politics/2013/sep/22/what-is-global-race-conservatives-ed-miliband, accessed 31 January 2014.

Berman, M. (2014) 'The American Sage'. *Dark Ages America*, 16 November 2014, available at: morrisber'man.blogspot.co.uk/2014/11/the-american-sage.html, accessed 27 October 2015.

Berners-Lee, M. and Clark, D. (2013) *The Burning Question*. Profile Books, London.

Bisadi, M., Mozaffar, F., and Hosseini, S. B. (2012) 'Future research centers: the place of creativity and innovation'. *Asia Pacific International Conference on Environment-Behaviour Studies* (AicE-Bs2012 Cairo), Giza, Egypt, 31 October–2 November 2012. Published in *Procedia – Social and Behavioural Sciences*, Vol. 68, pp. 240–241.

Blake, W. (1790) 'The marriage of heaven and hell – A memorable fancy' in *The Selected Poems of William Blake* [1994]. Wordsworth Editions Ltd. Ware, Hertfordshire, UK.

Blake, W. (1825) *Illustrations of the Book of Job*, Plate 2: 'Job and His Family'. Blake Archive, available at: www.blakearchive.org/exist/blake/archive/object.xq?objectid= bb421.1.spb.03&java=no, accessed 26 July 2015.

Blinder, A. (2015) 'Georgia: 28-year sentence in tainted peanut case'. *New York Times* (New York), 21 September 2015, available at: www.nytimes.com/2015/09/22/us/ georgia-28-year-sentence-in-tainted-peanut-deaths.html?_r=0, accessed 21 September 2015.

Borgmann, A. (1984) *Technology and the Character of Contemporary Life* [1987]. The University of Chicago Press, Chicago, IL.

Bourguignon, F. (2015) *The Globalization of Inequality*. Princeton University Press, Princeton and Oxford.

Bouteneff, P. C. (2015) *Arvo Pärt: Out of Silence*. St. Vladimir's Seminary Press, Yonkers, NY.

Breton Connelly, J. (2014) *The Parthenon Enigma*. Head of Zeus Ltd., London.

Brock, S. (1979) 'JOHN THE SOLITARY, "ON PRAYER"'. *The Journal of Theological Studies*, Vol. 30, No. 1, pp. 84–101.

Brooks-Pollock, T. (2015) 'Volkswagen ordered to recall 500,000 cars after software masks emissions'. *The Independent* (London), 19 September 2015, available at: www. independent.co.uk/life-style/motoring/motoring-news/volkswagen-ordered-to-recall-500000-cars-after-software-masks-emissions-10508892.html, accessed 20 September 2015.

Brotton, J. (2006) *The Renaissance*. Oxford University Press, Oxford.

Brown, S. M. (1981) *Higher and Higher: Making Jewish Prayer Part of Us*. United Synagogue of America, Department of Youth Activities, New York.

Browne, J. (2015) *Connect: How Companies Succeed by Engaging Radically with Society.* W. H. Allen: London.

Bryars, G. (1993) 'Jesus' Blood Never Failed Me Yet'. Audio CD Liner Notes. Point Music, Universal Music Group, Santa Monica, CA.

Buchanan, R. (1989) 'Declaration by design: Rhetoric, argument, and demonstration in design practice' in Margolin, V. (ed.) *Design Discourse: History, Theory, Criticism.* The University of Chicago Press, Chicago, pp. 93–94.

Bureau of Democracy, Human Rights and Labor (2014) 'China (includes Tibet, Hong Kong, And Macau) 2014 Human Rights Report'. United States Department of State, pp. 55–59, available at: www.state.gov/j/drl/rls/hrrpt/humanrightsreport/index.htm?year=2014&dlid=236432#sthash.doCRuhjM.dpuf, accessed 10 August 2015.

Business Times (2014) 'Tech giants settle suit over no-poaching deal'. *The Business Times* (Singapore), 25 April 2014, available at: www.businesstimes.com.sg/print/1073763, accessed 27 April 2014.

Caesar, I. and Youmans, V. (1924) 'I Want to Be Happy'. *JazzStandards.com*, available at: www.jazzstandards.com/compositions-2/iwanttobehappy.htm, accessed 11 August 2015. Song lyrics available at ST Lyrics: www.stlyrics.com/lyrics/teafortwo/iwanttobehappy.htm, accessed 11 August 2015.

Cain, S. (2012) *Quiet.* Penguin Books, London.

Caminoteca (2015) 'Number of pilgrims arrived to Santiago from 1985'. *Pilgrim's Office in Santiago*, available at: caminoteca.com/en/about-the-camino/statistics, accessed 6 September 2015.

Campbell, J. (2014) *Roy Jenkins: A Well-Rounded Life.* Jonathan Cape, London, referring to an article in the *Times* (London) 8 April 1988.

Cather, W. (1927) *Death Comes for the Archbishop* [1990]. Vintage Classics, Random House, New York, NY.

Cavafy, C. P. (2013) *Selected Poems.* Connolly, D. (trans.), Aiora Press, Athens, p. 25.

CBC (2011) 'Canada pulls out of Kyoto Protocol'. *CBCNews*, 12 December 2011, available at: www.cbc.ca/news/politics/story/2011/12/12/pol-kent-kyoto-pullout.html, accessed 9 July 2013.

Chaibong, H. (2000) 'The cultural challenge of individualism'. *Journal of Democracy*, Vol. 11, No. 1, pp. 127–134.

Chesterton, G. (1908) *Orthodoxy.* Image Book, Doubleday, New York, NY.

Chidester, D. (2000) *Christianity: A Global History.* HarperCollins, New York, NY.

China Labor Watch (2014) 'iExploitation: Apple's supplier Jabil Circuit exploits workers to meet iPhone 6 demands'. China Labor Watch Report, *China Labor Watch*, 24 September 2014, available at: www.chinalaborwatch.org/upfile/2014_09_25/2014.09.25%20iExploitation%20at%20Jabil%20Wuxi%20EN.pdf, accessed 5 January 2014.

Chomsky, N. (1997) 'The passion for free markets'. *Z Magazine*, May edition, available at: www.chomsky.info/articles/199705–.htm, accessed 11 March 2014.

Chudasri, D. (2015) 'An investigation into the potential of design for sustainability in the handicrafts of Northern Thailand.' Poster for the Design PhD Conference 2015 Lancaster, Lancaster Institute for the Contemporary Arts, Lancaster University, 30 April 2015.

Clark, M. J. (2014) *The Vision of Catholic Social Thought: The Virtue of Solidarity and the Praxis of Human Rights.* Fortress Press, Minneapolis, MN.

Common Cause (2011) *The Common Cause Handbook – A Guide to Values and Frames for Campaigners, Community Organisers, Civil Servants, Fundraisers, Educators, Social Entrepreneurs, Activists, Funders, Politicians, and Everyone in Between.* Public Interest Research Centre, Machynlleth, Wales.

255

Comte-Sponville, A. (2007) *The Book of Atheist Spirituality: An Elegant Argument for Spirituality without God*. Huston, N. (trans.), Bantam Books, London.

Cooper, T., ed. (2010) *Longer Lasting Products: Alternatives to the Throwaway Society*. Gower Publishing Limited, Farnham, UK.

Cordeiro, W. P. (2003) 'The only solution to the decline in business ethics: ethical managers'. *Teaching Business Ethics*, Vol. 7, No. 3, pp. 265–277.

Corfield, P. J. (2008) 'All people are living histories – which is why history matters'. *Making History*, School of Advanced Studies, Royal Holloway, University of London, available at: www.history.ac.uk/makinghistory/resources/articles/why_history_matters.html, accessed 10 February 2014.

Cornwell, J. (2014) *The Dark Box*. Profile Books, London.

Cottingham, J. (2005) *The Spiritual Dimension: Religion, Philosophy and Human Value*. Cambridge University Press, Cambridge, MA.

Cottingham, J. (2014) *Philosophy of Religion: Towards a More Humane Approach*. Cambridge University Press, New York, NY.

Coutts, L. M. and Gruman, J. A. (2012) 'Applying social psychology to organizations' in Schneider, F. W., Gruman, J. A., and Coutts, L. M. (eds.) *Applied Social Psychology: Understanding and Addressing Social and Practical Problems*, pp. 217–244. Sage, Los Angeles, CA.

Cox, S. (2014) 'Sebastian Cox: Designer and Craftsman', available at: sebastiancox.co.uk, accessed 10 June 2014.

Cumming-Bruce, N. (2014) 'Vatican tells of 848 priests ousted in decade'. *New York Times* (New York), 6 May 2014, available at: www.nytimes.com/2014/05/07/world/europe/vatican-tells-of-848-priests-ousted-in-last-decade.html?_r=0, accessed 7 May 2014.

C. W. and A. J. K. D. (2013) 'Was tulipmania irrational?'. *The Economist* (London), 4 October 2013, available at: www.economist.com/blogs/freeexchange/2013/10/economic-history, accessed 11 November 2014.

Daly, H. (2007) *Ecological Economics and Sustainable Development: Selected Essays of Herman Daly*. Edward Elgar, Cheltenham, UK.

Davenport, C. and Ewing, J. (2015) 'VW is said to cheat on diesel emissions; US to order big recall'. *New York Times* (New York), 18 September 2015, available at: www.nytimes.com/2015/09/19/business/volkswagen-is-ordered-to-recall-nearly-500000-vehicles-over-emissions-software.html, accessed 20 September 2015.

Davies, C. (2011) 'David Chaytor jailed for 18 months over false expenses claim.' *The Guardian* (London), 7 January 2011, available at: www.theguardian.com/politics/2011/jan/07/mps-expenses-david-chaytor-jailed/print, accessed 7 May 2014.

Davies, W. (2015) *The Happiness Industry: How the Government and Big Business Sold Us Well-Being*. Verso, London.

Davison, A. (2001) *Technology and the Contested Meanings of Sustainability*. State University of New York Press, Albany, NY.

Davison, A. (2013) 'Making sustainability up: design beyond possibility' in Walker, S. and Giard, J. (eds.) *The Handbook of Design for Sustainability*. Bloomsbury Academic, London.

Deloitte (2014) 'London Futures – Agiletown: The relentless march of technology and London's response', *Deloitte LLP*, London, available at: https://www2.deloitte.com/content/dam/Deloitte/uk/Documents/uk-futures/london-futures-agiletown.pdf, accessed 14 September 2015.

Donne, J. (1990) 'Meditation XVII: Nunc lento sonitu dicunt, morieris' in Carey, J. (ed.) *The Major Works including Songs and Sonnets*. Oxford University Press, Oxford, p. 344.

Doward, J. (2014) 'Tobacco giant "tried blackmail" to block Ugandan anti-smoking law'. *The Guardian* (London), 12 July 2014, available at: www.theguardian.com/business/2014/jul/12/bat-blackmail-uganda-smoking-law-tobacco, accessed 13 July 2014.

Dubois, L. (2011) *Haiti: The Aftershocks of History*. Metropolitan Books, New York, NY.

Duchamp, M. (1957) 'The creative act'. Session on the Creative Act, Convention of the American Federation of Arts, April 1957, Houston, TX, available at: www.wisdomportal.com/Cinema-Machine/Duchamp-CreativeAct.html, accessed 25 November 2014.

Duffin, J. (2009) *Medical Miracles: Doctors, Saints, and Healing in the Modern World*. Oxford University Press, Oxford, available at: inters.org/religion-medicine-and-miracles, accessed 28 November 2014.

Duffy, E. (1992) *The Stripping of the Altars: Traditional Religion in England 1400–1580*. Yale University Press, New Haven, CT.

Duffy, E. (2004) *Faith of our Fathers: Reflections on Catholic Tradition*. Continuum, London.

Durbin, R. J., Waxman, H. A., Harkin, T., Rockefeller IV, J. D., Blumenthal, R., Markey, E. J., Brown, S., Reed, J., Boxer, B., Heitkamp, H., Merkley, J., and Pallone, F. (2013) 'Gateway to addiction: a survey of popular electronic cigarette manufacturers and target marketing to youth', available at: media.cleveland.com/health_impact/other/Report%20-%20E-Cigarettes%204%2014%2014.pdf, accessed 10 July 2014.

Dworkin, R. (2013) *Religion Without God*. Harvard University Press, Cambridge, MA.

Eagleton, T. (2008) *The Meaning of Life*. Oxford University Press, Oxford.

Eagleton, T. (2014) *Culture and the Death of God*. Yale University Press, New Haven, CT.

EAston (2015) 'Hitachi developed a wearable device that can measure happiness'. *WT VOX*, 2 September 2015, available at: https://wtvox.com/2015/02/hitachi-developed-a-wearable-device-that-can-measure-happiness/, accessed 20 June 2015.

Ebert, R. (1967) 'Casino Royale'. *RogerEbert.com*, available at: www.rogerebert.com/reviews/casino-royale-1967, accessed 11 November 2014.

Edwards, B. (2012) *Drawing of the Right Side of the Brain: A Course in Enhancing Creativity and Artistic Confidence*, 4th Edition. Souvenir Press, London.

Edwards, P., ed. (1999) *James Cook: The Journals*. Penguin Books Ltd., London.

Ehrenfeld, J. and Hoffman, A. (2013) *Flourishing: A Frank Conversation about Sustainability*. Stanford University Press, Stanford, CA.

Eisner, E. W. (2002) *The Arts and the Creation of Mind*. Yale University Press, New Haven, CT.

Elfenbein, E. (2014) 'Wear are we going? The future of wearable happiness'. *The Coca-Cola Company*, 15 May 2014, available at: www.coca-colacompany.com/innovation/wear-are-we-going-the-future-of-wearable-happiness, accessed 23 June 2015.

Eliot, T. S. (1963) *Collected Poems 1909–1962*. Faber and Faber, London.

Elkington, J. (1997) *Cannibals with Forks: The Triple Bottom Line of 21st Century Business*. Capstone Publishing Ltd., Oxford.

EPA (2012) 'The Great Lakes today: concern – four toxic contaminants'. *US Environmental Protection Agency*, Washington, DC, available at: www.epa.gov/greatlakes/atlas/glat-ch4.html, accessed 10 June 2014.

Evans, M., Walker, S., Cassidy, T., and Twigger Holroyd, A. (2014) 'Design routes: envisioning the future of culturally significant designs, products and practices'. AHRC Funded Research Project, available at: imagination.lancs.ac.uk/activities/Design_Routes, accessed 25 November 2014.

Evans-Pritchard, A. (2015) 'Greece is being treated like a hostile occupied state'. *The Telegraph* (London), 13 July 2015, available at: www.telegraph.co.uk/finance/economics/11735609/Greece-news-live-Crucified-Tsipras-capitulates-to-draconian-measures-after-17-hours-of-late-night-talks.html, accessed 10 August 2015.

Farhi, P. (2014) '*Washington Post* wins Pulitzer Prize for NSA spying revelations; *Guardian* also honored'. *Washington Post* (Washington, DC), 14 April 2014, available at:

www.washingtonpost.com/politics/washington-post-wins-pulitzer-prize-for-public-service-shared-with-guardian/2014/04/14/bc7c4cc6-c3fb-11e3-bcec-b71ee10e9bc3_ story.html, accessed 7 May 2014.

Farell, H. (2015) 'The euro zone was supposed to strengthen European democracy. Instead, it's undermining it'. *Washington Post* (Washington, DC), 13 July 2015, available at: https://www.washingtonpost.com/blogs/monkey-cage/wp/2015/07/13/the-euro-zone-was-supposed-to-strengthen-european-democracy-instead-its-undermining-it/, accessed 3 July 2016.

Feist, G. J. (1999) 'Autonomy and independence', in Runco, M. A. and Protzker, S. R. (eds.) *Encyclopedia of Creativity*, Vol. 1, 2nd Edition [2011], Academic Press, Elsevier, London, pp. 157–162.

Fernández-Armesto, F. and Wilson, D. (1996) *Reformation*. Bantam Press, London.

Figgis, M. (2013) 'Why British film is all kitsch 'n' sink'. *The Observer* (London), 22 June 2013, available at: www.guardian.co.uk/film/2013/jun/22/mike-figgis-defeatist-british-film-industry, accessed 23 June 2013.

Fioramonti, L. (2014) *How Numbers Rule the World: The Use and Abuse of Statistics in Global Politics*. Zed Books, London.

Fischer, A. (2015) Personal communication, 24 September 2015. Andrea Fischer, Director, *Andrea Fisher Fine Pottery*, Santa Fe, NM.

Fischer, D. (2013) '"Dark money" funds climate change denial effort'. *Scientific American*, 23 December 2013, available at: www.scientificamerican.com/article/dark-money-funds-climate-change-denial-effort/, accessed 13 February 2015.

Fischer-Kowalski, M., Swilling, M., von Weizsäcker, E. U., Ren, Y., Moriguchi, Y., Crane, W., Krausmann, F., Eisenmenger, N., Giljum, S., Hennicke, P., Romero Lankao, P., Siriban Manalang, A., and Sewerin, S. (2011) 'Decoupling natural resource use and environmental impacts from economic growth – A report of the working group on decoupling to the International Resource Panel'. *United National Environmental Programme*, available at: www.unep.org/resourcepanel/decoupling/files/pdf/decoupling_report_english.pdf, accessed 27 November 2014.

Fisk, R. (2015) 'Greece debt crisis: EU "family" needs to forgive rather than punish an impoverished state'. *The Independent* (London), 6 July 2015, available at: www.independent.co.uk/news/world/europe/greece-debt-crisis-live-referendum-eu-family-needs-to-forgive-rather-than-punish-an-impoverished-state-10370181.html, accessed 9 August 2015.

Fletcher, K. (2013) 'Sustainable fashion' in Walker, S. and Giard, J. (eds.) *The Handbook of Design for Sustainability*. Bloomsbury Academic, London.

Foley, M. (2010) *The Age of Absurdity: Why Modern Life Makes It Hard to Be Happy*. Simon & Schuster Ltd., London.

Franck, F. (1973) *The Zen of Seeing – Seeing/Drawing as Meditation*. Vintage Books, New York, NY.

Franklin, U. M. (2006) *The Ursula Franklin Reader: Pacifism as a Map*. Between the Lines, Toronto, ON.

Fulcher, J. (2004) *Capitalism*. Oxford University Press, New York, NY.

Furlong, M. (1971) *Contemplating Now*. Hodder & Stoughton, London.

Furlong, M. (1980) *Merton: A Biography*. Harper and Row Publishers, San Francisco, CA.

Galer, S. (2015) 'Health, wealth and happiness: are we just a wearable away from having it all?' *Forbes*, 2 April 2015, available at: www.forbes.com/sites/sap/2015/04/02/health-wealth-and-happiness-are-we-just-a-wearable-away-from-having-it-all/, accessed 21 June 2015.

Gamble, R. (2016) 'Traditionalist liturgies attract record numbers during Easter premium'. *The Tablet* (London), 14 April 2016.

Gardener, C. and Sheppard, J. (1989) *Consuming Passion: The Rise of Retail Culture*. Routledge, Abingdon.

Gaver, W. (2012) 'What should we expect from research through design?' Proceedings of the SIGCHI Conference on Human Factors in Computing Systems, 5–10 May 2010, Austin, TX.

Gay, P. (2007) *Modernism: The Lure of Heresy from Baudelaire to Beckett and Beyond*. Vintage Books, London.

Gitlin, T. (2014) 'Where are the Occupy protesters now?' *The Guardian* (London), 17 June 2014, available at: www.theguardian.com/cities/2014/jun/17/where-occupy-protesters-now-social-media, accessed 11 November 2014.

Gorz, A. (2010) *Ecologica*. Seagull Books, London.

Graham, M. (2014) *Four Thought*, BBC Radio 4, British Broadcasting Corporation, 18 May 2014, available at: www.bbc.co.uk/programmes/b0435j93, accessed 19 May 2014.

Graham, M., Hogan, B., Straumann, R. K., and Medhat, A. (2014) 'Uneven geographies of user-generated information: patterns of increasing informational poverty'. *Annals of the Association of American Geographers*, Vol. 104, No. 4, pp. 1, 5, available at: www.oii. ox.ac.uk/people/?id=165, accessed 19 May 2014.

Gray, L. (2012) 'Rio +20: Nick Clegg defies Tories again by pledging environment key to growth'. *The Telegraph* (London), 15 June 2012, available at: www.telegraph.co.uk/earth/earthnews/9332404/Rio-20-Nick-Clegg-defies-Tories-again-by-pledging-environment-key-to-growth.html, accessed 31 January 2014.

Green, R. P. H., trans. (1997) *Saint Augustine: On Christian Teaching*. Oxford World Classics, Oxford University Press, Oxford.

Greene, G. (1938) *Brighton Rock*. Vintage, London.

Greene, M. (1995) *Releasing the Imagination: Essays on Education, the Arts and Social Change* [2000]. Jossey-Bass, Wiley, San Francisco, CA.

Grey, C. (2015) 'The future is not where the older generation seems to think it is'. *The Tablet* (London), 12 December 2015.

Griffith, T., trans. (2000) *Plato: The Republic*. Ferrari, G. R. F. (ed.), Cambridge University Press, Cambridge.

Hague, W. (2007) *William Wilberforce: The Life of the Great Anti-Slave Trade Campaigner*. HarperCollins Publishers, London.

Halliday, J. (2013) 'Police could have stopped Jimmy Savile in the 1960s, says official report'. *The Guardian* (London), 12 March 2013, available at: www.theguardian.com/media/2013/mar/12/jimmy-savile-metropolitan-police, accessed 7 May 2014.

Hampson, N. (1968) *The Enlightenment*. Penguin Books, London.

Hansell, A. L., Blangiardo, M., Fortunato, L., Floud, S., de Hoogh, K., Fecht, D., Ghosh, R. E., Laszlo, H. E., Pearson, C., Beale, L., Beevers, S., Gulliver, J., Best, N., Richardson, S., Elliott, P. (2013) 'Aircraft noise and cardiovascular disease near Heathrow airport in London: small area study'. *British Medical Journal* (*BMJ*), 347: f5432, available at: www.bmj.com/content/347/bmj.f5432, accessed 9 October 2013.

Hargett, J. M., trans. (1989) 'On the road in twelfth century China: the travel diaries of Fan Chengda (1126–1193)', Steiner Verlag, Wiesbaden, pp. 46–47, available at: bactra.org/Poetry/Su_Tung-po/Record_of_Stone_Bell_Mountain.html, accessed 2 February 2016.

Hartley, L. P. (1953) *The Go-Between*. Penguin Books, London.

Hawken, P. (2007) *Blessed Unrest*. Penguin Group, New York, NY.

Hawken, P. (2009) 'Commencement: healing or stealing'. Commencement speech, University of Portland, available at: www.up.edu/commencement/default. aspx?cid=9456&pid=3144, accessed 9 July 2013.

Heidegger, M. (1971) *Poetry, Language, Thought*. Hofstadter, A. (trans), HarperCollins, New York, NY.

Hemingway, E. (1964) *A Moveable Feast* [2000]. Vintage Books, London.

Herro, A. (2013) 'New bans on plastic bags may help protect marine life'. *Worldwatch Institute*, Washington, DC, available at: www.worldwatch.org/node/5565, accessed 31 May 2014.

Hick, J. (1966) *Faith and Knowledge*, 2nd Edition. Fontana, Collins, Glasgow.

Hick, J. (1989) *An Interpretation of Religion: Human Responses to the Transcendent*. Yale Unity Press, New Haven, CT.

Hickey, W. (2013) 'Apple avoids paying $17 million in taxes every day through a ballsy but genius tax avoidance scheme'. *Business Insider*, 21 May 2013, available at: www.businessinsider.com/how-apple-reduces-what-it-pays-in-taxes-2013-5?IR=T, accessed 5 January 2014.

Hobsbawm, E. J. (1969) *Industry and Empire*. Penguin Books, London.

Holden, M. (2015) 'Cameron's conservatives vow tough new strike laws'. *Reuters* (London), 10 January 2015, available at: uk.reuters.com/article/2015/01/10/uk-britain-conservatives-unions-idUKKBN0KJ0EJ20150110, accessed 10 January 2015.

Howes, G. (2007) *The Art of the Sacred: An Introduction to the Aesthetics of Art and Belief*. I. B. Taurus, London.

Howse, C. (2014) 'A peek at the catechism would be useful for any commentator on religion'. *The Tablet* (London), 5 July 2014.

Hughes, R. (1980) 'Episode 8. The future that was'. *The Shock of the New*, BBC TV Series, London, 56:34–57:13 minutes, available at: https://www.youtube.com/watch?v=AFc1BeS0vKI, accessed 20 December 2015.

IPCC (2014) *Climate Change 2014 Synthesis Report Summary for Policymakers*. Available at: https://www.ipcc.ch/pdf/assessment-report/ar5/syr/AR5_SYR_FINAL_SPM.pdf, accessed 25 August 2015.

Irwin, E. G. and Clark, J. (2007) 'The local costs and benefits of Wal-Mart'. *Downtown Economics*, Center for Community & Economic Development, University of Wisconsin Extension, Madison, WI, available at: fyi.uwex.edu/downtowneconomics/files/2012/07/local-cost-and-benefits-of-walmart.pdf, accessed 25 November 2014.

Jackson, T. (2009) *Prosperity Without Growth: Economics for a Finite Planet*. Routledge, London.

James, W. (1902) *The Varieties of Religious Experience*. The Modern Library, Random House, New York, NY.

Jeong, S., Kim, H., Yum, J., and Hwang, Y. (2015) 'What type of content are smartphone users addicted to?: SNS vs. games'. *Computers in Human Behavior*, Vol. 54, pp. 10–17, available at: www.sciencedirect.com/science/article/pii/S0747563215300467, accessed 7 September 2015.

Jones, O. (2015) 'We must stop Angela Merkel's bullying – or let the forces of austerity win'. *The Guardian* (London), 28 January 2015, available at: www.theguardian.com/commentisfree/2015/jan/28/syriza-merkel-economic-greece-europe, accessed 9 August 2015.

Jones, R. (2014) 'Wonga's fake legal letters passed to police'. *The Guardian* (London), 26 June 2014, available at: www.theguardian.com/business/2014/jun/26/wonga-fake-legal-letters-passed-police, accessed 10 July 2014.

Kara, S. (2014) 'Tainted carpets: slavery and child labor in India's hand-made carpet sector'. *FXB Center for Health and Human Rights*, Harvard School of Public Health, Harvard University, Boston, MA.

Kayfetz, J. L. (2013) 'Poetry – and medicine'. 13 October 2013, available at: janetkayfetz.wordpress.com/2013/10/17/poetry-and-medicine/, accessed 27 January 2014.

Klein, N. (2014) *This Changes Everything: Capitalism vs. The Climate*. Allen Lane, London.

Korten, D. C. (2006) *The Great Turning: From Empire to Earth Community*. Berrett-Koehler Publishers Inc., Oakland, CA.

Kristeva, J. (1995) *New Maladies of the Soul*. Guberman, R. (trans.), Columbia University Press, New York, NY.

Lanier, J. (2006) 'Digital Maoism'. *Edge*, May 2006, available at: edge.org/conversation/digital-maoism-the-hazards-of-the-new-online-collectivism, accessed 5 October 2014.

Lanier, J. (2010) *You Are Not a Gadget: A Manifesto*. Allen Lane, Penguin Group, London.

Lanier, J. (2013) *Who Owns the Future?* Allen Lane, Penguin Books, London.

Lansley, S. (1994) *After the Gold Rush – The Trouble with Affluence*. Century Business Books, London.

Latour, B. (2004) 'Why has critique run out of steam?' in *The Norton Anthology of Theory and Criticism*, 2nd Edition. W. W. Norton & Co., New York, pp. 2272–2302.

Lawson-Tancred, H. C., trans (2004) *Aristotle: The Art of Rhetoric*. Penguin Books, London.

Leonard, A. (2010) *The Story of Stuff*. Constable and Robinson Ltd., London

Leopold, A. (1949) *A Sand County Almanac and Sketches Here and There*. Oxford University Press, London.

Lepp, A., Barkley, J. E., and Karpinski, A. C. (2014) 'The relationship between cell phone use, academic performance, anxiety, and satisfaction with life in college students'. *Computers in Human Behavior*, Vol. 31, pp. 343–350.

Lester, L. (2012) 'Risks and rewards of quantifying nature's "ecosystem services"'. *American Association for the Advancement of Science*, available at: www.eurekalert.org/pub_releases/2012-06/esoa-rar062112.php#, accessed 5 August 2013.

Levitan, L., Cox, D. G., and Clarvoe, M. B. (2014) 'Avoiding pollution and saving farmers money by recycling agricultural plastic films'. CALS Impact Statement, Cornell University, Ithaca, NY, available at: vivo.cornell.edu/display/individual16665, accessed 31 May 2014.

Lewis, C. S. (1947) *Miracles*. HarperCollins, London.

Lillford, P. (2015) 'The Secret Life of Packaging'. *The Food Chain*, BBC World Service, broadcast 23 January 2015.

Longley, C. (2013) 'Being very wealthy can, as Jesus pointed out, be bad for the soul'. *The Tablet* (London), 10 August 2013.

Longley, C. (2014) *Thought for the Day*. British Broadcasting Corporation, Radio 4, first broadcast 10 February 2014. Transcript available at: www.bbc.co.uk/programmes/p01s272q, accessed 15 March 2014.

Lutter, S. and Giljum, S. (2012) 'The issue'. *World Resources Forum*, Global Material Extraction and Resource Efficiency, available at: www.worldresourcesforum.org/issue, accessed 14 August 2013.

Lloyd, S. (2013) 'RE: The truth unmasked – The supply of and support for religious education teachers: an inquiry by the All Party Parliamentary Group on Religious Education'. *Religious Education Council of England and Wales*, London, March 2014, available at: religiouseducationcouncil.org.uk/images/stories/pdf/APPG_RE_The_Truth_Unmasked.pdf, accessed 3 March 2014.

Macalister, T. (2015) 'Joseph Stiglitz: unsurprising Jeremy Corbyn is a Labour leadership contender'. *The Guardian* (London), 26 July 2015, available at: www.theguardian.com/politics/2015/jul/26/joseph-stiglitz-jeremy-corbyn-labour-leadership-contender-anti-austerity, accessed 27 July 2015.

MacCulloch, D. (2013) *Silence: A Christian History*. Allen Lane, Penguin Group, London.

MacIntyre, A. (2007) *After Virtue*, 3rd Edition. Bristol Classical Press, Bloomsbury Academic, London.

MAKLab (2015) 'Design. Prototyping. Making'. *MAKLab Limited*, available at: maklab.co.uk/, accessed 3 September 2015.

Malkina-Pykh, I. G. (2015) 'Effectiveness of rhythmic movement therapy: case study of subjective well-being'. *Body, Movement and Dance in Psychotherapy*, Vol. 10, No. 2, pp. 106–120.

Manzini, E. (2013) 'Against Post-It design: to make things happen'. Personal correspondence, available for DESIS Lab Coordinators and Operations Managers at: www.desis-network.org/sites/default/files/newsletters/10/DESISnewsletter10.html.

Marco Polo and Rustichello of Pisa (ca. 130) *The Travels of Marco Polo*, Volume 1 [2004]. Available at: hudsoncress.net/hudsoncress.org/html/library/history-travel/marco-polo-vol1.pdf, accessed 25 October 2015.

Margolin, V., ed. (1989) *Design Discourse: History, Theory, Criticism*. The University of Chicago Press, Chicago, IL.

McGilchrist, I. (2009) *The Master and His Emissary: The Divided Brain and the Making of the Western World*. Yale University Press, New Haven, CT.

Meroni, A., ed. (2007) *Creative Communities: People Inventing Sustainable Ways of Living*. Edizioni Poli.design, Milan.

Merton, T. (1969) *Contemplative Prayer*. Doubleday, Random House, New York, NY.

Miller, H. (1957) *Big Sur and the Oranges of Hieronymus Bosch*. New Directions Publishing Corporation, New York, NY.

Milton, J. (1674) *Paradise Lost*. Penguin Books, London.

Moore, R. K. (2014) 'The localization movement. Creating a viable local economy. Challenging the new world order'. *Centre for Research on Globalization*, 27 February 2014, available at: www.globalresearch.ca/the-localization-movement-creating-a-viable-local-economy-challenging-the-new-world-order/5371155, accessed 13 February 2014.

Mortley, R. (1986) *From Word to Silence*. Bond University, Australia, available at: epublications.bond.edu.au/word_to_silence_I/, accessed 13 June 2013.

Mukherjee, R., ed. (1993) *The Penguin Gandhi Reader*. Penguin Books India (P) Ltd., New Delhi, India.

Myers, A. (2012) 'A different drummer: Stanford engineers discover neural rhythms drive physical movement'. Stanford University, Stanford, CA, 3 June 2012, available at: engineering.stanford.edu/print/node/36844, accessed 16 July 2014.

Nagel, T. (2012) *Mind and Cosmos: Why the Materialist, Neo-Darwinian Conception of Nature is Almost Certainly False*. Oxford University Press, Oxford.

Nardelli, A. (2015) 'IMF: austerity measures would still leave Greece with unsustainable debt'. *The Guardian* (London), 30 June 2015, available at: www.theguardian.com/business/2015/jun/30/greek-debt-troika-analysis-says-significant-concessions-still-needed, accessed 9 August 2015.

Needhidasan, S., Samuel, M., and Chidambaram, R. (2014) 'Electronic waste – an emerging threat to the environment of urban India'. *Journal of Environmental Health Science and Engineering*, Vol. 12, No. 36, published online 20 January 2014, available at: www.ncbi.nlm.nih.gov/pmc/articles/PMC3908467/, accessed 29 January 2015.

Neumark, D., Zhang, J., and Ciccarella, S. (2008) 'The effects of Wal-Mart on local labor markets'. *Journal of Urban Economics*, No. 63, pp. 405–430.

Nicoll, M. (1950) *The New Man* [1972]. Penguin Books, Baltimore, MD.

Norman, D. A. and Verganti, R. (2014) 'Incremental and radical innovation: design research vs. technology and meaning change'. *Design Issues*, Vol. 30, No. 1, pp. 78–96.

Nugraha, A. (2012) 'Transforming tradition: a method for maintaining tradition in a craft and design context'. PhD dissertation, Aalto University, School of the Arts, Design and Architecture, Helsinki, Finland.

Nunn, T. M. (2001) *Sin Nombre: Hispana and Hispano Artists of the New Deal Era*. University of New Mexico Press, Albuquerque, NM.

O'Carroll, L. (2013) 'Senior Met officer sentenced to 15 months for phone-hacking leak'. *The Guardian* (London), 1 February 2013, available at: www.theguardian.com/media/2013/feb/01/april-casburn-sentenced-15-months-phone-hacking, accessed 7 May 2014.

Odent, M. (2013) *Childbirth and the Future of Homo Sapiens*. Pinter & Martin Ltd., London.

262

Oliver, J. G. J., Janssens-Maenhout, G., Muntean, M., and Peters, J. A. H. W. (2014) *2014 Report*. PBL Netherlands Environmental Assessment Agency, The Hague.

Overell, S., Mills, T., Roberts, S., Lekhi, R., and Blaug, R. (2010) 'The employment relationship and the quality of work'. Provocation paper 7, The Good Work Commission, *The Work Foundation*, London, pp. 72–73, available at: www.goodworkcommission. co.uk/Assets/Docs/ReportsWithCovers/07.EmploymentRelationshipQualityOfWork.pdf, accessed 14 September 2015.

Pagels, E. (2003) *Beyond Belief*. Vintage Books, New York, NY.

Pagels, E. (2006) 'The Gospel of Thomas: new perspectives on Jesus' message' [Recorded lecture]. Sounds True Inc , Boulder, CO.

Pagh, J. (2011) 'Sustainability by design: crafts'. Ministry of Foreign Affairs of Denmark, Copenhagen, Denmark, available at: www.denmark.dk/en/menu/About-Denmark/ Danish-Design-Architecture/Design/Sustainability-By-Design/, accessed 6 November 2015.

Palmer, M. and Wagner, K. (2013) 'ValuesQuest: the search for values that will make a world of difference'. Discussion paper, *Club of Rome*, p. 11, available at: www. clubofrome.org/cms/wp-content/uploads/2013/02/VALUESQUEST-The-search-for-values-that-will-make-a-world-of-difference.pdf, accessed 8 September 2013.

Panksepp, J. (1998) *Affective Neuroscience: The Foundations of Human and Animal Emotions*. Oxford University Press, Oxford.

Paradiso, M. (2015) 'Chiara Vigo: The last woman who makes sea silk'. *BBC News Magazine Online*, 2 September 2015, available at: www.bbc.co.uk/news/ magazine-33691781, accessed 2 September 2015.

Paton, G. (2014) 'Religious education subjected to "rank discrimination"'. *The Telegraph* (London), 24 February 2014, available at: www.telegraph.co.uk/education/ educationnews/10656555/Religious-education-subjected-to-rank-discrimination.html, accessed 3 March 2014.

Perry, G. (2014) 'Making meaning in the arts: Grayson Perry in conversation with Prof. Charlie Gere'. Lancaster Institute for the Contemporary Arts, Lancaster University, 28 November 2014.

Phillips, T. (2015) 'China ends one-child policy after 35 years'. *The Guardian* (London), 29 October 2015, available at: www.theguardian.com/world/2015/oct/29/china-abandons-one-child-policy, accessed 20 October 2015.

Peston, R. (2015) 'Why has the ECB punished Greece?' *BBC Business News Online*, 5 February 2015, available at: www.bbc.co.uk/news/business-31148199, accessed 9 August 2015.

Piketty, T. (2014) *Capital in the Twenty-First Century*. Harvard University Press, Cambridge, MA.

Porritt, J. (2007) *Capitalism as if the World Matters*. Routledge, London.

Powell, A. (2012) 'Trouble afloat: ocean plastics. Even in the most remote locations, the buildup of timeless debris grows'. *Harvard Gazette*, 10 February 2012, available at: news.harvard.edu/gazette/story/2012/02/trouble-afloat-ocean-plastics/, accessed 31 May 2014.

Pozzo di Borgo, P. (2014) Interview in 'To Die with Dignity?' *Heart and Soul*, BBC World Service, London, broadcast 30 September 2014.

Pratt, V., Brady, E., and Howarth, J. (2000) *Environment and Philosophy*. Routledge, London.

Protess, B. and Silver-Greenberg, J. (2014) 'Credit Suisse pleads guilty in felony case'. *New York Times* (New York), 19 May 2014, available at: dealbook.nytimes.com/ 2014/05/19/credit-suisse-set-to-plead-guilty-in-tax-evasion-case/?_php=true&_ type=blogs&hp&_r=0, accessed 19 May 2014.

Rebanks, J. (2015) *The Shepherd's Life: A Tale of the Lake District.* Allen Lane, Penguin Random House, London.

Reid, K. (2013) 'From fragmentation to wholeness'. *Resurgence & Ecologist*, No. 279, pp. 32–35.

Renton, A. (2015) 'What would you pay to be happy?' *The Observer* (London), 10 May 2015.

RFF (2016) 'RFF's decision to divest'. *The Rockefeller Family Fund*, available at: www.rffund.org/divestment, accessed 23 March 2016.

Rice University (2010) '"Mitochondrial Eve": mother of all humans lived 200,000 years ago'. *ScienceDaily*, 17 August 2010, available at: www.sciencedaily.com/releases/2010/08/100817122405.htm, accessed 15 March 2014.

Riley, J., Corkhill, B., and Morris, C. (2013) 'The benefits of knitting for personal and social wellbeing in adulthood: findings from an international survey'. *British Journal of Occupational Therapy*, Vol. 76, No. 2, pp. 50–57.

Rilke, R. M. (1903) *Letters to a Young Poet.* Soulard, R., Jr. (ed.), Scriptor Press, Malden, MA, p. 14, available at: https://kbachuntitled.files.wordpress.com/2013/04/rainer-maria-rilke-letters-to-a-young-poet.pdf, accessed 12 April 2015.

Rodwell, J. (2013) 'Aesthetic & spiritual responses to the environment: a two-day BESS workshop at York'. Biodiversity & Ecosystem Service Sustainability (BESS) Research Programme (2011–2017), Natural Environment Research Council (NERC), 3 July 2013, available at: www.nerc-bess.net/documents/BESS_NIA_Cultural_Ecosystem_Services_Workshop_Report.pdf, accessed 5 August 2013.

Rollo, K. (1997) 'Agricultural plastics – Boon or bane?' *Cornell Waste Management Institute*, Cornell University, Ithaca, NY, available at: cwmi.css.cornell.edu/agwaste.html, accessed 31 May 2014.

Rowson, J. and McGilchrist, I. (2013) 'Divided brain, divided world: why the best part of us struggles to be heard'. *Royal Society of Arts*, London, available at: www.thersa.org/__data/assets/pdf_file/0019/1016083/RSA-Divided-Brain-Divided-World.PDF, accessed 14 November 2013.

Ruddick, G. (2015) 'VW scandal: carmaker admits 11m vehicles are involved'. *The Guardian* (London), 22 September 2015, available at www.theguardian.com/business/2015/sep/22/vw-scandal-escalates-volkswagen-11m-vehicles-involved, accessed 22 September 2015.

Ruskin, J. (1838) *The Poetry of Architecture.* Part I 'The Cottage', pp. 8, 19–20, available at: www.gutenberg.org/cache/epub/17774/pg17774.txt, accessed 30 November 2014.

Ruxton, D. (2015) 'Media reaction to Syriza's victory in Greek general election'. *The Irish Times* (Dublin), 28 January 2015, available at: www.irishtimes.com/news/world/europe/media-reaction-to-syriza-s-victory-in-greek-general-election-1.2079844, accessed 9 August 2015.

Said, E. W. (1978) *Orientalism* [2003]. Penguin Books, London.

Salt, K. N. (2015a) Quoted from 'Haiti aid: throwing good money after bad?' *Newshour Extra*, BBC World Service, London, broadcast 7 August 2015.

Salt, K. N. (2015b) 'Ecological Chains of Unfreedom: Contours of Black Sovereignty in the Atlantic World'. *Journal of American Studies*, Vol. 49, No. 02, pp. 267–286.

Schama, S. (2009a) *A History of Britain, Volume 1: At the Edge of the World? 3000 BC–AD 1603.* The Bodley Head, London.

Schama, S. (2009b) *A History of Britain, Volume 2: The British Wars 1603–1776.* The Bodley Head, London.

Schama, S. (2009c) *A History of Britain, Volume 3: The Fate of Empire 1776–2000.* The Bodley Head, London.

Scheffler, S. (2013) *Death and the Afterlife.* Oxford University Press, Oxford.

Schwaabe, C. (2011) *Max Weber – The Disenchantment of the World*. Uhlaner, J. (trans.), Goethe-Institute. V., available at: www.goethe.de/ges/phi/prt/en8250983.htm, accessed 14 February 2014.

Schwartz, B. (2004) *The Paradox of Choice*. HarperCollins, New York, NY.

Scollard, J. R. (1987) *The Self-Employed Woman*. Pocket Books, Simon and Schuster, New York, NY.

Scruton, R. (1994) *Modern Philosophy: An Introduction and Survey*. Reed International Ltd., London.

Scruton, R. (2012) *Green Philosophy: How to Think Seriously about the Planet*. Atlantic Books, London.

Scruton, R. (2014) *The Soul of the World*. Princeton University Press, Princeton, NJ.

Scruton, R. (2016) *Confessions of a Heretic*. Notting Hill Editions, London.

Sennett, R. (2008) *The Craftsman*. Penguin, London.

SFMOMA (2011) 'Less and more: the design ethos of dieter rams'. San Francisco Museum of Modern Art, 29 June 2011, available at: www.sfmoma.org/about/press/press_exhibitions/releases/880, accessed 3 November 2014.

Sheldrake, R. (2012) *The Science Delusion*. Coronet, Hodder & Stoughton, London.

Shiva, V. (2013) 'The seeds of suicide: how Monsanto destroys farming'. *Asian Age and Global Research*, 5 April 2013, available at: www.globalresearch.ca/the-seeds-of-suicide-how-monsanto-destroys-farming/5329947, accessed 30 May 2014.

Shortt, R. (2016) *God Is No Thing: Coherent Christianity*. Hurst & Company, London.

Siegel, L. (2009) 'Did Frank McCourt invent James Frey?' *The Daily Beast*, 20 July 2009, available at: www.thedailybeast.com/articles/2009/07/20/the-mother-of-all-memoirists.html, accessed 25 November 2015.

Sim, S. (2007) *Manifesto for Silence: Confronting the Politics and Culture of Noise*. Edinburgh University Press, Edinburgh.

Skidelsky, R. and Skidelsky, E. (2012) *How Much is Enough: Money and the Good Life*. Other Press, New York, NY.

Smith, H. (2001) *Why Religions Matter: The Fate of the Human Spirit in an Age of Disbelief*. HarperCollins, New York, NY.

Strauss, C. F. and Fuad-Luke, A. (2008) 'The slow design principles: a new interrogative and reflexive tool for design research and practice' in Cipolla, C. and Peruccio, P. P. (eds.) *Changing the Change Proceedings*. Politecnico di Milano, Italy, pp. 1440–1453, available at: www.allemandi.com/university/ctc.pdf, accessed 25 November 2014.

Tarnas, R. (1991) *The Passion of the Western Mind*. Harmony Books, New York, NY.

Taylor, C. (2007) *A Secular Age*. The Belknap Press of Harvard University Press, Cambridge, MA.

Teather, S. (2014) 'Interview with Sarah Teather MP on the Sunday programme'. *BBC Radio 4*, Salford, 2 February 2014.

Thackara, J. (2005) *In the Bubble: Designing in a Complex World*. MIT Press, Cambridge, MA.

Thomas, R. S. (1993) *Collected Poems 1945–1999*. Phoenix, London.

Thompson, J. A. K., trans. (1976) *The Ethics of Aristotle: The Nicomachean Ethics*. Penguin Books, London.

Thompson, R. C. (2013) 'Written evidence submitted by Professor Prof. Richard C. Thompson (WQ17) [Water Quality 17]'. *Science and Technology Committee – Written Evidence*, House of Commons, UK Parliament, London, 28 February 2013, available at: www.publications.parliament.uk/pa/cm201213/cmselect/cmsctech/writev/932/contents.htm, accessed 13 July 2014.

Todhunter, C. (2013) 'Genetically engineered "terminator seeds": death and destruction of agriculture'. *Global Research*, Montreal, Canada, available at: www.globalresearch.ca/

genetically-engineered-terminator-seeds-death-and-destruction-of-agriculture/5319797, accessed 6 August 2013.

Torrecilals, F. L. (2007) 'Four in ten young adults are mobile-phone addicts'. *The Medical News*, 27 February 2007, available at: www.news-medical.net/news/2007/02/27/22245. aspx, accessed 20 October 2010.

Toye, R. (2013) *Rhetoric – A Very Short Introduction*. Oxford University Press, Oxford.

Treanor, J. (2012) 'UBS corrupt payments exposed as bank pays £940m to settle Libor claims'. *The Guardian* (London), 19 December 2012, available at: www.theguardian. com/business/2012/dec/19/ubs-pays-libor-fixing-claims, accessed 27 April 2014.

Turkle, S. (2011) *Alone Together: Why We Expect More from Technology and Less from Each Other*. Basic Books, New York, NY.

TV Guide (n. d.) '"Casino Royale" 1967 review'. *TV Guide*, available at: movies.tvguide.com/ casino-royale/review/110477, accessed 3 November 2014.

Tweed, K. (2013) 'Global e-waste will jump 33 percent in the next five years'. *IEEE Spectrum*, 17 December 2013, available at: spectrum.ieee.org/energywise/energy/ environment/global-ewaste-will-jump-33-in-next-five-years, accessed 29 November 2014.

USGS (2014) 'Environmental health, toxic substances – Biomagnification'. United States Geological Survey, *US Department of the Interior*, Washington, DC, available at: toxics. usgs.gov/definitions/biomagnification.html, accessed 10 June 2014.

UNEP (2009) 'Facts and figures: global materials extraction (Fig. 2.1)'. Resource Panel, *United Nations Environment Programme*, available at: www.unep.org/resourcepanel/ FactsFigures/tabid/106638/Default.aspx, accessed 14 August 2013.

Utsch, H. (2007) 'Knitting and stress reduction'. PhD Study, Department of Clinical Psychology, Antioch University New England, Keene, NH.

Van Nes, N. (2010) 'Understanding replacement behaviour and exploring design solutions' in Cooper, T. (ed.) *Longer Lasting Products: Alternatives to the Throwaway Society*. Gower Publishing Limited, Farnham, pp. 107–131.

Van der Ryn, S. and Cowan, S. (1996) *Ecological Design*. Island Press, Washington, DC.

Variety Staff (1966) 'Review: "Casino Royale"'. *Variety*, 31 December 1966, available at: variety.com/1966/film/reviews/casino-royale-1200421405/, accessed 3 November 2014.

Volkswagen (2015) 'CSR projects'. *Volkswagen Group*, available at: www.volkswagenag. com/content/vwcorp/content/en/sustainability_and_responsibility/CSR_worldwide.html, accessed 20 September 2015.

Wadsworth, M. (2007) 'IKEA exposed over "child labour" and green issues'. *The-Latest*, 22 May 2007, available at: www.the-latest.com/ikea-exposed-over-child-labour-and-green-issues, accessed 5 January 2014.

Wakefield, J. (2016) 'Apple, Samsung and Sony face child labour claims'. *BBC News Online*, 19 January 2016, available at: www.bbc.co.uk/news/technology-35311456, accessed 2 February 2016.

Walker, S. (2006) *Sustainable by Design – Explorations in Theory and Practice*. Routledge, Abingdon, Oxford.

Walker, S. (2011) *The Spirit of Design: Objects, Environment and Meaning*. Routledge, Abingdon, Oxford.

Walker, S. (2014) *Designing Sustainability: Making Radical Changes in a Material World*. Routledge, Abingdon, Oxford.

Walker, S. and Giard, J., eds. (2013) *The Handbook of Design for Sustainability*. Bloomsbury Academic, London.

Ward, B., trans. (1973) *The Prayers and Meditations of St. Anselm with the Proslogion*. Penguin Books, London.

Ward, G. (2014) *Unbelievable: Why We Believe and Why We Don't*. I. B. Tauris, London.

266

Whittier, J. G. (1892) 'The Brewing of Soma'. *The Poetical Works in Four Volumes*, available at: www.bartleby.com/372/197.html, accessed 29 July 2015.

Wilkinson, R. and Pickett, K. (2009) *The Spirit Level: Why More Equal Societies Almost Always Do Better*. Allen Land, Penguin Books, London.

Williams, R. (1983) *Keywords: A Vocabulary of Culture and Society* [2014]. HarperCollins, London.

Williams, R. (2014) 'Divine understanding: an exploration of the fundamental connection between faith and human perception spans neuroscience, philosophy and theology'. Book review of *Unbelievable: Why We Believe and Why We Don't* by Graham Ward, *The Tablet* (London), 20/27 December 2014.

Wilson, A. N. (2015) *The Book of the People*. Atlantic Books, London.

Wittgenstein, L. (1922) *Tractatus Logico-Philosophicus*. Kegan Paul, Trench, Trubner & Co., Ltd., London.

Wittgenstein, L. (1953) *Philosophical Investigations*, 3rd Edition. Basil Blackwell, Oxford.

Wolin, R. (2013) 'Emmanuel Lévinas'. *Encyclopædia Britannica*, available at: www.britannica.com/EBchecked/topic/337960/Emmanuel-Levinas, accessed 10 April 2014.

Worldwatch Institute (2013) 'The state of consumption today'. *Worldwatch Institute*, Washington, DC, available at: www.worldwatch.org/node/810, accessed 14 August 2013.

Wright, O. (2012) 'King blasts bankers over pay, service – and morality'. *The Independent* (London), 30 June 2012, available at: www.independent.co.uk/news/uk/politics/king-blasts-bankers-over-pay-service--and-morality-7900039.html#, accessed 7 May 2014.

Yonge, C. D., trans. (1993) *The Works of Philo: Complete and Unabridged*. Hendrickson Publishers, Peabody, MA.

Young, R. J. C. (2003) *Postcolonialism*. Oxford University Press, Oxford.

Yunus, M. (2007) *Creating a World Without Poverty*. Public Affairs, New York, NY.

Zarrilli, P. B. (2011) 'Psychophysical approaches and practices in India: embodying processes and states of "being–doing"'. *New Theatre Quarterly*, Vol. 27, No. 3, pp. 244–271.

Zeckhauser, R. (2013) 'The wisdom of crowds and the stupidity of herds'. Presentation to School of Information, Harvard Kennedy School, University of Michigan, 21 March 2013, available at: stiet.cms.si.umich.edu/sites/stiet.cms.si.umich.edu/files/The%20Wisdom%20of%20Crowds%20and%20the%20Stupidity%20of%20Herds%20Presentation%20Results.pdf, accessed 29 September 2014.

Zipes, J., trans. & ed. (2014) *The First Complete Edition: The Original Folk & Fairy Tales of the Brothers Grimm*. Princeton University Press, Oxford.

Index

Note: **bold** page numbers refer to figures and accompanying text; numbers in brackets preceded by *n* are note numbers.

278

May